MONIKA KRAUSE
QUEEN OF CONDOMS

1. *Monika Krause* (1941–2019)

MONIKA KRAUSE
QUEEN OF CONDOMS

Memoir of a Sex Educator in Revolutionary Cuba

EDITED BY
Dictys Jiménez Krause &
Julian Daniel Jiménez Krause

TRANSLATED BY
Regina Anavy

MIAMI & BERLIN

Copyright © 2022 by
Dictys Jiménez Krause and Julian Daniel Jiménez Krause

From Monika Krause's original work:
Cuba, mi infierno y mi paraíso (Iliada Ediciones, 2020)
Machismo? No, gracias (Ediciones Idea, 2007)

Translation from the Spanish
© 2022 by Regina Anavy

First paperback edition (March 2022)

Iliada Ediciones

www.iliadaediciones.com

ISBN 978-0-578-34013-5

Library of Congress Control Number: 2021925533

CONTENTS

		Page
FOREWORD	. . . . . .	xi

PART ONE
IT'S OVER

Chapter		
1.	GOODBYE, CUBA	3
2.	HELLO, GERMANY	14

PART TWO
THE SIXTIES

3.	IN THE BEGINNING.	31
4.	CULTURE SHOCK	47
5.	PACO AND MARY	69
6.	FILMING WITH THE GERMANS . . .	79
7.	THE MISSILE CRISIS	84
8.	THE BIRTH OF OUR FIRST SON . . .	87
9.	AN ALMOST FATAL ACCIDENT	109
10.	MY PARENTS IN HAVANA. . . .	114
11.	THE EUROPEAN REFRIGERATOR . . .	118
12.	BACK IN HAVANA	131

13. DICTYS THE PING-PONG BALL . . . 137
14. OUR FAMILY WILL BE COMPLETE . . . 142
15. IN NEW YORK 150
16. DANI IS BROUGHT BACK TO LIFE . . . 162
17. VACATION WITH THE GERMAN GRANDPARENTS 167
18. DICTYS TRAINS TO SWIM AND DANI ALMOST DROWNS 172

PART THREE
THE SEVENTIES

19. THE BOYS ARE GROWING 181
20. I COMPLETE MY STUDIES 192
21. THE YEAR OF THE TEN MILLION . . . 199
22. A PERMANENT POSITION 203
23. ALLENDE'S CHILE 207
24. A BITTER EXPERIENCE WITH CUBAN HOMOPHOBIA 221
25. THE FEDERATION OF CUBAN WOMEN . . 225
26. SEX EDUCATION BEGINS 233
27. MY CAPTAIN DISAPPEARS AND THE HOUSE FLOODS 243
28. WHAT DOESN'T KILL ME MAKES ME STRONGER 247
29. MY CAPTAIN RETURNS FROM THE WAR . . 260
30. THE NATIONAL SEX EDUCATION WORKING GROUP 264
31. A PILOT PROGRAM IN THE BOARDING SCHOOLS 267

PART FOUR
THE EIGHTIES

32. BOOKS ON SEXUALITY HIT THE MARK . . 277
33. MÓNICA, QUEEN OF CONDOMS . . . 283
34. STAR OF RADIO AND TELEVISION . . . 289
35. THE UNEXPECTED VISIT OF A WOUNDED MALE 296

36.	MISADVENTURES OF THE BOYS IN BOARDING SCHOOLS	299
37.	MY FATHER'S DEATH AND MY MOTHER'S LAST VISIT	310
38.	AT THE PEAK OF MY CAREER	314

PART FIVE

THE NINETIES

39.	THE SPECIAL PERIOD: *MACHISMO* AND UNDERDEVELOPMENT	323
40.	THE BOYS BECOME MEN	328
41.	MY LAST STAND AGAINST INSTITUTIONALIZED HOMOPHOBIA	332
42.	THE CIRCLE IS CLOSED	336
	AFTERWORD	340

PHOTOS

1. Monika Krause (1941–2019) ii
2. Monika with her sons Dani and Dictys in Berlin in the early 1990s 21
3. Monika marrying Cuban–Spanish captain Jesús Jiménez Escobar, at the club of the Warnow shipyard, April 1962 45
4. Ana María, Monika's mother-in-law . . . 57
5. Monika holding baby Dictys in Havana . . 102
6. Dani (Julian Daniel), three months old . . . 145
7. Dictys and Dani celebrating Dani's first birthday, New York, December 1967 159
8. Dani, Dictys, and two classmates at Ciudad Deportiva, the pick-up point for the Camilo Cienfuegos swimming school 174
9. Dani and Dictys with Uncle Gonzalo and Aunt Pilar 187
10. Monika, left of Castro, translating for a high-ranking official from East Germany, with Vilma Espín, president of the Cuban Women's Federation. . 229
11. Monika and Dora Carcaño, a senior FMC executive, at a discussion panel preparatory to the II Congress of the Federation of Cuban Women, 1974 . . . 235

12. *Monika and Vilma Espín, President of the Cuban Women's Federation, at the* UN *World Women's Conference, Mexico City, 1975, International Year of Women* 240
13. *Monika wearing a cervical brace (Minerva) after the horrific car accident, 1976* 253
14. *Monika, Dr. Siegfried Schnabl from East Germany, Dr. Celestino Álvarez Lajonchere, and journalist Natacha Herrera* 258
15. *Monika in her office at the National Sex Education Work Group (*GNTES*), Havana, late 1970s* . . . 265
16. *Monika on Cuban* TV *demonstrating the diaphragm* 291
17. *Monika on Cuban* TV *advocating condom usage* . 293
18. *Grandpa Herwig and Grandma Berta with Dani, Dictys, and Monika in Germany, Summer 1979, the last time they met Herwig alive.* 311
19. *Monika, Havana, late 1980s* 317

FOREWORD
BY JACQUELINE LOSS
Professor of Latin American Literary and Cultural
Studies at the University of Connecticut.

IN THE EARLY 1990S, Monika Krause entered my orbit through a quote in a book by Marvin Leiner about Cuban male sexuality and the AIDS pandemic. Her statement—"the one area revolutionaries and counter-revolutionaries have in common is homophobia"—stuck out to me for its unique manner of bringing together ideologies frequently cast as diametrically opposed. Similar bold assertions penetrate *Monika Krause, Queen of Condoms, Memoir of a Sex Educator in Revolutionary Cuba*, a memoir whose female protagonist emerges as deeply human, flawed, evolving, and dedicated to impacting individuals' outlooks on sexuality, however resistant they and their contexts may be to change.

Rare though it is in twenty-first-century critical writing in English to refer to authors by their first names, "Monika Krause" compels us to do so, by the degree of intimacy she forges between herself and readers, achieving it through startling honesty about her professional, personal, and romantic life. While often the modern subject may conceive such realms to be isolated from one another, Monika's story of her life in Cuba demonstrates the ways in which these realms overlap. At times, such an interwoven social fabric may be repressive, and yet, at others, it can evoke feelings of deep community. I'll refrain from calling Monika "Mónica," spelling her name as Cubans did, when they adopted her as their own, or at least, as their own East German. And, with reason. For, between 1962-1990, Monika put great effort into transforming aspects of sexuality in the country that she also called home, but *Monika Krause, Queen of Condoms, Memoir of a Sex Educator in Revolutionary Cuba* is more than an account of a sexual reformer. She directed the National Sex Education Working Group (GNTES) that years later, in 1988, became the National Center for Sex Education (CENESEX), an institution that presently is led by Mariela Castro and is sometimes criticized by the church for being too permissive and by others as being far too close to official positions on many matters.

Monika's memoirs are also the account of a woman who possessed a tenacity and drive, in the face of multiple and major personal, familiar, and historical obstacles. One could only hope to emulate her manner of approaching them. While the Cuban with whom Monika fell in love and wed soon after was in the a merchant marine, whom Monika refers to as "my captain," Monika did everything to steer her own ship, while being a sturdy anchor for her family. As a student of Latin American Studies—a new field at the University of Rostock meant to prepare Germans for forays into the widening socialist world, she was already an avid follower of the Cuban revolution. Her persistent desire for education permeates her life; her doctoral defense in 1983 in Rostock, East Germany, for instance, seems as if it were just a springboard for bolder investigations and confrontations with others in defense of them.

The book is a stunning portrait of a woman who faced more than one massive upheaval in her life as well as near-death experiences endured by her sons and herself. Monika's remarkable strength emerges in the book's initial pages, as she voyages from Cuba back to her native Germany, a nation in the process of reunification. Her self-portrait as a forty-nine-year-old woman reinventing herself in a country where even those who led the most stable of lives are all undergoing an immense overhaul is inspiring. Equally so is Monika's revelation of how it feels to face the loss of a professional identity that she constructed alongside some of the most prominent Cuban doctors and revolutionaries, such as Vilma Espín, in a far-away developing world. While comparisons between the communist bloc and imperialism are extensive and fraught, this autobiographic tale about the travails of a young, impassioned traveler contributes as much to a study of those links as it does to the genre of the feminist *bildungsroman*. Its contribution to studies of the Cuban healthcare system is also unique, because we don't just see the details of Monika's process, working with professors of gynecology such as Dr. Celestino Álvarez Lajonchere, but we also see her diverse experiences navigating the field as a patient and mother of two young sons. Her experiences with the education of her children and herself in Cuba are equally insightful.

Monika Krause, Queen of Condoms, Memoir of a Sex Educator in Revolutionary Cuba also testifies to the importance of translation on many levels. This aspect is of particular importance to me, as someone who continually engages in different forms of translation as a scholar of Cuban cultural studies based in the United States (a country for which, I should say, Monika felt little empathy). The author confesses to having once thought of homosexuality as a "problem," not yet conscious of the extent to which the revolutionary state had institutionalized homophobia. Nevertheless, that very ignorance, she reveals, is what led her to cherish the discussion of the many contours of human sexuality found in works such as *Man and Woman in Intimacy* by East German Siegfried Schnabl, a manuscript that she later helped translate and adapt for Cuban audiences. While its chapter on homosexuality was first censored in the Cuban version, it was ultimately included in a second edition, achieved through Monika's team's efforts to "circumvent the censorship." This is one of several anecdotes that also illustrate some unusual outcomes of the "ideological proximity" between Cuba and the Soviet Bloc, which are sometimes obscured by the more repressive influences of the Soviet Union on Cuba. That is to say, the book reveals how actual translators were also sometimes able to exert their influence over the body of literature that was being published and disseminated. We can surmise that the impact of such translation on readerships—copies of the book's first edition ran out fast, leading to a large second run and subsequent editions—was not just on policies toward sexuality, which over time have largely improved in Cuba, but also on individuals' behavior and treatment of others.

It would be erroneous to conceive of Monika as some kind of perfect transculturated subject. Monika is regularly confounded by Cubans and their government. And, to some twenty-first-century readers, used to particular ways of speaking about race, ethnicity, and sexuality, her expressions of befuddlement and annoyance may seem a tad chauvinistic or alarming. She sometimes uses out-of-date modes of expression for U.S. English speakers. She can be "heard" uttering, "Well, he IS Latino," and yet, to a degree, Monika transforms from being a foreign observer to active participant, to such an extent that she even uses the first person plural when discussing Cubans. Furthermore—and this is something that we cannot forget—she can be just as biting, if not more so, toward Germans and the Dutch as she is toward Cubans.

That the sexual is always political even in the most seemingly discreet of contexts cannot be denied, but the spheres of experiences which Monika's memoirs open up to us are even more infinite and difficult to categorize. They speak to how one individual can exert her will in favor of making transformations within the psychological make-up of generations and suggest that transcultural contact can lead to unknown horizons leading to disasters, as much as to spontaneity, surprise, and goodwill.

With women's rights under attack in my own homeland, I can't think of a better time to embrace Monika's commitment to education, pleasure, and liberation.

JACQUELINE LOSS, *New York City, November 12, 2021*

PART ONE
IT'S OVER

CHAPTER ONE
GOODBYE, CUBA

It's four in the afternoon on November 10, 1990. I take one last look at the courtyard, the bedrooms, the hundreds of books, our precious paintings, a collection of works by contemporary Cuban artists—almost all personal gifts. Rumba, our fox terrier puppy, is following me everywhere; she knows something strange is happening. Perhaps she senses the sadness and fear we're feeling on the eve of our next adventure. Fortunately, there's no time to think now. After one final review of all our documents, we leave for the airport. I've made this trip so many times that I know every pothole.

We have to be at the airport three hours before the plane's scheduled departure; three hours feels to me like three years. My Lada, broken down and snorting like a centenarian rhinoceros, a state it entered as a result of a terrible collision with a bus, comports itself like a hero. It doesn't fail once on the long road to the airport. Our companions aren't allowed to enter the building in the terminal area. Jesús, my ex-lover, ex-husband, and now a friend for life, says goodbye to me and Dani, our little boy. I'm putting an end to almost thirty years of life in Cuba.

For friends, colleagues at work, and family members, we're going, Dani and I, to spend a month of vacation in my mother's house in Germany. But first, before being able to continue on to my childhood home, I have to attend a congress. Dani and I know we're not coming back; our round-trip tickets will be used only one way.

The others don't know, and we mustn't tell them, because that way they can't be held accountable for not preventing our exit. My older son, Dictys, who was on permanent mission in Nicaragua, left a month ago "on vacation" and is waiting for us to arrive in Germany. At that point, our plan will have been successfully completed.

I feel like I have bright letters on my forehead saying *We're not coming back*. I'm nervous: If they do a thorough check, they're going to find all my documents, diplomas, and certificates, including books that aren't in my suitcase for my supposed trip to a congress, much less for going on vacation. They're going to find my German passport.

"Why," they could ask, "do you have two passports?"

And I'm not sure that any possible answer will convince them.

The requisite formalities include three basic steps: baggage handling, passport control, and customs. At each one there could be a catastrophe. We're checking our baggage. The Cuban officer notices the weight.

"Your suitcase has ten kilograms more than is permitted; you have to take things out that aren't essential, because that's not allowed."

"Is the plane full?"

It's a desperate question. The officer doesn't answer, he's looking at my papers. I note that his face lights up, but he doesn't answer my question.

"Mónica, finally I have you in front of me! I want you to know that your last radio program stirred things up like crazy, this idea that a woman has needs the same as a man. It seems to me you exaggerated, although, of course, there are men who are clumsy and pretty gross."

I'm not in the mood to listen to his analysis of my last radio program about the supposed and real differences between men and women in the sexual sphere. I want, simply, to know if my full suitcase, with everything packed inside, can make the trip with me or not. Finally the officer realizes that we're in the airport, that it's his job to deal with the suitcases for my flight, and that he has to make a decision about the baggage.

"Mónica, this will be resolved right away, don't worry. I've really enjoyed meeting you. What will be the next subject of the radio program? You'll be back in time?"

"Of course," I answer and, now very worried, ask him again about the suitcase. "So what can we do about my luggage? I can't take out anything, and I need the things that are inside."

"Mónica, for you I'd do anything. Your suitcase weighs twenty kilograms. I'll dispose of the extra ten with the passenger behind you. It's perfect, he's taking only one suitcase, and the plane is going to fly with less than half its cargo capacity. There's no problem. I wish you a good trip and please return soon. I never miss your programs. Why don't you expand a bit on last week's subject? Or, better yet, I'll write to you, and you can answer me directly. You'll answer me personally, right?"

"Of course, I always answer questions from the public personally."

I feel I have to lie to this friendly officer who has just gotten me out of a tight spot. Next we head to the immigration department, the most difficult hurdle to jump. A lieutenant asks Dani for his passport. *I hope the kid doesn't confuse his pockets, because if he takes out his German document, that's it for us*, I think, feigning indifference. It seems to me that the clocks have stopped, that the time it takes for the lieutenant to review my son's papers is endless. Finally, she lets Dani pass to the next hurdle, customs. And now it's my turn to be scrutinized by the lieutenant.

In my right pocket I have the Cuban passport, which I must present now; in the left, the German, which I must keep hidden. The lieutenant flips through the pages judiciously, as if she were attending to the only passenger on the flight to Berlin. Occasionally she raises her head to thoroughly examine my face. Thousands of thoughts go through my mind. The lieutenant stands up and goes off, taking my passport with her. The nervous tension is unbearable. It's because of that damned photo they took of me in the House of Monsters (what people call the only place at that time in Havana where you could get passport photos), I think, since certainly you have to resort to fantasy to be able to find any resemblance between the photograph and the original.

Luckily, this tortured wait comes to an end. The lieutenant returns and hands my Cuban passport back to me. She doesn't know that I will never in my life use it again.

"Have a good trip."

She presses a button inside her cage that activates the most important door at this moment. Theoretically, there is no longer any obstacle to getting on the plane to Germany. I feel a tremendous relief, but deep down in a corner of my mind, I retain a dose of distrust and fear, and I think over and over, I won't feel secure until the plane has at least crossed over the Bahamas. (I've made more than one work trip where the plane had to turn around and go back to Havana because of some mechanical defect, after having been in the air for more than half an hour.)

Two hours have passed since Jesús left us in the terminal. The customs check shouldn't take long. The large suitcase was cleared at the beginning of our pilgrimage; now it should be in the container next to the plane. All that remains is the screening of the carry-on luggage and the ability to withstand the meticulous body search that is practiced with zeal when the customs officers encounter a suspicious person who may be concealing something prohibited.

The customs control post this afternoon is in the hands of a group of young officers. They seem more like kids in a secondary school than public employees. They're laughing, making jokes, and exchanging stories about what's been going on in their private lives. They dispatch Dani in no time. Now it's my turn. I see two of them nudging each other. One tells the other my name, and she whispers:

"Ask her, Manolo, take advantage of the opportunity."

Like a little boy caught playing a prank, Manolo looks at me sideways and asks his colleague to ask the question he doesn't dare articulate. She approaches me with a nervous laugh, looking at the floor, searching for words, enveloping the subject in obscure vocabulary, trying to help her friend. I'm used to having to guess when the subject concerns sex. And just as I do on my radio program, I repeat, in simple words, the question that she's asked. The group of young people look at me with faces of satisfaction and relief. In order to be sure that I've correctly grasped his concern, expressed in such a complicated way that we could be playing hide and seek, I ask the question again.

"Is this what you want to know?"

A dissonant chorus of "Yes!" again accompanied by laughs. The ice is broken. We talk for a long time. I've always liked the exchange of ideas with young people.

For a moment I've completely forgotten that I'm not in the airport to give a talk about the problems of cohabitation and generational conflicts. When they're asking the fifth or sixth question, I realize that there's a long line of passengers behind me waiting to pass through customs control to take their respective flights. The young people say goodbye to me very effusively, thank me, wish me a good trip, and ask me to come back soon.

"Of course I'll come back soon," I lie, and continue loading my conscience down with guilt.

We still have a one-hour wait. We go up to the cafeteria. The air conditioning isn't working; there's a sticky heat and a smell of sweat, different kinds of suntan lotion, *café con chícharos* (coffee stretched with dried peas), burned toast, and greasy fried food. There are tourists roasted by the Varadero sun, some with sunburn blisters that will bring back memories weeks after they return to the inhospitable cold of Nordic countries. "The glory of the tropical sun," they'll report. They drink Hatuey beer or sip one last mojito before returning to their daily lives. I hear words in Dutch, German, French, and English. I try to follow the thread of one of the conversations. I can't concentrate. So many memories and so many thoughts pass through my mind that I'm overwhelmed.

And fear imposes itself constantly, the fear that someone might approach us to say that we're not permitted to travel, we must return home; there we'll be told the reasons.

I can't take this smelly, noisy atmosphere anymore.

"Let's go look at the shops downstairs," I suggest to Dani.

The shops are empty of customers but full of salesclerks conversing in groups. They barely allow me to look at the meager display of goods for sale when they pounce on me, bombarding me with questions. They address me as if I were their confidante, using the familiar *tu* form.

It seems that my last radio program, in which I discussed a subject especially difficult for Cubans, met with approval from most of the female public. I remember that it created a heated debate and aggressive telephone calls from some listeners as well as applause and congratulations from others. It was about the sexual needs of men and women and the rights of both to satisfy them. Some men called during the program to express their indignation, insulting me.

Others, apparently for the first time in their lives, had pondered the acceptability of my approach that women have the same sexual needs as men, that expression varies individually, and that satisfaction depends enormously on circumstances and environmental characteristics. I remember that I put a great deal of emphasis on such aspects as true love in place of mechanical competence, the exchange of caresses, tenderness, the need for mutual respect and consideration, and the prohibition on unacceptable demands and coercion in a couple's relations.

I had touched on a sore point for those men who follow a rigorous sexual agenda no matter what, without compassion for themselves or their partner, in accordance with the idea that men need to have sex every day, even if they don't feel like it or are sick, and the woman has to serve the man as an object. For a large part of the masculine population, sex is a mechanical function and a demonstration of manliness. If there's an unwanted pregnancy (for her), the man is confirmed as a potent stud and sends the woman to a hospital where she can get an abortion. After all, it's a routine operation that doesn't cost anything and that the doctors know how to perform well. The risks, dangers to the health, and, sometimes, the life of the mother: that's pure fabrication.

Ethical and moral considerations about abortion don't exist in the mind of men with macho attitudes and behavior, for whom "making love" means practicing a sexual sport, fulfilling a quota on a mattress, at the beach, in the grass, lying down, standing up, or floating in the water, and for whom the best "lover" is the guy who has on his list the greatest number of acts performed and names of the women he's conquered. I had launched a version of this content at a man who called me during this last radio show, boasting about having unmatched qualities in the amatory arena, complaining at the same time about the infantile desires— "absurd and immature," he put it—of many women who prefer cuddling to the magisterial function of "Mr. Penis."

The shop clerks are having a lively discussion about my arguments and those on the other side. There are differences, but no aggression. When I say goodbye, two women in the shop signal me to wait for them. The interested party, in need of counsel and orientation, obviously has delegated the other woman to represent her. With much dissimulation, she whispers her colleague's problem in my ear: she'd had an abortion a short time ago and now was pregnant again before the necessary time had passed to recover from the surgery. Of course, she doesn't want to bring this pregnancy to term either; her husband couldn't wait for the wounds caused by the abortion to heal, and being submissive and without strong willpower, she had given in to his demands.

And they keep me there again, only a few minutes away from ending my stay in Cuba, confronting the most frequent problem, the most contradictory and difficult to handle of the multiple problems I have encountered in my daily work of these last ten years: abortion. I feel sorry for this woman and at the same time indignation and frustration. How can so many Cuban women play with their health like that, knowing perfectly well that they risk grave harm, including the loss of their lives? And they always resort to magical thinking, worthy of a little kid: nothing's going to happen to me.

On a small piece of paper I write down the name, address, and telephone number of one of my ex-colleagues, a gynecologist who is not only competent but also experienced in helping women overcome conflicts of this importance. With one foot on the plane, I can't do anything now but delegate the whole task of trying to diminish the harm already done to this poor woman. I wish her much luck. Indeed, she's going to need it. With tears in her eyes, she thanks me and says goodbye.

There's still a half-hour before we're called to the departure gate. The woman in the kiosk that sells cigars, cigarettes, and books has observed my conversation with her colleagues in the shop and now wants her turn. After an affected panegyric, presented with elaborate words and exaggerated gestures (it seems she's using these oratorical flourishes in order to "enter into confidence"), María Antonia tells me about her matrimonial woes in a wealth of detail. Once more I am shocked by the familiarity and lack of inhibition of people I've never met and don't know who tell me about their most intimate experiences, wishes, adventures, and misadventures.

"My husband has nervous disturbances, and he takes several pills of Valium every day to stay calm. This helps him a lot, but when we want to make love, nature fails him, and he can't do it."

"If he could, it would be a miracle," I reply. "Did the doctor prescribe this amount of tranquilizer for him?"

"No, you're joking. You know they're in short supply. He's only getting a treatment based on blah-blah-blah, do this, do that, and the other, but without the medication he can't get better. Luckily he has a pharmacist friend who gets him the pills."

"I would say that unfortunately, since he's taking medication without medical supervision, far from solving his problem, this is making it even worse, and eventually it'll make it more difficult for him to get out of this vicious circle that's already been created.

Because Valium, in fact, prevents an erection, which means that even though he wants to do it, 'nature,' as you call it, will keep failing him."

María Antonia remains perplexed. She doesn't want to believe me. I explain to her how tranquilizers work.

"How awful! Then we're doing the exact opposite of what we should be doing!"

There's still a hint of incredulity in her voice. I point to the book *Man and Woman in Intimacy* (the publishing of which was one of my greatest professional accomplishments) on display in her kiosk, which she sells in dollars to foreign tourists. I suggest that she read the exact chapter on the matter of her interest.

"Show it to your husband too, so he knows he's not the only one with this problem, and the two of you together can overcome this difficult situation, which doesn't need any kind of medication, only a good dose of knowledge, will, sensitivity, and professional help."

Here I note down the name and telephone number of a good friend who can help them.

"She's very competent and discreet, and if you tell her I sent you, I'm sure she'll give you an appointment at short notice. And now I have to say goodbye because they're calling passengers to board the flight. I wish you much luck!"

"Hold on a second, Mónica, don't go yet. I want to ask you one more favor. Sign this book for me."

She removes one of the copies from the shelf and hands me a pen.

"But, María Antonia, this book isn't yours; it's merchandise that should be sold."

"Now that I know it also discusses our problem, this book is mine. You don't know how happy I am to have met and spoken with you. Come on, *muchacha*, I have to crown this luck with your signature on my book."

I do María Antonia the favor she requests so insistently. And she babbles words of thanks and gives me an effusive hug.

With this last signature on a book published in Cuba, with

the sensational circulation of 300,000 copies across the length and breadth of the country thanks to my persistent and tenacious struggle against the army of prudes, hypocrites, and bureaucrats who saw it as a capital menace to morals, a detonator of sexuality (as if in Cuba sexuality didn't explode every day), I am suddenly aware that an important stage in my life has ended, that I will never again have so much satisfaction in my professional life, nor suffer so many disappointments, fears, and disgust as those I've experienced since the work of sex education, counselling, and therapy became my daily battleground.

Nevermore would I be called "terrible," a "corruptor of minors," "sexually obsessed," "the defender of women," "queen of condoms," or, simply, "the Mónica of sex education," as I've often been called in place of my proper name. I would never again have to answer hundreds of letters or telephone calls from the most remote places in the country from people of the most diverse social strata, representing a spectrum of extraordinarily versatile sexual ideologies, quintessentially contradictory, and, frequently, truly folkloric.

I would no longer receive letters with insults and horrendous accusations that went beyond the pale. No one would find it necessary to resort to the most absolute anonymity to communicate his morbid fantasies to me by cutting letters from newspapers and creating genuine works of collage. Nor would I continue receiving requests for help, or announced and unannounced visits. Now no one would ask me questions during the brief time before a streetlight changed, on the way to the cafeteria, or in line at the grocery store. Never again would I enter a television or radio studio to have a live, person-to-person dialogue with a large audience. "Mónica" with a *c* would cease to exist and become again "Monika" with a *k*: a small difference but one that involves a change like night into day.

My metamorphosis from a lion to a rat has now occurred. A terrible ambivalence seizes me as I pass from the bus to the plane. I suddenly begin to feel a nostalgia for the island that still today, many years after my exit, has not left me. I believe it will never abandon me. I continue dreaming in Spanish as well as in German. When I speak with my sons, we mix the two languages, jumping from one to the other without realizing it. Friends who are present at these encounters are amazed. They can't understand such a radical, magical change they see in us when we go from German to Cuban Spanish, when from a slow, well-articulated language that doesn't allow making faces or the athletic use of arms and legs to establish an understandable communication, we fall into our *cubano*, increasing the volume and speed of our voices as if we are talking machine guns, accompanying our verbosity with movements of our whole bodies.

The most insignificant news from Cuba provokes intense dreams at night. I wake up exhausted, sweating, sometimes crying, sometimes laughing, and with relief I tell myself, They're only dreams. I get up, and in the shower the voltage has changed from 110 to 220. I leave for work a German woman from head to foot, as if Cuba had never existed in my life. But the island is omnipresent. When I'm least expecting it, Cuba overtakes me, tortures me, pursues me, makes me happy and sad at the same time, and exercises an enchantment over me that permits me now to understand the vacillating attitude of Spanish-Cubans: If I die in Havana, bury me in Madrid, and if I die in Madrid, bury me in Havana.

CHAPTER TWO

HELLO, GERMANY

Finally, after so much time wasted, with my nerves on edge, we're boarding the plane. We're on one of the last flights of the former East Germany's Interflug. Weeks later, this company will become part of Lufthansa, leaving hundreds of employees laid off and suffering. After the euphoria over the reunification of Germany will come the head-on collision with the dark side, for them, of the still-unknown capitalist system.

Some friendly flight attendants (had they received an intensive course in taking care of the public?) welcome us and distribute brochures and German newspapers. My first reading of the dailies from unified Germany! Everything is new, everything is different. Preparing for take-off, the crew introduces itself to the passengers. With names, surnames, and the specification of their corresponding responsibilities. Who has seen such a thing on previous flights? They inform us in detail about the trip's features.

"Right now we're flying over Varadero, the most beautiful beach in the world."

This tells me that in approximately half an hour we'll be coming to the Bahamas. Until we're there, we can't feel secure about having accomplished our getaway, because who's going to tell us then that because of a technical defect the plane has to return to Cuba? Once we fly over the Bahamas, we'll drink a toast, since there's no return. Even if a failure occurs, or a situation that requires an emergency landing, it will happen on North American territory, since Interflug flights coming from Cuba are now allowed to land anywhere.

I'm still tense. Dani tries to distract me. I'm not paying attention. He could be talking to the wall for all it matters. I still can't believe that we carried out our project without any mishap, I, who was nicknamed "Jinx" for the innumerable accidents—some almost fatal—I suffered during my almost three decades in Cuba, with my friends from work warning everyone not to go out with me anywhere ("With Mónica, you won't even make it to the next corner."); it's unbelievable that I could pull off such a grand undertaking. And to top it all off, this time it involved a totally individual act of self-determination, of violating the established norms, of betrayal and deception. I abused important people who helped me, who got Dani and me the exit permits thinking we were going to spend our vacation with my mother, not knowing that we would remain abroad. And this was the thanks they get. I'm sure they'll think I'm disgraceful and despicable.

By now I was so adapted to being a Cuban with a herd personality, having to think and act in plural (the use of "we" was institutionalized), that I had become a person with a collective opinion, who followed Party guidelines, who even had feelings of guilt, of ingratitude, of being a freak, of being disloyal for having decided all by myself, without asking permission from anyone, to go down this path.

I confess that my guilt complex lasted a long time, until finally, with the help of family and friends, after truly psychotherapeutic discussions with them, I began to reestablish my ego and act on personal matters without authorization from "the higher authorities." I came to understand that resorting to tricks, deception, and breaking the rules are legitimate actions if one finds oneself in a situation in which individual rights and self-determination are restricted. I consigned my shame to hell and stopped disparaging myself and self-censoring. Now I didn't care what my Cuban ex-bosses might say. Once your reputation is ruined, you might as well do what you want.

"The lights you can observe from both sides of our plane belong to the Bahamas," announces the captain of our Airbus, and he continues to inform us in detail about the next stretch of the flight.

"Dani, it worked! Do you realize that we've done it?"

I open all the escape valves. After months of tension, fear, uncertainty, and ambivalence, an enormous exhaustion, physical and mental, comes over me. I feel terribly tired, yet for the first time in years, calm and relaxed. The flight continues smoothly. We land in Berlin, right on time, the day after our departure.

It's November, the saddest, darkest, wettest month of the year in Germany. The bare trees stretch their black and naked branches to the sky. It rains and rains—a drizzle that never seems to stop. Microscopic drops of frozen water stick to my face, and I hurry to find shelter under an overhanging roof.

So many years of sun, heat, permanent sweat day and night, have charged the batteries of my organism with reserves of fuel for the long term. I feel like new, with energy to take on the world. I am going to need this strength, and it begins with my arrival in Germany, almost thirty years after moving to Cuba. Uncertain years lie ahead of me, difficult and full of surprises, surprises that will certainly bring me joy and satisfaction at times (I am an optimist by nature and believe in the good in people and in happiness), but also many problems and difficulties. However, I have made this decision, and there's no point in crying over spilled milk.

The first days in Berlin are filled with the search for solutions for the three of us: my older son Dictys, Dani, and me. Dictys had been staying with my brother for three weeks. His authorized vacation from his former employer, the news agency Prensa Latina (PRELA), has ended, and he is expected to return to Havana. Because he didn't, they performed against him, in *absentia*, with the required participation of all his colleagues at PRELA, an "act of repudiation" for treason, for selling out his country, for surrendering to the capitalist enemy, and he received the "honorary" title of "scum," reserved for those who dare to make their own decisions, not dictated by the higher authorities. A few weeks later, a colleague who had taken part in that act of repudiation went into exile in Canada and told him about it in detail.

For a year, Dictys had been head of the agency in Nicaragua, in the midst of a civil war and with the country preparing for the first elections authorized by Ortega's government. He had a work passport with entry visas for Nicaragua and permanent permission to leave Cuba, so it was easy for him to abandon the island. Instead of returning to PRELA, he stayed in Berlin, where, after weeks of polishing doorknobs, making the rounds of agencies, institutions, companies, and businesses of the most diverse nature to offer his services, he had to accept a frustrating reality: There already existed in Berlin an army of highly qualified journalists without employment. So he'd come to the conclusion that he would have to steer his working life in another direction, thereby verifying the opinion he'd expressed at the beginning of his studies in the inhospitable city of Moscow that "My degree is sanctimonious shit, but that's what was indicated for me in my ration book. I had no choice; I was to study what was destined for me or nothing at all." Nevertheless, it was painful for him to have to give up his profession and start over.

Dani has made his own plans: He will return to his university in Dresden, where he studied mathematics, and apply to continue with PhD studies. When this kid was born he hit the ground running. A few days after our arrival in Berlin, he presented himself before the Scientific Council; they granted him a scholarship, and his immediate future was assured.

As for me, my professional problems take an ugly turn, and sooner than I expected, I'm forced to accept the irreversible fact that I've gone from being someone who is known in the most remote corners of Cuba to total and complete anonymity. My work tools—a specialized book and video library, research protocols, pre- and post-graduate medical education programs; in a nutshell, everything I needed for the normal exercise of my profession—was left behind in Havana. When I made the decision to return to my roots, I feared that this decision would put an end to my professional life and that I'd have to earn a living doing something else, relying on my knowledge of foreign languages and forgetting the rest.

"You have to offer your education, skills, aptitudes, and assistance (even if it's more lie than truth) on a golden platter," counsel the connoisseurs of this subject, and they teach me a series of things to do that should be sure prescriptions for finding work. Almost thirty years in Cuba have made me useless as far as any real knowledge of a capitalist system goes. I know absolutely nothing about taxes, insurance, labor laws, rights, and possibilities. How ignorant I am; I miss many opportunities that are available only to someone who knows how to seize them.

I become a specialist in writing job applications. Dozens of letters, with corresponding documents attesting to my qualifications, former professional activities, and accumulated experience, land on the desks of corporate personnel departments, research and assistance centers, and other places involving some form of work I know how to do.

I am experiencing the sad reality that even with all the university degrees to my credit I'm not going to get anywhere. The unemployment rate in Germany is skyrocketing as a result of the merger of East and West. There's an interesting documentary about unemployed German academics—a physics professor making potato fritters and selling them in a kiosk, a biologist working for a company that collects litter in public areas, and a lawyer working half-time as a secretary. And then this character comes along, who has two doctorates and knows seven languages that are not good for anything and earns only enough to rent a room that's more like a rabbit hutch.

The reality sweeps away any illusions and shows me the extent of my problem, and to all this I have to add the fact that I'm about to turn fifty. Who would even think about finding a job at this age? German women who have worked a normal amount of time are retiring at sixty. Only an ignorant person, like me, fallen from the moon, has the illusion that what's important is knowledge, not age. Don't we have a head of state who is ten years older than I am, who is confident that he will be reelected again in the next elections?

The universities reject me for not having had teaching experience in Germany. My beloved University of Rostock, where I began my degree and passed my doctoral defense successfully, is immersed in a painful process of restructuring, dissolving institutes of international renown, and dismissing academics who have brought it fame. There's no place for me there.

And Cuba remains so far away, awakening in people only associations with beaches, sun, rum, cigars, music, and beautiful mulattas. Nobody has ever heard of an extensive national program, systematic education, guidance, and sex therapy on the island. People don't want to believe what I tell them, and finally the answer to my inquiries about the possibility of employment is summed up by: "Here in Germany, the focus, laws, philosophy—actually everything—is different."

There are no openings in welfare work for family planning, education, counseling, or sex therapy; they belong to the unproductive sector. There aren't enough resources to be able to supply the consultation and assistance needs of the poor, and the rich have their own private therapists. They don't need a German-Cuban who doesn't know anything about the new world into which she's just arrived.

Someone recommends that I find a source of financing to become independent, so I can open my own consulting service. I'm realistic enough to know that this idea could never become reality, since the required source of financing doesn't exist. Hoping to win the lottery seems too uncertain to me, since I've never in my life won anything in organized school raffles, in the neighborhood, or in charitable activities. In Cuba, playing the lottery is prohibited. They threw my sister-in-law in jail for one day because they caught her playing Monopoly with a neighbor. Instead of money they were using black beans, which were worth more than the Cuban pesos in circulation at that time. So in Cuba I forgot how to play the lottery, and here in Germany I lacked the money to do it. The few times I participated, they discriminated against me systematically. Never, ever, have I won, save for one time when the amount of the prize covered exactly the cost of the ticket.

"You don't have any inheritance in sight?" ask friends who want to see me better off. On the horizon no fortune is visible, and analyzing my German family's situation realistically, I understand that I can't hope for miracles.

The employment office in Hamburg, where I've moved, recommends that I take a job as a German-language teacher for refugees, the unfortunate citizens of the world, and for Russian-German and Polish repatriates who, before receiving permission to work in Germany, have to learn the language. I accept gladly, even knowing that the salary—one-fourth of the official rate I should be receiving—doesn't even begin to be enough.

My students are divided into two groups, one composed of people who already speak the language somewhat fluently but have to perfect their knowledge in order to set about finding work, possibly in a sector at least similar to the trade they were practicing in their earlier lives. The other group consists of men and women who are illiterate or don't know the Latin alphabet, all of them on a low cultural level, each and every one born and brought up under inhuman, authoritarian, and despotic regimes that crush individuality. As a consequence, their psyches are severely damaged, and they don't understand the concept of tolerating differences. They suffer immeasurable tortures now that they're immersed in a world that is open, multicultural, and with freedoms that they don't understand and to which they are not accustomed.

The first group of students presents no problem; they just follow the rigorous program established by the principal's office. The work with the second, the illiterates, however, becomes an

2. *Monika with her sons Dani and Dictys in Berlin in the early 1990s*

enormous challenge. In Cuba, I arrived too late to be able to take part in the literacy campaign. I had never even considered the possibility of making a contribution as a literacy teacher in one of the most developed countries in the world. It appears that fate has assigned me missions that are truly bizarre.

The school isn't prepared to give special attention to my group and thus free itself of the inconvenient commitment to give these marginalized people German language classes. It grants me almost total power over the content of my classes, as long as I achieve the goal: the students must at a minimum learn how to write their name, read rudimentary texts (street names), identify modes of public transportation, read the prices of products in the market, and articulate in a way that will let them manage the most elementary communication without the help of an interpreter.

We're having a lot of fun in my group of illiterates. I improvise and constantly invent engaging approaches. My pupils speak Kurdish, Polish, Russian, Afghani, Bulgarian, Persian, Turkish, Arabic, and Chinese. None of them knows the customs, traditions, or language of the others, and they all idealize their far-away homelands that caused them so much suffering.

The youngest is forty-five years old; the oldest, seventy. All have endured the most unimaginable vicissitudes: tortures, persecution, banishment, war, terror, and exile. All of them are ill, their nervous systems destroyed; the few nerves that keep them healthy are irremediably damaged in the daily struggle against the insurmountable, unattainable, world-renowned, and implacable German bureaucracy. I, who was born in this country, learned from tender infancy the rules of the game: the ability to coexist, the language, the culture. I feel like I'm on another planet, because three decades in the Cuban ambience have warped me. How, then, must these poor unfortunates feel, my illiterate students who don't speak the language or understand absolutely anything, but from whom the host country requires full compliance with all its norms and laws?

Every day brings another document from the employment office, from social security, from immigration, from the police, from the department for non-citizens. I was never interested in studying law, but now I see the need to read a stack of regulatory provisions, and then, whether I know them or not, without apologies or excuses, adhere to the codes, laws, and existing regulations, as Germany demands. In Cuba, the same as everyone around me, I was used to solving problems by resorting to some ploy, trick, or finding a back door with the help of some colleague, friend, or friend of a friend ("he who has a friend has everything" is true in Cuba), to clear the road of landslides, legal impediments, and—many times—the petty minds of self-important bureaucrats. But in Germany this doesn't work.

Fines can ruin the richest person if he dares transgress the law. Even today I can't explain how this German system possibly works, but it does (gossips say that the French incubate the law, the Italians die laughing when they learn about it, and the

Germans comply with it). My students are perhaps having horrible nightmares about what they experienced under bloody and dictatorial regimes, and the torture and physical misery are now replaced by papers that carry implicit threats and punishments. With trembling hands they bring me a letter whose sender is one of the country's (to them) fearsome institutions. Without exception, the letters contain some accusation, fine, or condemnation because the addressee didn't comply with one or another rule. I become my students' lawyer; I fight with the authorities whose job, to all appearances, consists of always being right and guaranteeing order among these people who, for bureaucrats, constitute chaos perfected.

I now include psychotherapy in my teaching program. That way, my gray cells don't atrophy, and I make sure my students feel protected from bureaucratic persecution. At least during German classes they can set aside their legal problems. The classroom feels like an oasis to them; they are unworried, secure, and—sometimes the most important thing—understood and respected by their professor, whom they adore. We understand each other without anyone speaking the other's language. When there is aggression in the atmosphere because one side makes fun of the other—telling them they stink of garlic or hurling racial slurs at the ones who eat pork—I do everything possible to keep the discussion civil, so it doesn't end in physical assaults.

From Monday to Friday they have to endure six hours of daily classes. They are used to tough physical labor, but picking up a pen between their fingers and writing some words makes them sweat, and sometimes they have true attacks of depression. When Yuri's hand stiffens, he emits a cry that enters my bloodstream. He contemptuously throws the pen across the classroom, and in Russian, mixed with some German words, he stammers:

"I can't take this torture anymore. My whole life I worked in the fields. I was plowman and horse at the same time. In forty below zero weather I had to be outside, and in order not to die of cold, I had to work, move, carry heavy loads. And here they're having me scribble stupid letters that I don't need."

It's not easy for me to console Yuri. I take his stiff hand, massage it, and whisper to him in the three words of Russian I still remember from my school days, managing to make him laugh. We stop what we're doing, and everyone does relaxation exercises, accompanied by a children's song that they like a lot and learn with enthusiasm, like kids in a childcare center. Every night, when I'm preparing the next day's class, I create guessing games to make learning more fun, more bearable. We play the game of remembering images. I share the praise and placate the angry, who sometimes despair when their memory betrays them or when their clumsy hand doesn't want to write legible letters.

Yuri now knows how to write his name, and he can sign documents in his own hand. I find that this old peasant, a field worker descended from Germans, recruited by Tsarina Catherine the Great to cultivate the virgin lands and shores of the Volga, later expelled from his new land by Stalin's followers, tortured, sent to extermination camps or to Siberia during the Second World War, and now returned to Germany, learns more quickly than I would have imagined. When I give him the assignment to write his last name (composed of eight letters) five times, I see him put his initials five times.

"Yuri, why don't you write down your complete last name?" I ask.

"It's too long; it's enough like that," he answers. "Otherwise, it will go over the line."

Meanwhile, I've learned how to live comfortably and affordably. The owner of a house in one of the most exclusive neighborhoods in Hamburg gives me the whole lower floor. Her condition is that I do not change anything and leave all the furniture and knick-knacks in their places. The woman is ninety years old and has lived through the terror of two world wars and the world economic crises that have ruined the country. She has known the reemergence of a strong nation, but she still has her suspicions and fear. In the cellar, she keeps a stash of canned goods produced shortly after the war—that is, in the middle of the century—"just in case." She doesn't even let her son, who takes care of the routine repairs and garbage collection, touch her store of reserves.

Yet again, I feel I'm faced with a regime of despotism and subordination, almost like in Cuba. Of course I'll pay the rent, because the house where I'm living is almost ideal, but I have to admit that the cheap, worn-out furniture that smells old and dirty would be an insult to anyone. I try, diplomatically, to persuade *Madame* to allow me to introduce some changes. She stands firm. Never in my life have I had to resort to tricks, deception, and other unconventional resources in order to make my dwelling minimally pleasant.

I take advantage of her absence for a few days to sand the wood floor. My son and a cousin, a German who is almost seven feet tall, red-bearded, with blue eyes and the strength of a bull, join the conspiracy. We rent a sanding machine that weighs more than I do, makes a racket that could wake the dead, and devours—if I don't operate it correctly—the complete floor. I try to guide it, but it lifts me like a feather. I have to ask my helpers to maneuver the machine, which is hungry for pine, and in a matter of three hours I have shiny a new floor that smells like a forest.

If I could dump the junk that passes for furniture in the trash, my living quarters would be perfect, but I can't risk a war with the landlady. I have to fire up my imagination, make some calculations, and buy fabric, chairs, and lots of plants to camouflage the ugliness. Naturally, I also want to throw some of the more geriatric items in the basement, certain that *Madame* will never remove them—hoping that if I'm lucky she won't notice my transgressions.

Days later, after my masterwork is completed, *Madame* returns from her vacation. It seems that some tattletale neighbor has told her about the noise, the people going in and out with tools, and the junk that had been tampered with during her absence. She greets me coldly and wants to see the living space. Her eyes widen.

"But what is this? Everything has changed—the floor, what did you do to the floor?"

"*Madame*, don't you see how nice the floor looks?" I reply, like a little girl caught with her hand in the cookie jar.

"Yes, but I didn't give you authorization, and you didn't inform me about anything. You took advantage of my absence to do all this behind my back."

Only after I assure her that I'll take care of the entire cost does she comment, with her head raised arrogantly.

"Who would ever want this blue color? It costs too much."

"Yes, exactly," is the only thing I can think of to say.

My "home" begins to fill up little by little. Friends give me dishes, kitchen gadgets, and, above all, books. A stereo radio and record player is the first big gift from my sons for Christmas. I begin to create—how many times have I done this by now?—a library and a collection of records. If it weren't for the miserable salary from the language school, which doesn't allow me even to breathe, I would be happy.

In the school, rumors are spreading that they're thinking about closing, because the employment office isn't extending the contract. My inquiries induces me to look for another job, since I don't have money to live if they lay me off. In addition, I need to accumulate more years of work to be able to receive, at age sixty-one, the minimum pension, since my three decades of work in Cuba don't count toward retirement.

In the Hamburg newspaper I find an offer of employment at a company that supplies products for ships. They need a translator-interpreter and secretary for the general management and technical management offices. In the advertisement, they specify that the candidate doesn't need to have technical knowledge, that command of Spanish, English, German, and French is required, and that all the rest will be taught on the job. This job has been created for me! I write my routine application letter and send it, along with all the rigorous documents required, to the address given in the ad. Hardly has my letter been delivered when the manager of the company calls and invites me to come in for an interview.

The head of personnel speaks with me briefly, and I sense a strange movement behind me—I'm seated with my back to the open door of the meeting room. Of course, I can't turn around to see what's happening. Later, they tell me that my request for the job of translator, interpreter, and secretary immediately raised a cloud of curiosity and surprise among the directors of the business. The technical director, who is the manager most interested in my becoming his underling, speaks to me as if I'm his collaborator. Suddenly a woman comes in and introduces herself, but I don't get her last name, so I don't realize that she's the manager and owner of the business. She looks and speaks to me as if I'm a rare bird. Several times she repeats the same question.

"Are you sure you lived for almost three decades in Cuba? My God, how could you spend so much time in that country?"

Also present is the fourth member of management, a specialist in finance, whose head is full of numbers printed on hard-currency bills, and who is also dying of curiosity to see this phenomenon who wants to work in his company.

After a little while we're already talking about the content of my new mission. My future bosses die laughing when I explain to them that I've never worked with a computer, that I have no idea what a fax is, and that never in my life have I used a rotary telephone to make an international call since that was the responsibility of the operator in Cuba. They assure me, chuckling and good-naturedly ribbing me, that there's no need to worry, they'll teach me everything.

The first day of work is such a huge nightmare that never, even if I live to be as old as Methuselah, will I forget it. Every other minute some colleague comes through my office on some pretext to see this strange creature; they whisper, laugh, and look at me. I feel like a monkey in the zoo—at least I imagine an animal would feel this way in such circumstances. The technical director, the finance officer, the owner, and perhaps worst of all, a business consultant with a warped personality (a jealous man, fearful I could learn too much and dethrone him) invent problems and overwhelm me with tasks that are mainly absurd and contradictory, totally outside my area of competence, and drive me mad. Before the first day ends, I already want to leave and never return. The promises to teach me my new job go up in smoke; instead they give me orders, most of them impossible to fulfill.

I've never before known an atmosphere at work where there is such a great desire to pick on, humiliate, and make life impossible for another person. I know now that there are institutions, associations, and therapy centers that repair the psychological harm done to people by the attitudes and aggressive, destructive behavior of bosses or work colleagues.

Once again I hear the whisper of the inner demon that tells me to throw in the towel, but I resist, since I have a firm contract and a salary that allows me to live with dignity, with all my needs met. Those who know more about a free-economy environment reassure me:

"You'll get used to it, and soon you'll be on top of things and be able to laugh at the people who are now torturing you."

I don't want to believe them. I can't imagine that I'll be capable of taking this tension for long, but we human beings have unsuspected reserves and resources to protect ourselves. On the way to work I now start to prepare myself psychologically for the struggle. I spend a whole minute hating each one of my torturers. I imagine them in ridiculous situations and feel stronger. And it happens, just as my friends predict: I'm on top of things.

I develop the hide of an elephant. I accept orders, but now I'm the one who decides whether or not to carry them out, at my discretion. I delegate to other colleagues those matters which aren't my responsibility, and we establish a level of endurable coexistence. In order to stay sharp, I take advantage of every available minute to write my story. I remain in the office at night to have a catharsis, hammering on the keyboard. It feels like this is the best response to my sufferings at work. The proverb "every cloud has a silver lining" becomes my mantra.

PART TWO
THE SIXTIES

CHAPTER THREE
IN THE BEGINNING

THE NEW ACADEMIC YEAR began on September 1, 1961. Two weeks earlier, on August 13, the Berlin Wall had been constructed. I was pursuing my third year in Latin American Studies, a specialty recently established by East Germany in order to prepare specialists for the expansion of socialist Germany's political, economic, and socio-cultural relations in Latin America.

Our group, six students at the national level, five women and one man, were true guinea pigs, since we were the first privileged academics, *la crème de la crème*, selected to study this totally new specialty: five years of intensive study, in which the most ridiculous experiments conducted by ambitious professors, under the permanent supervision and vigilance of the Party Central Committee, turned our dreams into interminable nightmares. As far as I knew, at this time there were no antecedents for a course of study so charged with subjects: Spanish, Portuguese, and French language and literature; the history of Spain and Portugal; the history of Latin America; economic policy; Marxism-Leninism; philosophical currents from Spain and Latin America; sociology, translation, and interpretation; editing and composition—just to mention the most important. Everyone envied us, since our studies were associated with the dream of being able to travel, see distant countries, and escape from the narrow circle of the socialist community.

When I began my studies, Fidel Castro had been in power for a little over half a year. At that moment I could not even remotely imagine that for three decades, the Cuban Revolution would determine my direction and my life.

During the first two years of our basic studies we barely heard the word "Cuba." The island was associated with a terrifying song I had learned as a child from street friends. It went like this:

"The Negroes in Cuba are rebelling / Gunshots break the afternoon's silence / The drumbeats are announcing death / The cries of the dying are heard everywhere / Bloody, massacred bodies remain in the streets."

I remember that when my friends sang that song, with gestures and fearful voices, with the morbid desire to terrorize me, my hair stood on end, and I screamed with fear at night.

When the Rebel Army and the Popular Militias, led by Fidel Castro, triumphed at the Bay of Pigs, the University of Rostock organized an assembly with the students from Latin America. At a screening of the famous documentary about this battle filmed by the Cuban Institute of Cinematographic Art and Industry (ICAIC), I saw—for the first time in my life—the temperament, the fire, and the enthusiasm of Latinos. In Germany, you would never yell or applaud at the movies. Once the documentary began, the audience screamed at the top of their lungs; the applause and the uproar—totally normal phenomena for Latinos, I later learned—had us Germans confused and giddy. I felt like I was among people from another planet. I think this unforgettable encounter set the stage for my intensive interest in Cuba.

Every student in our microcosmic group had to individually analyze and study particular aspects of two countries in Latin America. We could choose the two countries and determine the order of priority. I chose Cuba as the first country of importance in my study program.

During the completion of a semester's work in Berlin, which lasted several weeks, I spent many days in the state library, searching for information on the island. I reviewed hundreds of magazines, newspapers, and books from many different sources. At that time they still allowed us to review publications coming from the West, under the supervision and strict control, of course, of the library's employees. I filled at least a dozen notebooks with notes, and I wrote my first short monograph about Cuba.

By the time I met the youngest captain in the world (he was twenty-two, a founder of the merchant marine in revolutionary Cuba) in that month of September 1961, a few days after the beginning of the new academic year, I was already a "specialist and connoisseur" of the Cuban revolutionary process.

The captain was working in the Rostock shipyard, in my city, supervising the final construction on the flagship of the Cuban merchant marine. He and a small group of his officers frequented our institute's library, which was endowed with the most important and prominent works of literature, philosophy, and history of Spain, Portugal, France, and Latin America. It was unrivaled by anything in the shipyards for satisfying a thirst for reading in their native tongue.

One of our professors, in his time off, played the role of interpreter for the shipyards' management. It was he who devised a plan for us to practice our Spanish with the Cuban officers. By the way, all of our Spanish professors were German; they spoke an outdated Spanish and were as much in need of practicing the language with people coming from Spanish-speaking countries as we students were.

We were thrilled with the proposal.

Never before had a meeting been organized in such a short time. We invited the captain and his small group of officers to come to our institute to converse, and then later, to go dancing. We didn't have to worry about our budget; the university premises were at our disposal for free, and the restaurants at that time didn't offer any fancy dishes, only a few inexpensive plates, as economical as they were basic and boring. The two or three better restaurants in Rostock had combos, which began performing at five in the afternoon and played music that was danceable and typically provincial. This seemed wonderful to us.

The first part of our improvised meeting began quite stiffly.

Both groups were curious, nervous, and insecure. Seated in a circle, we introduced ourselves and forced ourselves to keep an understandable conversation going in Spanish. During this activity, I began to doubt for the first time whether what our guests were speaking was Spanish. These doubts would continue—later in Cuba—for months. We couldn't find any similarity between the Spanish of our guests and what we were speaking and had learned in five semesters of intensive study. So it was hard to follow the thread of the conversation. However, very soon we felt as if we were among friends. We didn't understand the jokes they told, but when they laughed, so did we, like little kids who applaud the antics of older ones.

At my right was seated the captain; at my left, the official interpreter for the shipyards, in charge on this day of handling our guests. That interpreter is the man who was responsible for my living in Cuba for almost thirty years. He was skinny and ugly, with huge ears and rabbit's teeth, but in addition to these physical defects, which weren't his fault, he was appallingly clingy. He had chosen me to practice his pick-up routine on, pretending he was in love with me in the most ineffective way imaginable. It all landed on me like a lead balloon, and his crude perseverance, in poor taste and unequaled boorishness, annoyed me. I wasn't willing to continue putting up with this individual, so I started talking to the captain, ignoring the interpreter. Don't ask me how I managed to understand the captain and make myself understood, but we understood each other beautifully in "Germish." Naturally, we showed our best sides to each other and had a lot of fun.

The moment to go dancing arrived. We waited for the tram. When it came, the interpreter and two friends from our group got on. We managed to play a trick on the big-eared interpreter, and he was trapped on the tram while the other two got off before it pulled away.

"Get on, hurry up!" the poor interpreter yelled, and when we noticed that the tram began to move and he couldn't leave, we yelled back.

"We'll see you at the zoo stop!"

The stop for the zoo was the last one. We walked to the restaurant, which was two blocks away from the institute. The captain and I sat down in a corner, far away from the dance floor. The officers and the rest of our group danced all evening and into the night. For me, this first encounter with the captain was the most intensive Spanish class I'd experienced up to then, and I knuckled down like never before in order to look good.

We fell in love very quickly. I began to experience a state of mind totally unknown to me before. For the first time in my life, I forgot that I was studying, that I had obligations. We met every day after class. We walked for miles around the university village, through the woods and nearby parks. The rain didn't bother us; neither did the cold or the dark. I thought no one had ever existed before who would change the world so radically and rapidly, who would transform Cuba into a true paradise, like we all imagined at that time—fantasizing, talking, debating, and feeling we were participants in a truly revolutionary and humanistic process.

And so passed the end of summer and autumn, and winter began. The test voyage of the new ship was scheduled for the week of Christmas, and then it would sail to Cuba.

The captain said goodbye. We were engaged. We agreed to get married during his next stay in Rostock, in April of 1962.

Our romance might have been called a modern-day Romeo and Juliet, and fortunately, it didn't end like the two young lovers in Shakespeare. I walked around like a zombie, in a daze of hope and happiness. I took classes and attended seminars, but I was only physically present, while my fantasies took flight. I was very lucky during that trance that I didn't have an important exam since I don't think I would have passed it.

Near our philosophy classroom was an old church that possessed a treasure, a jewel from Nordic artisans: an eighteenth-century organ. The theology students practiced their ecclesiastical music there, bringing forth from this instrument majestic, moving sounds. How I enjoyed those free concerts that helped me enter my world of fantasy, pouring fuel on my burning soul.

My professors' lectures slid by without entering my brain. For weeks, I didn't learn a thing in my classes. While they spoke, inebriated with their own erudition, I was inebriated with love, filling dozens of sheets of paper, writing letters to my captain, dreaming in broad daylight about my wedding and my new life in Cuba.

On December 24, 1961, in my parents' house, I was helping my mother prepare dinner for Christmas Eve and the holidays that came after, when the doorbell rang for a long time, forcefully. At this hour on this day, no one was expected who wasn't already present, so my mother gave me a sidelong glance, as though asking me if I knew who could be interrupting our work. I looked through the window and saw a taxi moving away through a mountain of snow, clearing a path behind it. I opened the door, and there was the captain, standing in front of me. He had been on the test voyage with his new ship, and now it had returned to the shipyard for a few days to have some things corrected. My love took advantage of this unforeseen stay to get to know the place and the house where I was born, and to introduce himself to my parents.

My parents hadn't been aware of our adventures, our wanderings, our love affair, or our romance of, by now, some months. Two years ago, my father had committed an unforgivable indiscretion, telling his friends about a very intimate matter that I had confided to him, and since that time I had never again spoken to him about my personal life. My brother, the only family member who knew about my plans, had agreed with me and kept his mouth shut.

The captain asked to speak to me alone. He told me that he wanted to ask my parents if they would permit us to marry. It wouldn't have mattered if I had answered that in Germany, a grown woman (like I was) didn't need to ask permission of her parents to get married, that this was our decision, his and mine, and no one else's. He insisted. *Well, he IS Latino*, I thought.

I didn't have the slightest idea how the captain was going to phrase his request. We took a long walk—the last for many years—through the woods, my dear childhood forest, which had been transformed into a beautiful, white, enchanting landscape. The trees were flocked in thick coats of snow, and we sunk up to our knees in a carpet of dazzling flakes. While we walked, in a temperature of twenty degrees, we debated in detail about how and when he would ask my parents for permission to marry me.

On our return to the house, everything was prepared for the Christmas Eve celebration. Before my father could give the signal to start our traditional ceremony, my captain asked to speak with him and my mother. On top of the oddness of all this, I had to act as the interpreter. I didn't know where to look; I wanted the earth to swallow me, but nothing of the sort happened. The captain warned me:

"Don't even try to invent something that I'm not saying. You have to translate literally and, above all, fully!"

After the revelation, there was a crushing silence. My parents looked at me as if they didn't know me. What they had just heard left them dumbfounded and stunned.

"To tell you the truth, this is a big surprise. Of course, I can't stop you from marrying my daughter, but how do you plan to procced? She's in the third year of her university courses; she needs two more to finish her studies. I don't think that everything we've done for her and for us should be thrown away just like that so she can leave and marry you. I'm imposing one condition: that my daughter finish her university courses, no matter where, either in Germany or on the other side of the Atlantic. Right now, she's blinded by love; who knows when she'll recover her sanity. She has to be able to support herself, and for that she has to have a career. So give me your word and promise me that this will happen."

My captain accepted and fulfilled his promise.

Thus passed the most extraordinary Christmas Eve of my life. My parents had discovered that we were thinking seriously about getting married, and that with this decision, one day in the near future, I would be leaving Germany and them to start a new life five thousand miles away, across a big pond that wasn't easily jumped.

I was excited, crazy in love, a brainless being lacking any type of reasoning power.

On my first day of work after the Christmas holidays, I went to the civil registry office to take care of the paperwork required to allow me to get married and leave the country.

"I want to get married next April. What do I have to do to get everything ready for a specific day? My fiancé is a ship's captain, and he can only be here two days before the date."

"There's no problem. You're of legal age. You just have to present your birth certificates and identity cards, and it can all be organized on short notice. For sailors we make exceptions. The paperwork won't take long. Everything will be taken care of much sooner than for people on land who have more time," replied the officer at the civil registry office.

I hadn't imagined it would be so easy. To be completely sure that I heard everything correctly, I repeated in my own words all the details that the official had just explained to me and, in passing, mentioned that the captain couldn't present his identity card because he only had a passport.

"But that's not a problem, right?"

"What do you mean he doesn't have an identity card?"

"Well, he really does have one, but he doesn't bring it with him; when he's on the ship he has to carry his passport, so he leaves his card at home."

"Okay, you can get the card and show it to me later, but now I'll go ahead with this matter. Here are some forms that I need you to fill out with your information and that of your fiancé, so we can save time, since the paperwork will be done while he's out to sea. When he returns, he only needs to sign the documents, and, a day later, you can get married. Of course, for the ceremony, the formal marriage certificate, he has to be present."

I sat down and began to fill out the forms. I knew the captain's information by heart. It didn't take me long to complete the documents. I handed the papers to the official, and he started to read them. Suddenly, he frowned, shook his head, and his face turned bright red like a giant poppy flower. He couldn't contain himself and yelled at me.

"Are you making fun of me? I'm a public official, not a circus clown! Do you realize where you are?"

I was really scared and babbled like the neighborhood idiot.

"But sir, what did I do, what happened?"

"Don't act stupid. You didn't tell me that the person you want to marry is a foreigner."

He spit out this last word as if it caused him physical harm to pronounce it.

"Yes, he's a Spanish and Cuban citizen; he lives in Cuba, and his documents are totally in order."

"I don't give a rat's ass about his documents."

And after filling his lungs with air, a lot of air, the officer began to give a speech in which he gesticulated and raised his voice to give full rein to his indignation.

"And you pretend to be a university student. You're a fool, as if you didn't know that marriage with foreigners is prohibited. Berlin's anti-imperialist wall has existed since the middle of last year. Any trip to a capitalist country is prohibited."

I dared to interrupt him.

"But Cuba is a socialist country."

"You don't say. Do you know that the wall is still open there? That every day hundreds of Cuban citizens go to the U.S.? You could well be one of those who under the pretext of getting married to a Cuban is looking for a way to escape to Miami. If you insist on wanting to marry this man, it'll be the end of your university career, and you'll end up cleaning public toilets. You'll NEVER get out of East Germany. You'll NEVER get married to this man, you'll NEVER, NEVER, NEVER...!"

The once-sympathetic official had become a raging ogre. He sounded like a broken record. He was so furious that he couldn't stop shrieking. Never before had I been insulted in such a way; never before had I felt my university career in such danger. My sane, solid world, my luminous future was crumbling. The same friendly, attentive man who had explained the process for marrying my captain with such patience and, I would almost say, warmth, was now announcing my ruin, the loss of my civil rights, the end of my studies, and the impossibility of achieving my goal, and all that simply because I wanted to marry a foreigner.

In my desperation, I started to reply, presenting arguments I had learned in my philosophy and Marxism-Leninism classes. Indignant, I asked him if he had never heard of the principles of solidarity and aid among friendly countries, of friendship among the peoples, and other things along that line. Stupid me. What was the point? The man made gestures like someone who had just been slapped. Clenching his jaw, he screamed his final phrase.

"What we do in matters of international solidarity and friendship with the peoples is determined by the PARTY, not by you! Get out of here! GET OUT!"

For the first time in my life, I was thrown out of a government office. I was in a very delicate situation, and I was afraid. My captain was so far away in his brand-new ship, not suspecting that our plans were falling apart, bursting like a soap bubble. I sent him a cablegram, explaining in great detail the situation that had me on the brink of insanity, and he responded quickly, also by cable.

"Don't worry, everything is taken care of. They promised me they would give permission for us to get married."

Certainly, during his half-year of residence in the shipyard, not a single day had passed that there wasn't something in the press or on the radio about the progress of the ship's construction, about the youngest captain in the world and his officers. Information about Cuba was on the rise, although there still weren't full diplomatic relations, but now there was a trade office and a Cuban consulate in Berlin. They couldn't treat the captain as rudely as they had treated me. In addition, he knew how to go up the chain of command to get the help we needed. Our marriage had been turned into a diplomatic matter of high importance. The German side opted to demonstrate its generosity, promising the Cuban side that it would allow me to marry the captain.

When I received confirmation that everything was going to be all right, that they would grant us permission to marry, the German authorities responsible for the official paperwork held onto the information and left me up in the air. They kept responding:

"We don't have any information. There's nothing new."

The day planned for the wedding was approaching, and I still had received no official notice. My captain was sending me cables from the ship, assuring me over and over that everything would be all right. What a schizophrenic world; I was prepared for anything. Hanging in my university locker was a white wedding dress, a thing that was hard to find, since on the one hand, I permanently lacked resources—the money at my disposal wasn't enough to even begin—and on the other hand, items of this kind were scarce. People had to call professional seamstresses months in advance to have wedding dresses made.

I didn't have the necessary time or money. By pure chance I had found a white wedding dress that was very simple and pretty. I had the luck to also find a pair of dainty white shoes of very good quality, imported from Austria (I remember this detail vividly, because such a find was extraordinary). My luck in assembling this nuptial wardrobe was comparable to winning the lottery, but the most important thing was missing: the assurance that I would be able to actually wear these garments. I was in a state of constant desperation, and I was prepared to keep the wedding dress for what remained of my life, since my decision was to marry the captain or become a spinster. It was this man or no one, come hell or high water. There was no alternative.

During the long weeks of uncertainty, I sent dozens of letters to Cuba, of unheard-of length. Much later I found out that my captain had never received them, since his mother held onto them and "forgot" to deliver them. Sometime later, when my sister-in-law was giving the house a general cleaning, she found them in a corner of the closet.

Luckily, no one knew Spanish in my city's post office, so neither the mailman who was responsible for the personal delivery of cablegrams coming from the extraordinary, patient, and persevering work of the radiotelegraph operator of the ship, charged with the transmission in Morse code of his boss' missives, nor the rest of the post office's employees knew the reason for so much costly correspondence. The curiosity must have killed them; the subject must have generated unheard-of levels of gossip, drastically interrupting the monotony and daily boredom of the post office, not to mention the university administration, since at least once a day they got lucky tracking down a simple, insignificant student and delivering a foreign telegram to her. In those days, the mail carrier had to deliver cablegrams immediately to the recipient, on foot or, in the best case, on bicycle, with no excuse or pretext.

The uncertainty was driving me berserk. Less than a week was left before the planned date for the wedding. How could the captain assure me, again, that everything was resolved if the authorities weren't confirming it to me? Or were they so stupid that they knew absolutely nothing?

Three days before the scheduled date, I remember perfectly that when I returned to the university residence, the administration advised me to go immediately to the director's office. I shot out of there like an arrow. The director called me into his office.

"The provincial office of the Ministry of the Interior just advised me that you must be there this afternoon before six."

"Before six? It's twenty before six already!"

"Then you better run. If you're lucky, you'll get there on time."

I always was a good athlete, although marathon running was never one of my favorite sports. My strong point was short runs, but now I had to make record time without anyone's help. There was no taxi, and the tram took too long. I had to trust my legs and my lungs. I arrived at the office three minutes before it closed. An official with the face of a locked gate told me to wait in the waiting room. I wondered why I was asked to be present.

"Didn't you ask to leave the country?"

"Yes, but . . ."

"Yes, but what? It's here."

And he placed a blue passport on the table. Incredulous, I took it, opened it, and found a seal on the last page that said: "Date of exit: April 23, 1962. Valid until: April 26, 1962." I had permission to leave the country in three days, expiring three days later.

"Go as soon as possible to the Cuban consulate so they can give you an entrance visa, since without it, the passport is not valid," the officer warned me before closing the door in my face and putting me out on the dark street.

Indescribable feelings came over me: happiness mixed with astonishment and fear, and the knowledge that in three days I would be leaving my country. I had wished for this moment so many times, and now that it was happening, I was nervous, even ambivalent. The ship with my captain at the helm was approaching, but it would still be twenty hours or so before it arrived at the port in Rostock. There was no way to make telephone contact. I had to avail myself again of the radiotelegraph operator's services to send the good news to my captain. More importantly, I had to get the Cuban visa, and quickly. How was I going to settle so many matters in such a short time? Luckily, the consul had given me his private phone number, so I could reach him outside working hours.

"You can meet me in Berlin tomorrow night, at the journalists' club. I'll put the stamp and my signature on your passport there, because tomorrow the office is closed, and during the day I won't be in Berlin."

The next morning, I had to go again before the frenzied officer who had thrown me out of his office when I requested permission to get married. Now he received me with a smiling face, accepting with scarcely a word of protest all the copies of my captain's documents, translated by me, embellished simply with the stamps from my university instead of the official stamps of a lawyer and an institution that legalizes translations. *The world is crazy*, I thought, accepting without comment the congratulations of this slimy, hypocritical man.

"We hope that you will be a worthy representative of our socialist German State in Cuba."

What a despicable being. I wanted to scream terrible things at him, but the only thing I could say was "Thank you."

"You have to go this afternoon to the Party Provincial Committee. The Secretary General wants to speak with you," he said, before saying goodbye.

The Secretary of the Party of the province of Rostock had delegated to another official—a true expert on Cuba who had just returned from the island, where he had worked for several months—the task of dissuading me at the last minute from my resolution to go to Cuba. What a crazy situation. The more horrible he painted the picture of the situation in Cuba, the more stubborn and determined I became to go there. Needless to say that later, as I started a new life in Cuba, I saw for myself that the Secretary General's delegate had told the truth, that he hadn't invented anything, that major difficulties and problems confronting the Cuban population had already begun—difficulties and problems that were even more serious than this German, a foreign official in Cuba, could have appreciated, since he himself, assured of a regular supply of the food and products that were already becoming unavailable on the island, didn't have to forgo necessities or experience shortages.

"Inside three months you'll be back here begging on your knees for us to let you return to your studies," he told me.

And I thought to myself, *Keep talking, no one will make me change my mind about continuing my life in Cuba. Even if I get eaten by sharks, even if the sun scorches my skin, even if hunger makes me despair, and even if the mosquitos and cockroaches and other bugs, which you're describing to me in full detail, make me sick, I still won't come back to East Germany, at least not voluntarily.*

"I can see that you're beyond reasoning with. There's no use talking to you, but I have fulfilled my duty and will inform our Secretary General. Goodbye."

This obligatory interview seemed like a terrible waste of time to me. I hurriedly left Party headquarters for the train to Berlin, where I had to locate the Cuban consul so he could stamp and sign my passport and turn it—at last!—into a valid document. As I'd been instructed, I went to the journalists' club. I found him surrounded by dozens of bizarre people and enveloped in a dense cloud of cigar smoke. Before the astonished eyes of this crowd, the consul took out a small cedarwood box with the label "Romeo and Juliet," but instead of cigars, inside was a jumble of official stamps and an ink pad, the tools for exercising his function. He adorned my passport with the stamps *de rigueur* and wished me all kinds of luck in this new chapter of my life.

Running, I made it to the station in time to take the last train back to Rostock. There were three days left of marathon runs and depleted energy, which put my capacity for endurance and patience to the test—good practice for what awaited me in Cuba.

3. *Monika marrying Cuban–Spanish captain Jesús Jiménez Escobar, at the club of the Warnow shipyard, April 1962*

The day of my wedding arrived. My captain picked me up at the university. The ceremony took place in a club at the shipyards. My parents, friends, my fiancé's colleagues—everyone dressed up—and my professor, who acted as an interpreter that day, were already waiting in the vestibule. A quartet (I still don't know where they came from) was playing the wedding march when, escorted by the flagship officers from the Cuban merchant marine, we entered the assembly hall. All the rest happened so quickly that I barely had time to reflect.

We had a party at home after the ceremony, and instead of taking a trip for our honeymoon, we spent it on board the historic ship, crossing the Atlantic, our course set for Cuba, my husband working and I as a passenger, adapting to my new status as a woman married to the head of the crew, surrounded by men, technical equipment, buses, and agricultural machinery, and all around, the Atlantic: impressive, frightening, sometimes gentle and beautiful like a mirror with infinite dimensions, and sometimes savage like a demon, transforming our ship into a walnut shell, giving us living beings on board to understand the full magnitude of the brutal and devouring force of the sea that surrounded us.

CHAPTER FOUR
CULTURE SHOCK

My parents, brothers, university colleagues, and friends came on board the ship to say goodbye to me a few hours before departure. Around midnight we weighed anchor. The ship was on its way to the Baltic Sea. As we began our journey we were helped along by tugboats, until we arrived at open water. My first night on board passed without my being aware that I was in a totally different environment. The exhaustion accumulated over the last few weeks, the nervousness, the tension, the joy at having accomplished my goal, together with my sadness at being separated from my family, friends, and colleagues acted like a sleeping pill. I gave in and slept like a rock, while my captain took his turn on the bridge.

In the morning, looking out from under the covers, I saw something totally bizarre, and at first I thought I was dreaming. Was a springtime Fata Morgana waving goodbye from the European continent? Surely I was on board a ship, but we were moving through green meadows, adorned with millions of yellow, red, and white flowers, and black-and-white Holstein cows were filling their bellies in the middle of this sea of flowers and grass. My captain, seeing me open-mouthed and astonished, explained.

"We're going through the Kiel Canal that connects the Baltic Sea with the North Sea."

As a little girl, I had always imagined paradise to be like this.

At night we arrived in Hamburg, where another surprise was waiting for me. My father had sent a telegram to my cousin in Hamburg, telling her I would be passing through the city two days after the wedding. She interpreted the cable in her own way. For her, it was clear that I had managed to escape from East Germany and was planning to stay in Hamburg. She advised the port police, asking for help in escorting me to safe ground.

The police officials congratulated me and expressed their admiration for my having accomplished the monumental feat of escaping from the communist regime of Walter Ulbricht. I explained to these gentlemen that I had not the least intention of staying in Hamburg. They didn't want to believe me.

"Look at our uniform, madame, don't you see the difference? This is the uniform of the police of West Germany. You've reached freedom! If you dare to tell us frankly what you want to say, we can escort you to land. You'll be totally safe, and the henchmen from the other side won't be able to detain you."

The poor guys were disappointed when I told them that I really was going to Cuba, that I didn't need anyone to help me stay in Germany, not even with the most attractive and sophisticated promises. My cousin, uncles, aunts, and other family members in Hamburg agreed with the police and declared me crazy as a loon for rejecting all their proposals. They had already coordinated the continuation of my studies with the university and had prepared the conditions required for my remaining in Hamburg, and here I was, refusing their generous help and solidarity. They simply couldn't understand that I was so in love with my captain that all I wanted was to go to Cuba and become a participant in the revolutionary work of the island. To my way of thinking, everything had already been done in Hamburg, while there was still so much left to do, everything left to do, in Cuba. There was a need for enthusiastic people who were ready to take part in constructing a new society.

My relatives were convinced that my obstinacy and blindness

had totally clouded my judgment and that I was in no condition to objectively analyze the consequences of my decision. They were sure it was a recipe for disaster. And I thought, *Did they receive a message from a representative of the General Secretary of the Party?* Because I had heard all this already, a few days before, from the opposite camp.

Feeling like the queen of the world, I continued on my trip to Cuba. The passage through the Bay of Biscay gave me the first example of what it meant to have the temerity to brave the Atlantic, mounted on a shell and trying to land it on safe ground. Our ship was only "majestic" and "huge" when it was in calm waters; it was microscopic, fragile, and insignificant when it was navigating on the high seas. It leapt, shuddered, heaved, and rocked like a boat made of paper.

The buses, agricultural machinery, and other heavy equipment, covered and strapped down with thick steel cables, were creaking, and I thought that at any minute they would go flying into the sea, breaking free from the cables, which would snap like sewing thread. Almost all the crew members were ill, including the officers, whose neat, martial attire contrasted with their bright-green faces. On stormy days, fewer diners came to the dining room. After a week of bobbing up and down, day and night, I really wanted to get off the ship and feel terra firma under my feet again, but we still had two weeks before arriving in Havana.

In the two suitcases where I kept all my treasures—books and some personal items—nothing interesting remained. I poked around in the ship's library, where I found only manuals on political economy, Marxism-Leninism, and classic tracts like *History Will Absolve Me*, by Fidel Castro, plus magazines published by the Socialist Popular Party. These materials had been required reading at the university, and I had read them and chewed them up, using all my existing reserves of will and discipline not to throw them into the corner of oblivion. Now, even sick and desperately needing something powerful to distract me, I didn't fancy rereading them; it would have been an act of masochism.

I sat on deck, reclining against the mainmast, where the rocking of the ship wasn't as noticeable, and I daydreamed with open eyes, interpreting cloud formations, entering my world of fantasy, becoming a solitary adventurer. I remembered the stories I had devoured in my childhood—stories of pirates, daring adventurers, shipwrecks, lonely islands, and enchanting landscapes.

After two weeks aboard the ship, I had adapted to the pitching of the ship, the lack of terrestrial sounds, and the agitation of the sea. I could already feel the heat of the nearby tropics, day and night. The ship had no air conditioning, so I became trained during the Atlantic crossing to endure the climate that later, for nearly three decades, I would have to endure on the island.

There was one day left before we arrived in Cuba. As if to welcome us, dolphins and flying fish appeared. Never before had I seen such a beautiful spectacle. I don't remember how many miles separated us from Cuba when the first little birds appeared. They seemed to be sparrows, but sparrows in the Americas? Again, I experienced indescribable feelings. Seeing land after so much time, seeing my beloved Cuba, still unknown but already dear to me, my second homeland, was something that I would never forget.

We approached Havana around midnight. From the port side of the ship I could see the Malecón, the boardwalk in Havana. The lights of hundreds of cars, from that distance, were like an enormous sea of thousands and thousands of fireflies, or lightning flashes along the avenue. A starry sky competed with the city's electric illumination—an extraordinarily beautiful painting. I had never seen a metropolis from the sea, much less one that was so immense, so impressive and bathed in light.

My first vision of Havana: never again would I see it so beautiful, so gigantic, and at the same time so welcoming. What a contrast with the Havana in the nineties: dirty, dark, crumbling, and sad, as if it had been bombed.

We had to drop anchor and wait until the following morning to enter the Bay of Havana. I got up early. I'd packed my two suitcases the night before. By eight o'clock the sun was already as hot as it would have been at noon on an exceptionally warm European summer day. An hour later, the heat was unbearable, and our ship was still anchored. Finally, around ten in the morning, they gave us permission to enter the port, and we could tie up at the dock.

I still didn't know it, but this was the start of my assimilation of the Cuban condition. From this morning on, until the day of my exit from Cuba in 1990, I never stopped hearing the almost daily refrain: "Mónica! You're not in Germany; that's the way it is in Cuba. You have to be patient."

My captain explained to me the procedure that would be followed by the Cuban authorities who monitored the cargo and the crew, which included a health check. The port doctor checked my international vaccination certificate.

"So, you got married recently, no?"

"Yes, that's right."

"Congratulations."

"Thanks."

"We can't allow you to disembark, because your certificate of vaccinations is not complete."

"What do you mean it's not complete? The Germans vaccinated me against I don't know how many illnesses and assured me that everything was in order."

"It's missing the vaccine against smallpox."

"I've already had that one several times. They told me it's no longer necessary."

"Then they gave you the wrong information, because here it's necessary. You're not pregnant, are you?"

"No, I'm not."

"Then we can vaccinate you right now and you can go up on land."

"All right, if it's required, let's do it!"

And so I began my life in Cuba with a smallpox vaccination.

There was nothing else that prevented us from disembarking and going to our house. My captain had sent a cable to Ramón, his best friend, notifying him of our arrival, and Ramón agreed to pick us up with our car, which had been left in his care for personal use while the captain was gone.

More than an hour went by, and there was no sign of Ramón. My captain went to the street to try to phone him. Another hour passed before he returned. Ramón had been in a marathon meeting since the morning and couldn't leave to pick us up. My captain's brother was at work, but his car was in bad condition. First he had to take it to the shop and then he would come get us. It was now two in the afternoon.

"Antonio—my brother—will be delayed for at least two more hours. What do you think about going to have lunch at a restaurant in the port? We can leave the suitcases on the ship. I'm sure the restaurant on the dock will have something good to eat."

I gladly accepted the invitation. We went down the stairs. What a weird feeling. I was walking like a drunk. Now the firm ground felt abnormal; I missed the movement of the ship. As we walked toward the dock, the sun was implacable. Please forgive me, Cubans, so proud of your country, but the truth is that the stench of the port was nauseating. Why would anyone want to leave garbage cans uncovered in the tropical sun, their contents literally cooking? The water of the bay was thick and black, with dead animals floating on the surface. It contained the refuse of every continent, emitting very disagreeable odors. The stench, heat, and humidity—all of it disgusting.

"This is what ports look like in hot countries," was my captain's brief comment.

After a quarter hour of walking we came to the dock restaurant. My husband was fresh as a naturally-ripened mango, and I was a wilted flower, wishing I could crawl inside a refrigerator. We closed the door behind us and reveled in the cold air.

We sat down at a table. There were few people and an abundance of waiters, all in uniform, with black jackets and pants, white shirts, and black ties. *How can they stand the heat with long sleeves and heavy pants, and black no less?* I thought. *Maybe whatever protects against the cold also protects against heat.*

One waiter gave us water, another the menu, and a third wrote down what we wanted.

"There is only one item left on the menu," he warned us.

For lunch, I then had what I would eat every day for months to come: white rice with black beans and, as a distinguished extra, a fried egg.

While we waited for our food to arrive, I began to observe my surroundings. The bad smell still enveloped us. The tablecloths were stained with the remnants of food from previous diners, and the walls seemed to scream "Paint us!" My meticulous study of the unsanitary state of the restaurant was suddenly interrupted when a dog that was sitting calmly underneath its owner's table shot like an arrow toward ours. I saw him grab something black on the floor. He released it, and now I could see something revolting that from then on would pursue me every day in Cuba: the biggest cockroach I had ever seen in my life, with long antennae that moved up, down, to the right and the left, feet that looked like hooks, and a body so repulsive that it made me shiver. The cockroach running from the dog was headed toward my feet. I jumped up on the chair and began to scream in terror. The diners and waiters must have thought I was having a nervous breakdown. Disgusted, I held out my index finger to point out the cockroach.

"What kind of animal is that?" I managed to ask my husband, who then angrily ordered me to sit down.

"Don't be ridiculous! Making a spectacle out of yourself over a miserable cockroach! These animals are part of tropical folklore. They exist in all hot countries. They don't respect social class or rank. They're everywhere, and if you look at them objectively, they won't bother you."

Antonio, my husband's older brother, finally came to get us. He arrived in a prehistoric car, as big as a Sherman tank and intimidatingly noisy and clunky: his favorite toy. He greeted his brother effusively, giving him spectacular thumps on the back, accompanying this ritual with a welcome speech. He also greeted me. It seems he didn't know how to do it and, above all, what to say to me. After a brief "Welcome to Cuba, hope you like it" just to say something, he gave me a look that seemed to express serious doubts that this German woman would remain in Cuba for more than the blink of an eye. Then we got into the humungous vehicle, and Antonio took us to my mother-in-law's house, where we would live for several months before getting our own apartment.

In the course of my first week in Havana, I came to understand why my brother-in-law was skeptical about my ability to endure life in my new country. His wife, born in Madrid, had not adapted to the climate, or to the living conditions, or to the people, or to the Cuban environment, and she held a gun to Antonio's head: Either he returned with her to Spain, or she would divorce him. With these precedents and this experience he assumed that a German woman, after the hell-or-high-water wedding vows, would start moaning about wanting to go back to the north and might even try to swim across the Atlantic.

My first meeting with my Cuban family was, frankly, unpleasant.

It took another half-hour to drive, chugging mightily, from the dock to our temporary dwelling. We passed through frightfully ugly, dirty neighborhoods, with tin-roofed shacks made of cardboard and wood planks. On every block I saw cooking-oil containers functioning as garbage cans, crammed full of unhealthy waste that appeared to be exploding. From the back seat I could closely observe this spectacle, and I discovered that the garbage was moving because inside some of the cans there were rats, dogs and cats in others, and in their search for food, they were rolling around in the contents.

For the first time in my life I saw the little animals that are the most common breed of dogs in Cuba, at least in those times: Chinese dogs. It took work to identify them as belonging to the canine family; they seemed to me more a mix of a piglet with I-don't-know-what other animal. They had a pink belly and were white or light gray with black and gray spots; they were hairless, naked, with skinny legs of an indefinite color, more from grease than the color nature might have intended, and what most surprised me were their shaved heads, with small, pointed ears, also a white-pink color with black spots, and, on the top of their heads, a tuft of short hair, like the beard of a goat placed there by mistake. The best part of this cartoon animal was that tuft of hair that seemed to be cut meticulously by a barber who specialized in the style.

"What kind of animal is that?" I asked my captain when I saw those strange creatures for the first time.

"It's a Chinese dog," he replied.

He went on talking to his brother and seemed not to notice my disbelief.

"Listen, I'm talking about those animals in the garbage cans, the ones that look like newborn piglets," I said, trying to get his attention.

Laughter and then the affirmation.

"Well, yes, they are dogs, Chinese dogs that have only a bit of hair on their heads," my husband explained. "They must have mange or some other skin disease, poor things; the itching must drive them crazy," I said. More laughter.

"They're not sick; that's their breed. I'll show you a book with illustrations of the different dog breeds, and you'll find the Chinese dog there. The ones you see in garbage cans and running through the streets look exactly like the ones in the book. The only difference is that the Cuban dogs running loose without owners are dirty, and the ones in the book are perfumed, bathed, and wearing jeweled collars."

Finally we left behind the dilapidated shacks and dirty streets and entered a more prosperous residential area. Antonio parked the car in the carport of a nice five-story apartment building. Across the street was the new but not yet finished Ministry of Transport. Our building was on the corner of the impressively wide Avenida de Rancho Boyeros. Royal palms, oleander, hibiscus bushes, and—to my surprise—roses, carnations, and exotic plants I couldn't identify gave lovely splashes of color to the avenue and the neighboring houses' gardens.

If this lovely place is where I'm going to live, I thought, there shouldn't be a problem. We got out and entered the building. The heat was unbearable, and the summer hadn't even begun. Climbing the stairs to the second floor, I had to stop several times. It was hard to breathe, and I felt tremendous fatigue. I went up the stairs at a snail's pace. My husband waited for me politely. Antonio, performing the role of messenger, announced our arrival when we were still between the first and second floors. This triggered a colossal shouting, as the neighbors were now informed that their long-awaited hero was about to arrive. They were all at home, and the old, young, children, and elderly all came running to greet the captain's arrival.

When we got to our floor, a crowd had already gathered, and they all were talking at once. From the living room came strident music produced by a record player, and that racket mixed with the voice of an announcer on a radio station, with the television doing its best to compete in its own way. After spending three weeks crossing the Atlantic with a silence at times overwhelming, the noise coming from all corners stunned me and made my head buzz.

My mother-in-law embraced her son, my husband, as if he were a miraculous apparition. And she talked, talked, talked, her speech alternating with euphoric cries. My nephew, then a boy of six, had fastened himself to his uncle's leg. The neighbors, all teary-eyed and with big smiles, embraced him effusively. They gave him the same thumps on the back as Antonio had given him.

Naturally, they also greeted me, but in a very different way. From the first instant, all those present must have noticed that I didn't understand much of what they were saying, and they must have found it somewhat difficult to address me, someone they didn't know, a foreigner besides, with a skin as white as milk, who looked more like a college kid than someone who could be the wife of their beloved and esteemed captain. They all must have been terribly disappointed. I didn't fulfill any of the requisites of a wife for a person of my captain's stature. In place of the obligatory mane of hair, I had a short haircut, and only years later would it become popular in Cuba. Instead of high heels, I wore flat sandals. I wasn't wearing makeup, not even mascara. I didn't have on a tight skirt, just a loose one, and I was wearing a white blouse that looked like an elementary-school uniform. Nor did I wear gold chains, rings, bracelets, earrings, or loops. My mother-in-law probably thought *My son must have been blind drunk when he fell for her*. At least, that's how I interpreted

4. *Ana María, Monika's mother-in-law*

their reactions of rejection and scorn, which lasted every day we stayed in the apartment.

Our little nephew, tired of not getting the attention he wanted from his uncle, came over to me. Poor little guy, I didn't understand what he was telling me. I probably was saying "yes" when I should have been saying "no." I didn't laugh when I should have at his antics, because I couldn't understand them. Disappointed, he went off into a corner to play with the dog, Blaqui, a true monster that dropped hair long enough to make rugs out of and barked so loudly and annoyingly that I wanted to kill him every time I saw him.

Little by little, people returned to their apartments, and my sister-in-law, Maritza, my mother-in-law, my husband, the nephew, the dog, and I were left to ourselves on the large balcony, the coolest place in the apartment. My mother-in-law continued speaking with my husband. Maritza was taking care of the nephew who was upset about being neglected during the whole show. She threw me a few sympathetic looks. I think she was the only one who realized that I was feeling uncomfortable.

That first day in Cuba, so full of different impressions, left me feeling dizzy, confused, exhausted, and, frankly, disappointed. When we all finally went to bed, I found that even as tired as I was, I couldn't fall asleep. The heat, instead of decreasing, seemed to increase. The walls, overheated during the day, were now furnaces. The sheets stuck to my body after I took off my nightgown, which had made me sweat as if it were a bearskin coat. As dogs do to find a cool place, I got off the mattress and lay down on the tile floor, changing my spot every so often. I slept in spurts and had horrible nightmares.

My captain got up early to go to work. We agreed to arrange our room in his mother's apartment to our taste. He suggested that I go with Gonzalo, his brother-in-law, to buy furniture and all the other things we needed for our "home." Gonzalo, my captain's brother-in-law, a Spaniard by birth, had been in Cuba for two years. As a cabinet maker, he was the perfect person to help me choose the best furniture for our home.

Gonzalo became my teacher, my guardian angel. He spoke a Spanish that was more understandable than the rest of the family and friends I had met up to then. It's possible that he and his wife, Pilar, who later became a second mother to my sons, had experienced the same problems of adaptation as I had to overcome.

Gonzalo accompanied me on my pilgrimage through all the furniture stores in Havana. Already at this period—early 1962—there was little to choose from, and what was left was expensive. I made a calculation about buying with the resources at my disposal, and the money didn't stretch far enough to even begin. Gonzalo proposed that he make some of the furniture himself, and we proceeded to buy the materials he'd need. The following days went flying by, with Gonzalo working as a carpenter and I as his assistant. We painted walls and upholstered mattresses, turning them into couches, which could be pushed together at night and made into beds.

These pieces of furniture were so well made and so tough that they lasted until I left Cuba, almost thirty years later. They withstood two hurricanes that dumped masses of water on them and three moves. I left them in Havana when I went back to Germany, and they continue in their role as modern and acceptable pieces of furniture. The bookcase suffered a small mutilation when a thief broke its only locked door with a crowbar. Gonzalo patched it up with wood and replaced the broken lock with another one, which he bartered for.

My relationship with my mother-in-law never became harmonious, and in the first months I was on the brink of attacking her many times. She spied on me and monitored my movements. There was nothing I did that could meet with her approval. When I washed my husband's white uniform shirts, she stood by my side to criticize me. When I ironed, she called the neighbors in to see the show.

"Look at my daughter-in-law. She says she's ironing. You call that ironing? She doesn't even sprinkle starch on the shirts and leaves them looking like the iron didn't touch them. How awful! This woman doesn't know how to do anything useful."

I wanted to throw the hot iron at her head, and I had to muster my patience, even when it didn't exist.

My captain was traveling. My mother-in-law took advantage of any opportunity to discredit and reproach me for not acting like a good wife to her favorite son. She even told me that she didn't accept me as a daughter-in-law, since I didn't know how to do anything and never asked her opinion. Her son deserved a real woman.

Fortunately, I had a brief reprieve when my captain invited me to accompany him on a trip to Oriente province. I was happy! In a flash I packed my bag and went with him, leaving behind my mother-in-law, sister-in-law, the nephew, and the dog, fleeing the atmosphere that was making my life hell.

The crew was performing the maneuvers for leaving the Bay of Havana when a wind came up, so strong that it threatened to push the ship against the dock. My captain ordered the anchor to be thrown out to avoid a serious accident. Instead of crashing into the dock, an equally serious accident took place: the winch for the anchor didn't work when he gave the order to raise it. The anchor snagged on the Western Union cable, the only line maintaining Cuba's communication with the outside world. Today, there wouldn't be any repercussions, since satellites have taken the place of cables, but in 1962, this was a disaster. With tremendous effort, the sailors finally managed to disengage the cable and let it sink to the bottom. Everything seemed to indicate that the cable was intact, and there didn't appear to be anything that was torn. My captain gave the order to continue on to Nuevitas.

I felt peaceful. The wind blew fresh, salty air in my face. Flying fish accompanied us for a while, and dolphins greeted us in a lovely race with our ship. The heat was not as oppressive on the open water; even in my small cabin I didn't feel as hot as I did in the city.

Unfortunately, my new-found happiness after those first stormy and disappointing days in Havana was about to come to an abrupt, premature end. My captain received an order from Havana to inform the higher-ups in the security services, immediately and in full detail, about the accident with the cable. The order was blunt and threatening. Logically, I couldn't remain on board. We decided that I would go back to Havana.

I was expecting a big adventure, though for a Cuban it might be a normal, daily occurrence: a trip through a landscape that would remind me of movies about the African savannah. On both sides of the highway I saw only dry, yellowish grass, a foot in height, burned by the sun. The shaky car that took me to the station in Nuevitas threatened to leave us stranded on the road. Several times the motor broke down, and we had to get out and push the car. Luckily it started up after each push. Its snorts and starts filled me with terror. I imagined that I would be found days later, burned to a crisp by the sun, having suffered a horribly slow, tortured death. The more the car snuffled and bounced, and the thirstier I got, the more terrible deaths I imagined. Finally, we got to the train station in Nuevitas. The train was due to arrive in a half hour, which gave me enough time to drink something cold that would bring me back to life. But no such thing existed. There was nothing cold because the refrigerator in the station's cafeteria did not work: there was no electricity.

"Do you want something to drink? A glass of *guachipupa*?"

No, I certainly didn't. Better to be thirsty than drink a warm *guachipupa*, colored sugar-water, which would be like drinking my own pee.

An hour went by with no train.

I eventually asked for that drink. It was hot, excessively sweet, and made me want to vomit. The trip hadn't even begun, and I was already drained and about to collapse. Mosquitos, heat, dust, my dress sticking to my body, bad smells everywhere, hundreds of people who wanted to take the train that still hadn't arrived: an unbearable spectacle. I kept remembering the warnings of the Party official back home and his final comment: "After a few weeks you'll be begging to come back," which chimed in my ear like a bell.

The train arrived two hours late. Passengers, carrying bundles, suitcases, children, chickens, and goats, rushed to the train, elbowing their way in right and left. In the midst of the tumult, I was lucky to find a seat. In its salad days, the train must have been a model of luxury—a true Pullman—with air conditioning, comfortable reclining seats, bathrooms with running water, and spacious passageways. Very little remained of that past glory. The air conditioning didn't work. There was no water in the bathrooms; the walls were paneled with feces, and the floor was waterlogged with urine. The hallways were crammed with pieces of junk, people seated on their crates and suitcases, and goats pulling on the ropes used by their owners to restrain them. Chickens tied and held up by their feet flapped around, trying to free themselves, cackling and constantly releasing streams of shit. The seat covers were worn and full of holes, through which the innards protruded. I was sitting in the corner of the last row, glued to the window and the wall, half-drugged by the smelly, stifling, nauseating air. In my delirium, I tried to engrave this surrealistic scene on my brain because it was so extraordinary.

The trip lasted eighteen hours, three times longer than planned, double what I would need today to fly across the Atlantic. I must have fallen asleep several times, waking up suddenly from the atrocious nightmares that were torturing me. The cries of small children, the murmurs of their mothers trying to calm them, and the snores of the lucky ones who were able to sleep formed a rich stew that fed my nightmares. When we arrived at the train station in Havana, I was half-dead, walking like a zombie. My dear sister-in-law was waiting for me and took me home.

I ran to the bathroom, using the last of my strength. I stepped into the shower and let the cold water bring me back to life, with agreeable sensations of bliss and happiness. I lay down on the clean bed and didn't wake up until the next day.

My captain returned a day later. His trip took a whole day. On the way, the train had to stop for five hours. A maverick cow had become confused and walked onto the tracks; the train collided with her, and her blood and pieces of her body went everywhere. As the accident happened in the countryside, the police took their time, so by the time they finally showed up to investigate the case and record the event, the bits of skin and bones that were left of the poor animal were already in a state of putrefaction.

In Havana, my husband learned that the cable was still damaged.

Telecommunications with the world were interrupted for almost a week, and from then on, "the youngest captain in the world" was nicknamed "the captain who conquered the cable." That's how rapidly an idol's status can change and a reputation be lost. For days he was irritated, preoccupied, and also very disappointed, because although he had proved that it wasn't his fault, the broken cable began to follow him everywhere.

Summer was in full swing. The continuation of my studies was planned for the beginning of the new semester, in September of 1962. To occupy my free time during the recess, I landed a temporary job as a translator in the East German trade office in Havana.

My mother-in-law was indignant.

"This woman goes out in the street with long pants, in sandals. It's disgraceful! Do you expect me to attend to your husband? He earns enough to support his family. You don't need to go out at all."

"He's not a child, or an invalid. What kind of attention does he need? And what attention is he giving me?" I replied.

Scandalized, she answered time and again that a decent wife stays at home, taking care of her husband. Fortunately, my captain supported my position. He remembered the promise he had made to my father when we announced our marriage. On the contrary, he was content that I had found something useful that would make the tense situation with my mother-in-law more bearable.

At this time, food was growing increasingly scarce, so to supplement the meager portions allotted them by their ration book, people began to seek out relationships with farmers who produced meat and vegetables. Soon, a black market, or barter system, emerged; thirty years later this "informal" system would reach its peak during the infamous Special Period. I was intimately familiar with the rationing system established in Germany during the Second World War (which was still in place when I left for Cuba), so to my dismay, I was "privileged" to continue down the same road until my return to Germany in the late nineties.

When I started working in the trade office, I knew that the German officials regularly received supplies of food that came in on merchant marine ships: canned vegetables, meat, sausages, spices, and thousands of marvelous things that you couldn't find in the Cuban markets. I wasn't on the list of official personnel, so I didn't have the right to participate in the "booty." But sometimes there were products left over because the people who had requested them were on vacation. On those occasions, they offered me the surplus. At first, I felt indignant and humiliated; they were giving me to understand that they were only giving me something because they had too much. But soon I came to the conclusion that pride doesn't fill the stomach, and I decided to accept what they offered me. Ultimately, I was paying for it with my hard-earned money.

One day, when I hadn't seen anything in the house for weeks but rice and black beans, when the butcher had refused to give me my ration of meat, saying, "German woman, why don't you go back to your country? Don't you know there won't be anything left here in a little while?" I was delighted when the Germans allowed me to buy a tin of sausages.

I came home cheerful, carrying my treasure in my bag. At this point my mother-in-law had decided that I wouldn't be allowed access to the family's food.

"No, this woman who goes out in the street and doesn't dutifully take care of her husband, my dear son, let her prepare her own food, let her look for her own products, let her take care of this matter by herself. Really, she never stops complaining that every day it's the same thing: rice and beans. She's rude and ridiculous."

Maritza, my dear sister-in-law, always ready to help me and to violate the regulations imposed by her mother, had been able to get me two potatoes that I was keeping for a special occasion. Now, with the tin of sausages, the occasion had arrived. *I'm going to prepare a soup*, I thought. The ingredients would be Maritza's gift, plus the sausages, water, and salt. The smell of the cooking soup made my mouth water. I had what I learned the Cubans called *hambre vieja*, an old hunger, comparable to the hunger I felt many times during and after the war.

I took the pan of boiling soup off the stove. I was so eager to taste it that it was all I could do not to burn my mouth. Blowing on my treat, I raised my head and blew again, my eyes incredulous when they fixed on something green hanging from a vase on an altar.

"This looks like, looks like, looks like ... No it IS—parsley!"

And then I was holding it in my hand, like a dog with a bone. I took off a leaf and rubbed it between my index finger and thumb, smelling it, almost faint from surprise, joy, and happiness. Since my arrival in Havana some months ago, I hadn't found any spice or herb that I liked. I was convinced that there wasn't any parsley in Cuba, and suddenly, as if from Aladdin's lamp, in my hands was a sprig of parsley. Quickly, before someone could snatch it away, I washed it, took a bite, and threw the rest in the stew. Few times after the war had I eaten anything with such eagerness, pleasure, and haste—without leaving any trace.

I was washing the pot, plate, and silverware when I heard a scream.

"Who took the parsley? It's an offering to *Oshún*; where is the parsley? My God, how terrible! Who the hell would take the parsley? Mónica, do you know where the parsley is?"

"Maritza, please, don't panic, I took it."

"*Ay*, Mónica, don't do that to me. Give it back, I need it. I need it before my mother comes back."

"I'm sorry, Maritza, I can't. I ate it. It's inside my stomach, and just so you know, it was delicious."

Maritza gave a cry of astonishment.

"Mónica, I can't believe you would do such a stupid thing. It's not possible. It's sacrilege! You're going to drive me crazy! It took a lot of work to find a bunch of parsley in Chinatown, and now you've eaten it. I can't believe it, I really can't."

"Since when is it sacrilege to eat a sprig of parsley? I don't understand your shouting, your accusations—why are you saying I disgraced you?"

Making a visible effort to remain calm, Maritza explained the scope of my sin, my totally unacceptable act.

"Today—not tomorrow, not yesterday, but today—we are

offering to *Oshún*, that is to say *La Vírgen de la Caridad del Cobre*, Our Lady of Charity, this bunch of parsley. Do me a favor, Mónica, don't argue; you're not going to understand. Just suffice it to say that I'm telling you it's imperative that before my mother comes back there be parsley on that altar. And since you ate it, I can't fulfill my obligation."

I apologized to Maritza a thousand times and offered to go with her to find a Chinese man who might be able to sell us another bunch of parsley. I was vaguely aware of *El Barrio Chino*, Havana's Chinatown, but had never thought about going there; it was another world inside my new one. We rushed over to that neighborhood, and after some asking around we found a man about a hundred years old, resembling a prune, who after a long speech in Chinese, sprinkled every other minute with the word "parthley," surrendered his last bunch of parsley. We wanted to give the old fellow a hug.

"May *Oshún* bless you!" I told the wrinkled little man.

"Thank you for the blething," he sang.

After the lamentable incident with the parsley, which, luckily, didn't unleash a catastrophe with my mother-in-law, I never again touched anything on the altar. I didn't understand that in times of extreme shortages there would be glasses of wine, even eggs and apples, placed on the altar, when the whole world was going crazy to eat those rare delicacies that had come from Spain for the celebration of Christmas or the New Year. Repressing my sense of logic, I accepted that for some reason beyond my understanding this Lady, Our Lady of Charity, catholic and African at the same time, and furthermore Cuba's Patron Saint, had the right to share in the little we received. I even think she received more than we did. I also observed that our nephew, seven years old, naughty and spoiled, never missed a chance to raid the refrigerator and fill himself with the food that belonged to the whole family, but even he respected the altar and didn't touch anything dedicated to the saint. When my mother-in-law bought flowers, they were placed on the altar for *Oshún* without question, in beautiful Murano glass vases.

In the course of my thirty years in Cuba, I learned to respect the rites of *santería*, the syncretism of Catholicism and African religions, showered during the Revolution with Marxist-Leninist jargon, but during my period of adaptation, I would, sadly, often put my foot in it.

* * *

I had just returned from the office. It was incredibly hot. I wanted to take a shower, so I went into my mother-in-law's room, where we kept our clothing in an enormous armoire, to get a change of clothes and a towel. The four windows of the large room were closed. In the bathroom, on both sides of the mirror in the china cabinet and on the table were lighted candles. It was absurd in this period of perpetual blackouts and extreme shortages, when you couldn't find a single candle in the market, that in my mother-in-law's room, with a sun outside that could fry an egg on the pavement, all the reserves of candles that we had in the house were being wasted.

It can't be. I think the old lady's losing it, I thought. I put out all the candles and opened the windows and the door to get rid of the funeral home odor. I bathed calmly, dried off, got dressed, hung up the wet towel, and went into my mother-in-law's room again to get another towel to make our bathroom ready for my captain.

Damn it! The door's closed again, and I just opened it! Are we in Roman catacombs? Why don't they let in some fresh air? Good heavens, what's going on? The windows are closed again, and the candles . . . Just a minute ago I blew them out, and now they're burning again. This is a madhouse.

I cursed under my breath. My mother-in-law pretended not to notice me. She was on the balcony, rocking in a rocking chair. Maritza, my teacher, my protector, now used to my freak-outs, came to my rescue.

"Look, Mónica, today is the day we put candles to *Oshún*. My mother set out the candles, and—if you noticed—there are also images of Our Lady of Charity behind each candle. Leave them be. Don't worry about them. Today, even though there's sun and it's hot as blazes, the candles still must be lit, and the windows and door have to stay closed for the candles to have any effect."

"But, Maritza, those burning candles are the last ones we have. There's not a shop in the country that has them, and at the rate we're going there never will be. We need candles for the house when there are blackouts. It's absurd to light them during the day. Why not put the portraits of the saints in the sun? That way, they'll get natural light. And tell me, why do they have to have candles?"

"Mónica, really, anyone would lose patience with you. I can't explain the reasons, but do me a favor and don't put out any more candles. Don't keep opening the windows and the door, leave things in the room like they are, and don't keep looking for answers to your questions because you're not going to find any. If we run out of candles, it's true that we won't have any more. It doesn't matter. We'll be in the dark during the blackouts. But while we still have even the stub of a candle, *Oshún* will get it, broad daylight or not. When there aren't any, *she* will know why."

With the help of Maritza and her saints, little by little, I was making progress in assimilating Cuban folklore.

CHAPTER FIVE

PACO AND MARY

I FIND A LITTLE PIECE OF PAPER on my night table: "A message for you: at four p.m. tomorrow you will have an interview with the Rector of the University of Havana. Matter to discuss: continuation of your studies." My captain had requested the interview. They granted it to me promptly. I knew Professor Marinello, the Rector, through the press, from the hundreds of Cuban friends who knew him personally, and also through some of his literary essays.

He received me in his office. He was friendly and spoke slowly, so I could understand everything. We debated a good while about international politics—the relationship between East Germany and Cuba, in particular, and also about my being able to complete my degree at the University of Havana. He assured me that I could begin my program in September, when the new semester started. He had the kindness to coordinate an interview with the Dean of the Faculty of Humanities in order to clarify the program. Saying goodbye, he presented me with his most recent publication, signing it with a dedication to me. What a nice old man! What a charming gentleman!

The Dean of the Faculty inflicted my first disappointment with respect to my professional prospects. It was hard to believe that the Rector had assured me of the continuation of my studies the next semester.

"We're beginning a reform of the university. Your degree, or rather what appears to be your degree, is frozen, and it will be two or three years before we can add it back. You must realize that the ideological focus has completely changed. We have to prepare the professors and develop totally new programs in order to make the content agree with our new policy position."

And what did the university Rector tell me? He apparently had his head in the clouds, spinning around in the stratosphere. He's probably lost touch with reality, since he said nothing about university reform and all the rest, I thought, disgusted. *You've put him in the position of Rector, but it looks like he's only there for decoration. Really unbelievable.*

The Dean handed me a mountain of paper with information on present programs and future projects, recommending that I change my degree or wait for two to three years to complete what I had interrupted in my third year in Germany.

How was I to choose between the two alternatives? Had I suffered through three years of intensive study, sacrificing my youth, studying night and day, working when others were partying, only to now either start over or wait three years? Impossible. However, the director of the department confirmed everything the dean had said and advised me to wait three years and study at home or look for some work that would be useful at this time. It's so easy to give advice.

This situation, which was truly disastrous for me, coincided with an important change in our family: my sister-in-law, the wife of Antonio, my captain's brother, was on the edge of a breakdown. She didn't want to, and indeed couldn't, continue suffering through the shortages, the problems, the crushing heat, the humidity, and the constant restrictions imposed by the Revolutionary government. She didn't care one whit about the Revolution and wasn't interested in it. She wanted to see her family in Madrid and recuperate from the Cuban craziness. The two of them were going to Madrid, and they said they would let us stay in their house while they were gone.

In no time I had my suitcase packed, and we moved into

Antonio's house in Miramar. I had to turn a blind eye constantly to the hundreds of tasteless ornaments that were everywhere. I hated those decorations made out of glass and plastic with thousands of different colors, but the house was filled with them, and as we couldn't throw them out, I collected the most offensive and stuffed them in the closet so Antonio and his wife would find their "treasures" intact when they returned from Spain.

No more saints, no more altar with the temptation to take something that didn't belong to me, to steal it from *Oshún*. No more humiliating comments from my mother-in-law, no more meetings with the neighbors convened by *mamá* to demonstrate my failure as a housewife. No more stories for the little nephew, no more butchers unwilling to sell me my quota (although the one near my new home didn't have meat for me either). Freedom, air, and space, and the most thrilling of all: Paco, my captain's friend from the time of being underground, who spent the day at home, lived nearby. He still had his post of senior official in the Ministry of Foreign Relations and continued receiving his salary, but he was forbidden to go to work. He had been ousted. Paco was the son of a well-heeled aristocrat, the owner of several mansions on the Prado de Cienfuegos, who hadn't managed to "enjoy" the Revolution because he left before January 1959 and didn't have to see his family hand over to the rebels all the inherited property, accumulated for generations.

Mary, Paco's mother, was a journalist and writer, divorced, and the heir to the houses in Cienfuegos. Now she was busy getting food together in order to have something to offer Paco's many friends, unemployed but with salaries—yesterday underground fighters, today marginalized—who hung out in his house, exchanging the most recent national and international news. I, in the midst of these gatherings, was learning about the many different facets of the Cuban Revolution, things that didn't appear in any book, magazine, or newspaper.

Paco had earned three degrees at the University of Havana, in political science, social science, and psychology. As a brilliant student and the favorite of Raúl Roa, the Revolutionary government's first Minister of Foreign Relations, Paco moved to the Ministry to work beside his former professor. Roa maintained this position his whole life, exercising skills that guaranteed his permanence in such a high post, come what may. Paco didn't have the same skills (or cunning) for agreeing with the opinions of others, and instead of working in Roa's office in the Ministry building facing the Malecón, he stayed home, receiving dozens of former senior officials and ex-combatants.

In Paco and Mary's house I had the privilege of being able to study, in a fun way, and almost without realizing it, the Cuban Spanish that was so difficult for me to understand, Cuban folklore, and life itself in my new land. Mary was an excellent teacher for me. Paco's visitors were almost exclusively men. I, the only woman whose ear was still not sufficiently able to follow the visitors' speech, devoted myself, at first, to helping Mary and sitting with her to receive my daily dose of her verbal storm.

Every day, without realizing it, Mary repeated what she had said the day before. I didn't notice at first, either, because my Spanish was so enormously different from the Spanish spoken in Cuba. Mary was noted for speaking fast, and for using a cultured vocabulary that was occasionally quite archaic. She was so intoxicated by her own stories, such a prisoner of her memories, so happy to have someone who listened to her without interrupting that she wasn't aware that I could barely follow the thread of the conversation and that my responses had nothing to do with the subject, since many times I didn't even know what she was talking about. However, through her systematic and constant repetition, little by little I came to understand not only Mary but also every other Cuban. Never again in my life did I attend a school that was as entertaining, effective, cordial, and affectionate as the one offered to me by the noble and generous Mary.

It was eggplant month. The agro-markets offered nothing but eggplant. We ate rice with eggplant, eggplant with rice, fried eggplant, grilled eggplant, or eggplant in vinegar. I had had it up to my ears with eggplant. Arriving at Paco and Mary's house, I found her preparing eggplant in the oven.

"Get that out of my sight! What the hell, Mary, I feel like vomiting. It seems like there's nothing in Cuba but eggplant."

I couldn't stop complaining. Luckily, Mary didn't take offense at my expletives; I think she felt the same need to swear and grumble, only she did it in an elegant way. She began talking about the dishes in "her time," when there were still things to be had in Cuba. In a luxury of detail, she told me about exquisite dishes of Cuban cuisine. However, not even by resorting to prodigious fantasy could I free myself from the nausea produced by those eggplants roasting in the oven. My stomach and intestines were forming a duo of dissonant music, and it pained me that the others had to hear it. However, the eggplant didn't go slowly into my mouth: I gobbled it down. There was no other way, not with the great hunger that gripped me.

I don't remember how Mary managed to change in a matter of minutes from one subject— the most diverse facets of the culinary arts—to another, the clandestine struggle and her participation in it. I only remember that she suddenly asked me a question.

"Did you know I managed to mislead Ventura? That was so extraordinary that sometimes I wonder if I dreamed it or it really happened."

I already knew that Ventura occupied a senior position in the hierarchy of Batista henchmen and that he was one of the worst thugs in the dictatorship.

It seems that Paco, with the help of his mother, had moved for the tenth time to another apartment, this time to one that had a flat roof, one balcony overlooking the street and another overlooking the patio, two entrances, and big windows, so that fleeing to neighboring houses would be relatively easy. Never before had he needed this type of house, since at crucial moments he had always managed to stay hidden in places where no one was hunting for rebels.

The day of Ventura's visit, Paco was in the apartment. He had a bag full of rifles, ammunition, and other material in a closet, and that would have been enough for the thugs to kill anyone. A friend managed to sound the alarm. Paco grabbed the bag and vanished through the back door, jumping to the roof and from there to an alleyway, blending in with the people passing by.

Ventura personally opened the front door, and like flying cockroaches, his minions, who were armed to the teeth, swarmed into the house. Mary received them as if she were a princess eager to perform her role of hostess to perfection. Ventura stood, frozen, and—perhaps for the first time in his life—astonished, pointing a machine gun at Mary. Everyone knew him; everyone knew that if he appeared with armed assistants in a house it was to kill someone. Mary, knowing perfectly well who he was, received him with a big smile on her face, offering him coffee, and asking him courteously to what she owed this honored visit. His aides didn't dare raise a hand against Mary or tear apart the cupboards and other furniture without the approval of their boss. Ventura was dumbfounded by Mary inviting him to chat and have coffee with her.

On that day, the gift of hypnotizing one of the most feared assassins in Cuba must have fallen from the heavens onto Mary. She had paralyzed the monster with the same verborrhea she demonstrated in teaching me Cuban Spanish. I am convinced that she was so impressed with herself and that spectacle of outsmarting Ventura that it was recorded in her memory, and this recording was repeated to me so many times that, one day, I finally understood every little detail and could reproduce it by heart.

Paco took me to the house of some friends who had hidden him during the period of revolutionary struggle. Among them was old Candelaria, a black woman, as wrinkled as a raisin, charming, funny, well-informed, and spontaneous. She lived in a poor, dirty neighborhood, but her apartment was sparkling and full of *santería* artifacts. It was enough that Paco told her I was a friend of his family for Candelaria to treat me with deference and cordiality. She consented without question to Paco's request that she "throw the shells" for me. I didn't believe then and don't believe now in those things, but Candelaria did her work so seriously, so meticulously, that there was no doubt that she knew the art of divination. I don't remember the details of the consultation. I only remember that she predicted I would have five children. I fulfilled less than half of this program, but why quibble? In addition, Candelaria couldn't know that I was practicing, with satisfactory results, family planning. Over that, the shells had no power.

One morning my captain was away and as now was my custom, I was talking with Mary while she waited for her son to arrive for his Paconian gathering. She received a call from Paco for me.

"Mónica, do you want to learn about another face of our post-Revolutionary culture? I'm with some friends who told me there's a house near here where the new inhabitants are throwing away paintings they consider to be just garbage. If you want, you can come with me to see if there's anything good there."

Curious and more than a little happy to get out, I accompanied Paco. The garage of the house in question was crammed with junk, old boards, and rubble. But there, as advertised, leaning against a wall among sacks of debris, we found a painting by Mijares, a celebrated contemporary Cuban painter. It was a canvas of approximately sixty inches in length and forty in width. It was a bit dirty from mistreatment but otherwise in perfect condition. The person invited us to take it with us.

"Take it away, after all, that junk can be painted by anyone, even a little kid. That's not art. We don't want it in our new house. Not even the frame will work for mosquito netting."

Paco took the Mijares painting home, where it was cleaned and incorporated into his contemporary art collection, which to me was more exciting than the collection at the Museum of Fine Arts in Havana. During the two or three months that I frequented Paco and Mary's house, time and again I admired the incalculable value of their library, record collection, and art objects. Her vast knowledge of art and literature—not only Spanish-American but worldwide—and of philosophy and music impressed me greatly. Without exaggerating, I can say that every day I spent in the company of Paco and Mary became for me a day of learning. I think I took good advantage of the time that the university needed to reorganize its study programs, which for me was a time of recess from official activities in that other, unofficial, center of education.

Thanks to Paco's relationships with painters who still lived in Cuba, I got to know some of the icons of contemporary painting on the island. One day we were driving along the Malecón toward the Plaza de la Catedral in a Willys jeep that was dilapidated, noisy, and spewing a big cloud of black smoke from its tailpipe. Paco had put a cardboard box in the back seat and was driving, talking the whole way.

"Can you tell me where we're going?"

"It's a surprise, and I'm not going to tell you until we get there."

We arrived at the Plaza de la Catedral. Paco found a place to park, and we got out. He grabbed the box and walked toward one of the most beautiful buildings in Havana. When we went up the stairs, he finally told me.

"I'm going to introduce you to Victor Manuel."

Victor Manuel was my favorite Cuban painter. Some of his paintings were exhibited in the Museum of Fine Arts. I liked them, especially his portraits of women with large, dark, almond eyes, looking melancholy and gentle. Their long necks and thin faces made me think of Modigliani, another of my favorite painters.

I couldn't believe that in a few minutes I was going to personally meet Victor Manuel.

The building, which years later would be part of the Historic Center of Havana reconstruction and conservation program, was seriously damaged. Large pieces of stucco hung off the roof and walls, requiring the tenants to be permanently on alert, since if a piece of cement fell on someone's head, a concussion would surely be the result, and perhaps the least serious injury.

Paco rang the bell. As there was no response, he rang again, until finally he realized that the bell wasn't working because the electricity was cut off. He banged on the door with his fist. Steps could be heard, someone shuffling his feet. And then a refined, low voice.

"I'm coming, hang on."

Víctor Manuel, a slender little man with a languid gaze, greeted Paco effusively, like friends who hadn't seen each other in a long time. He appeared to be fatigued, and I realized that he was very ill. He wheezed, like an old accordion that was out of tune. I learned later that he had never been able to overcome a chronic lung illness, which in the end led to his death.

Paco introduced me as a "German artist of high caliber" and told him a lot of invented things about me, sprinkled with a myriad of lies. Victor Manuel looked me up and down. Walking backwards, still analyzing me, he murmured something I couldn't hear. Paco was dying of laughter, infecting Victor Manuel with his state of euphoria.

"Don't believe a single word Paco tells you. I'm not an artist, or anywhere near one," I clarified.

"Victor Manuel, she's modest, but she's a wonderful painter. I've seen her latest painting in her house. It's a marvel," said Paco, among laughs that almost suffocated him, alluding to a painting that I had recently painted on a bag of sugar, using up the last vestiges of a box of watercolors that was one of my remaining treasures brought from Germany.

The result of my attempt to create something decorative for the living room wall was a multicolored bird. Purely by chance what came out was the image of a tropical bird, although nonexistent in the catalogue of bird species of the world. It satisfied my need at the time to put something decorative on the wall that wasn't a plaster figurine like the horrors that abounded in the shops, or some tasteless artificial flowers. At that time I couldn't really afford to buy a painting.

Victor Manuel was delighted with my self-analysis and subsequent self-disqualification as a painter. I don't know if he believed me or Paco. I must have made a big impression on him, because after inviting me to a work session for him to paint my portrait (my extremely long neck fascinated him), he gave me two of his latest prints, dedicating them to me, and he also arranged to have them framed. A friend managed to get them out of Cuba. I have them here, in my apartment in Germany, as a timeless memory of this great painter.

The painting of "the German woman with an enormously long neck" was never painted. Death intervened in this last project of Victor Manuel.

CHAPTER SIX

FILMING WITH THE GERMANS

My regular get-togethers with friends, lessons for me about daily life in Cuba, became sporadic, because once again the Germans in the trade office needed my help. They wanted me to meet in Havana with a group of filmmakers from the East German state film company, headed by director Kurt Maetzig. I had seen actors like Armin Müller-Stahl, Günther Simon, and Gerry Wolf only in movies, and now suddenly they were asking me to work with them for several months in the filming of a Cuban-German co-production. That was my introduction to an interesting category of art: cinema. I helped organize the takes and prepare the timetables, and I traveled with the cast to locations in Havana and the interior of the country.

I also had the responsibility of taking members of the team to the hospital if they got hurt during the filming, or had to consult a specialist about digestive problems, or—as happened with the director's wife—had to see an obstetrician. She insisted on bringing her first son into the world in the city of Havana, a caprice that cost whatever patience her husband, who was at least twenty-five years older, still had left.

One of the most impressive scenes in the movie was filmed on and near the famous Bacunayagua Bridge, whose beautiful span is almost 400 feet above the river below. We worked there for several days, leaving early in the morning to travel by van to Matanzas. By the time we would arrive at the scene, the sun would already be so strong that we'd be feeling depleted of energy before we even began. The German technicians put on a show for the Cubans, taking their clothes off, working in their underwear or in pants that were so short they might as well have been nude. Most astonishing of all, they walked around in sandals.

They soon got what they deserved for such "shockingly immodest" behavior when they carried the camera and other hand-held equipment under the bridge and couldn't use their hands to clear a path through the weeds. *Guao*, an endemic Cuban plant (just touching its leaves causes a terrible rash) burned their skin so horribly that some had to be taken to the hospital in Matanzas to deal with the blisters on their backs, arms, chests, faces, and legs.

It was also my first experience ever with a dangerous plant, and my forearms were also covered with blisters that lasted several weeks and left dark patches for months. I had been saved from more extensive burns because fortunately I was wearing long pants, closed shoes, and a blouse, so the *guao* wasn't able to contact major areas of my skin, but this experience was enough for me to appreciate how my German associates must have been suffering. You only have to burn your skin once with *guao* to understand.

The highway that led to the Bacunayagua Bridge was full of military vehicles, ambulances, and cars in both directions. A group of "enemy invader" parachutists were supposed to parachute onto the bridge to attack a group of rebels (or the other way around, I don't exactly remember) who were hidden in the hills near the bridge. The pyrotechnicians had performed their last tests. Several ambulances with rescue equipment were stationed near the scene and the bridge to be able to go into action immediately should they be needed. Although they were filming only a "pretend" war, the work was still dangerous. Everything was ready for the helicopters to take off and drop the parachutists. Several cameras were set up, like machine-gun emplacements, at different points of the cafeteria—on the terrace and the roof—and on and underneath the bridge. It was an impressive spectacle.

The helicopters circled round and round. Every time the director gave the order to jump, a gust of wind, or cloud, or some other obstacle would prevent it. The director was livid, screaming like a madman, but he had to accept the situation, since the parachutists' safety took priority.

Finally, the helicopters dropped their human cargo. The sky above the bridge was seeded with parachutists. At first they looked like black dots, and then little by little they grew larger. Some managed to land on the bridge. Several landed in the palm trees and other vegetation and dangled in space. One got tangled on the bridge railing and he, too, dangled above the abyss. His buddies had to rescue him; the same with those who were hanging from the trees. The guy on the bridge must have had one of the most frightening moments of his life, suspended by a rope, fearing he might fall 400 feet into the river below at any moment. I'm sure it couldn't have been fun. The cameramen were happy with their filming, although they had to hurry and didn't have the chance to repeat their takes. The rescue of the accident-prone parachutists didn't allow for delay.

After the parachute jumps, we filmed a combat scene in the hills and under the bridge. From far away it looked real. Crowds of curious people tried to approach the bridge. An army unit in charge of keeping the way closed and preventing drivers and pedestrians from approaching guaranteed that no one could get through. The job in Bacunayagua was almost over when the German head of the sound equipment had an accident. He was walking around in Jesus sandals, which left his feet almost bare, and he stepped on a broken bottle and embedded a piece of glass in the sole of his right foot. I took him to the Matanzas hospital, where they already knew me in the emergency room. The surgeon on duty was getting ready to suture the wound, which was an inch deep and three long. The wounded man was as pale as a sheet of paper, and when I saw the doctor grab a curved needle, with a thread so thick it could sew up a truck, I was on the verge of fainting.

"Are you a butcher? Don't you dare suture this man without an anesthetic!"

I blurted this out, astonished and incredulous. The doctor gave me a look that said *Just what I need, an asshole giving me orders* and grabbed the injured foot with one hand to jab in the needle with the other.

"Man, are you crazy? Don't you have *that cooling thing*?"

I was so scared that I forgot the common name of this local anesthetic, which chills the tissue and makes it insensitive to pain; it was an essential medication for all hospitals and medical offices, or at least that's what I thought.

"Tell the nurse to find it; you must have it in the hospital. Don't tell me you're going to sew up this poor devil without an anesthetic. We're not living in the Middle Ages!" I screamed at him, almost feeling the same pain at the thought that they were going to suture him without an anesthetic.

The doctor listened to my diatribe and responded calmly.

"Look, it's been a year since I received the last vial of the anesthetic you're demanding. I have nothing that will help his pain. The wound is bleeding a lot. I'm sorry but I have to suture it without an anesthetic."

I barely dared to translate what the doctor just said to the patient. When he heard that they weren't going to give him any anesthetic, he screamed.

"Go to hell! Let go of my foot! I'm not having a suture, don't touch me!"

"This wound needs to be sutured. If you don't accept my work, you'll have to do something else, but I can assure you that you're not going to find another doctor here in Matanzas who has an anesthetic, because we don't have any."

It took some work to convince the wounded man that he had to submit to torture. But reason triumphed over fear and horror. The patient took a large handkerchief out of his pocket, made it into a ball, and stuck it between his teeth. With his two hands he held onto the seat of the chair and allowed the surgeon to proceed. Few times in my life have I seen a man sweat so profusely. Thick drops of sweat poured from his forehead; sweat ran down his arms and legs, leaving black tracks of dust. We carried him, half-fainting, to the car to return to the filming location.

"I hope I never have to submit to something like this here in Cuba." I told the doctor.

But just five months later, when I gave birth to my first son, they did things a thousand times worse to me than I had just witnessed.

Having finished the filming in Bacunayagua, Mariel, and the center of Havana, we had a few days left in the Hotel Habana Libre where the office of the director, Maetzig, was. The suite, converted into an office, was like an anthill; Cuban and German filmmakers came and went, and several times the famous Soviet poet Yevgeni Yevtushenko, at that time the poetry star of the socialist bloc, made an appearance. I was present at enjoyable discussions and felt extremely good in this atmosphere. I would have liked to continue working in this field, but before thinking about any serious job I had to finish my degree. In addition, I had only five months left before the birth of my son, and that—whether I liked it or not—would have to take priority.

As for the famous movie filmed by the Cubans and Germans in the summer and autumn of 1962, it seems it didn't pass the test of those who had to authorize its screening. I never heard anything more about it.

CHAPTER SEVEN

THE MISSILE CRISIS

Luckily I never knew the real extent of the danger to which the entire world was exposed during the fateful days of what the West knows as the "Cuban Missile Crisis." After finishing my project with the film crew I started working in a language school. The day the crisis was at its height, my captain came running from work to tell me that he needed to pack some things, he was mobilized to take charge of a ship, and he had only half an hour with me. He didn't know, he said, when he was coming back.

"Can you give me your telephone number so I can find you in case there's a problem?"

"I don't have a telephone; there's no way to find me. When your father was at the front during the war, could they find him by telephone?"

"Listen, this is different. Of course there's no communication with family members in a war, but we're not at war here."

"What do you mean, we're not at war? The Yankees have been at war with us for a while, and now the situation has worsened, and we don't know how and when it will end. I asked Carmen and Mañi (wives of friends also mobilized) to come around so you don't feel so alone. Take care of yourself and our half-a-son in your belly. And don't worry, everything will work out."

I didn't know how not to worry, how to believe that everything would work out, since he had just told me that we were at war. How did I end up in this crazy country?

The initial fear dissipated immediately after my captain left. I was still upset, but more because of the loneliness than the political situation of the moment. I think I had heard so much talk about the wolf that I stopped believing in him. I came to think that it was more a matter of bravado than serious danger and that talking about a state of war was an exaggeration. Indeed, since my arrival in Cuba, in early 1962, I had been seeing every kind of person—teenagers, young people, adults, and old people—with every type of weapon—pistols, revolvers, submachine guns, and rifles—in the street, as if those objects were part of their bodies. So "war" seemed to me to be just another ideological catchword.

The only thing that really, truly bothered me was the absence of my husband. Since the wedding, I had spent entire weeks without him. Every other minute, it seemed, he would be called away for an indefinite time. When we decided to get married he had warned me clearly, so I had no right to complain, and yet it was terribly hard for me to accept this reality. Theory is one thing and practice another.

Being in a country that for me was still full of mystery, alone, pregnant, with no one close by I could run to if I needed help was a difficult test of patience and endurance. Sometimes I would stroll along the Malecón watching the waves, thinking that if it were possible to walk across them to the other side of the Atlantic, I would do so in an instant.

On the day the news was published of the Soviets' unilateral decision to withdraw the missiles stationed on Cuban soil, the cries of the newspaper vendors woke me up.

"*Nikita, mariquita, lo que se da no se quita*! Nikita, little faggot, what you give shouldn't be taken away!"

Other insults against the Soviet Union, particularly against Nikita Khrushchev, could be heard everywhere. I dressed quickly and went down to the street. A spontaneous mini-rally had formed, without direction from the higher organizations—neither the

Committee for the Defense of the Revolution nor any official institution had called for a mobilization. People were grimacing, screaming, shouting angrily. Some were laughing; others were yelling "treason" and "no respect for Fidel," and even attacking the Soviets, calling them "cowards."

I bought a newspaper to find out the details. I believe it was the day after the Soviets urgently sent Andrei Gromyko, the Minister of Foreign Relations, to Havana to placate Fidel's anger. Days later, Fidel visited the u.s.s.r., and as I recall, during his stay there, the "unwavering friendship between Cuba and the u.s.s.r." was reaffirmed.

CHAPTER EIGHT
THE BIRTH OF OUR FIRST SON

I HAD BECOME PREGNANT two months after arriving in Cuba, but I didn't know it until my fourth month. In the midst of my efforts to adapt to my new tropical world, constantly made unpleasant by my mother-in-law; trying, with the help of my sister-in-law, to understand the mysteries of *santería*; doing temporary work with the Germans in the chargé d'affaires office and the film crew; and studying the past and present history of Cuba at Mary and Paco's house, I hadn't noticed the changes that were taking place in my body. The nausea and dizziness, the fatigue, and the paralyzing sleepiness caused by the tiny fetus lodged in my body was depriving me of energy and leaving me a sleepwalker. I didn't interpret these as the unmistakable signs of pregnancy that they were. I attributed them to the climate, which was diametrically opposed to the one I had known in my twenty-one years of life in northern Europe, and to the shortage of food, which became more catastrophic every day in the Cuba of 1962.

I continued menstruating, but it was only a light bleeding. In reality, this was a serious threat to my bringing the pregnancy to term, but I totally ignored the danger because it didn't occur to me that I might be pregnant.

"The only advantage of the change in climate that I can see is that menstruation now takes place every forty days instead of twenty-five, and the flow lasts for only one or two days and is lighter than ever," I commented to a woman friend, the only one I dared to talk with about such intimate matters.

"Mónica, you're pregnant," she told me. "You have to go to the doctor as soon as possible in case you have a serious problem. Look, if you want, I'll go with you. That way you can register in the hospital so they'll take care of you during the whole pregnancy."

I still wasn't totally convinced that my strange mental and physical state was because I was pregnant, but just to make sure, I agreed to go to the hospital with my friend and consult a specialist.

"Be ready at four in the morning. You have to go to the hospital early because they can only take so many people. You have to stand in line."

There were still doctors' offices and private clinics where you could receive complete attention, but you had to have a friend to get in. We had the money to pay for a private clinic, but it was a matter of principle:

"You're going to receive medical attention in one of the best hospitals run by the Revolution," my captain told me. "No way will you have privileges. Medicine is for all the people."

You had to stand in line to get in, and the lines were organized. At the agreed-upon time my friend and I were in front of the hospital. A long line had already formed. With the confidence of someone who knows, my friend yelled:

"Who is the last in line?"

"Here!" answered a young woman with a large belly.

We joined the line into the place assigned to us and began to wait. At noon I was registered and with that had the right to be seen in the hospital. The doctor confirmed my pregnancy and explained my "tropical menstruation" as a threat to my pregnancy: he said I might have a miscarriage. Fortunately, and without applying any therapeutic measures, not even rest, the bleeding stopped. The little one seemed to be clinging to me like a snail to its shell.

I went regularly to my appointments with the obstetrician. Each time I was seen by a different specialist, so I didn't know whether I would see a familiar face on the day I gave birth. Every appointment was an exhausting exercise in patience. I would spend hours and hours sitting in the waiting room, during which I learned a lot about gynecology and obstetrics, without knowing that years later I would be dealing with these issues professionally. Women from at least three generations—teenagers, their mothers, and their grandmothers—would be expecting offspring, and they would pass the time in the doctor's office exchanging experiences about being pregnant in a frank and uninhibited way that I had never heard before. What was evident in their conversations was the lack of contraceptives, medication, or information, and also of the possibility of an abortion. This last lack resulted in a "baby boom," an enormous number of births, but also, in the first half of the sixties, a high infant and maternal mortality rate.

Luckily, I was able to take the preparatory course for *parto sin dolor*—"childbirth without pain." I learned that giving birth doesn't hurt and that the uterus contracts until it stays dilated and opens the canal and the orifice for the baby to be born. In the course, the instructors constantly repeated that the word "pain" was incorrect; the word "contraction" should be used instead. I was satisfied with this definition, but subconsciously I heard the voice of my mother, who, on the few occasions that she spoke about giving birth, always referred to long hours filled with pain until "the bursting point"—and my mother wasn't one to complain easily. Also, my Cuban friends who had already experienced childbirth looked at me with faces that said, without having to say a word, *Poor thing, she doesn't know what she's talking about.*

My confidence continued as I observed the growth of my belly. My body had become a caricature. My legs and arms were thin; my belly was adorned in the center with an American football; and my face was so gaunt it looked like I had just come out of a concentration camp. I would spend the day dreaming about food that didn't exist in Cuba. Everyone made an effort to offer me something to eat—for example, malt drink mixed with condensed milk. I only managed to drink one glass of this concoction. As soon as it got to my stomach it came back up, to the dismay of the kind couple who had sacrificed their ration of condensed milk and malt.

One month before the delivery we were given an apartment in El Vedado. It was a cubbyhole adjoining a *solar*, a tenement house, where a large contingent of immigrants from Oriente Province—the new labor force in Havana—had moved. These neighbors of mine, illegal and omnipresent, with an enormous reproductive capacity, became my unwitting teachers of Cuba's lowlife slang. From early in the morning until late at night, I heard vocabulary which, my friends assured me, didn't belong to the Castilian lexicon but formed an unquestionable part of Cuban popular speech. Little by little, the most vulgar swearwords were engraved on my brain. When I asked my friends the meaning of those dreadful words, their mouths dropped open, and they didn't want to answer me.

"Mónica, don't say those words. They're obscene," they warned me.

"But they're screaming them all day long. Listen for yourself. The mother of the little boy who's running around naked in the courtyard, she calls her own boy a 'son of a bitch,' 'cunt,' 'shit,' and 'bastard,' and I don't know how many other epithets, as if they're terms of endearment. They don't sound unpleasant to me; besides, they're spoken with force and are surprisingly frequent," I told them.

"It's true, but you must know that this vocabulary is disgustingly vulgar. A decent person doesn't use it."

My neighbors in the *solar*, however, continued to communicate among themselves using this special language, and, little by little, I learned how to differentiate between the most offensive words and the ones that were less dirty, and on what occasions they were used, being very careful myself not to utter any of these indecencies, which were learned almost despite myself, and in unfortunate circumstances.

I was confident and excited as I prepared for the day of the great event—the birth of my son—and I paid strict attention to my exercises, especially the one where I took rapid breaths, as I had been instructed to do for the later contractions. I felt like a panting dog. I was still working as a teacher of German until the last minute, and I was so unbearably tired that I couldn't stand it anymore. I was ready to let go of my little bundle, which was now a heavy load.

Teaching languages was one of the hardest of the many jobs I had in my life. My students were militants of the Communist Youth, almost all without any cultural education, who were trainees or employees of the foreign service, so knowing a foreign language was indispensable for their work. The selection of my students turned out to be a true disaster. Only one had the required ability to learn such a difficult language as German; the rest didn't even know the basic elements of Spanish. Their vocabulary was extremely limited even in their own language, and when they wrote in Spanish, I had to decipher their salad of spelling mistakes.

We were learning the conjugation of German verbs. Since they didn't understand any of the terminology of grammar and I wasn't going to accomplish anything talking to them about infinitives, singular, plural, present tense, indicative, and subjunctive, I had to resort to other teaching methods that were more primitive but, for the moment, very effective. In order for them to understand me, I wrote on the left side of the blackboard the conjugation of a given verb in Spanish and on the right side the same thing in German. When I got to the form for "you talk," *vosotros habláis* in academic Spanish, a chorus of laughs and comments interrupted my work.

"Ay, no, prof, that ain't needed in 'Panish, this you invented it."

How happy they were, convinced that they had caught me committing errors in Spanish. My model student, upset, tried to help me.

"Look, guys, the professor is right. It does exist in Spanish, but we don't use this form in Cuba. Here we say *ustedes hablan* instead of *vosotros habláis*."

"Boy, that *vosotro*, maybe Germans say it, but not in 'Panish," was the challenging reply.

The following day they disrespected me again in a way that I wasn't ready to tolerate. Trying to explain another grammatical problem in German, gathering all my patience, I suddenly saw that some of my worst students were reading the newspaper. They were so absorbed in their reading that they didn't notice that I had stopped talking and was looking at them with disgust and amazement.

"Ay, profe! What's wrong? Are you upset? Please, don't get yourself upset. We don't understand nothing of what you're saying, so we're reading the paper and not bothering you."

I refused to keep giving German classes to this group and imposed the condition that students had to have at least full knowledge of their native language in order to be accepted into my class. That way I managed to get rid of the semi-illiterates in my program who had no interest in anything I had to teach them, but this didn't happen until after the birth of my son, the best gift I could possibly have.

The night before the delivery, my anxiety prevented me from sleeping. At one in the morning I woke up my husband.

"Listen, I need to walk. Come with me. It seems our son is bored; he wants movement."

We got dressed and walked along the Malecón. In the middle of February it was as hot as the middle of summer. In order to feel the breeze from the sea, I climbed up on the Malecón wall. My belly didn't hinder my acrobatics, worthy of a circus act.

We came back home and went to bed. At three in the morning I awoke from a tortured dream. I was having strong, sporadic cramps in my belly and was immersed in a lake of pink water. My bed had become a bathtub. I took off the wet sheet, washed it, and kept dribbling water, without understanding where it was coming from.

I was now standing in a pool of water. What did this mean? Where was so much water coming from? I hadn't drunk enough liquid to produce such a huge leak; had the boy given me a kick in the bladder? I tried to figure out the reason for this. I opened my consultation book and found all the stages of pregnancy and delivery described. At the end I found the explanation. Reading the paragraph about the beginning of birth, I found that I was making headway in the process of bringing a child into the world.

The children's song *Let's go, let's go, the dam is breaking,* came to my mind, suddenly acquiring quite a different meaning. I took another shower, dried off, plugged the leak with a pack of cotton, and again woke up my husband, who was sound asleep, exhausted from the loss of sleep on the Malecón. Around four in the morning we went to the hospital.

"I'm having contractions every three or four minutes and my water broke at three in the morning," I informed the doctor in the obstetrics emergency room.

I began the bureaucratic step of filling out forms when there suddenly was a racket and people running as if they were possessed. The doctor, after assuring me that my son would be born that day and there was still enough time for the required dilation to take place, left me alone with the nurse. His presence was required for a very sick patient. She was on a stretcher in the cubicle next to me, surrounded by two policemen and several family members. The police were yelling and repeating the same question over and over. They wanted the sick woman to give them the name of the person who had helped her to abort. The patient, now half-dead with pain and suffering, refused to answer. Her family begged her to tell them who it was. Nothing. The doctor intervened, ordering everyone out. They took her to the operating room, where—as I learned later—they had to remove her uterus in order to save her life. She had injected hydrochloric acid to get rid of an unwanted pregnancy and was now mutilated, at the age of eighteen, and unable to be a mother. This was my first experience with the problem of abortion. Many years later, the subject of abortion would become one of the key issues in my work.

I never again saw the doctor who had admitted me. A nurse took charge, moving me to a small room where she made me perform the work of "hatching my egg" for eight hours.

"The specialist in 'childbirth without pain'," they informed me, with evil faces, "isn't in the hospital today. You picked a bad day to give birth, so you must try to take care of this by yourself. You learned all the steps, so you won't have a problem," was the nurse's cynical comment.

She closed the door and left. She came back about every two hours, hours that for me were centuries of torture and suffering compared to nothing I had ever before experienced. During those eight hours of struggle to give birth and survive, I totally lost faith in the friendly therapy of "childbirth without pain." I felt betrayed, abandoned, mistreated, humiliated, and punished for something that I couldn't understand. What did this woman mean by "pain" I wondered, over and over between violent contractions that were shattering me. If this isn't pain, then either I'm abnormal or she doesn't know what she's talking about. Maybe something inside me broke; perhaps I'm dying and my son along with me, and no one here cares. They're not worried about what I'm going through. They've abandoned me, and my husband, instead of looking for help, is in his office, not realizing that we're dying.

I swore I would never look at him again, that I would punish him for what he had done to me, for being indifferent to my suffering, for not even knowing the state of distress and misery we found ourselves in, his son and I.

A half-hour before they took me to the delivery room, the nurse came for the last time to check the progress of my labor. She found me contorted, with my lips bleeding from the bites I had inflicted on myself so I wouldn't scream. Screaming seemed undignified; I didn't want to lose what little self-respect I had left.

"Don't be an idiot, stop biting yourself, that doesn't help anything," she told me angrily. "Did they tell you that this wouldn't hurt? Well, now you know. This is what giving birth is, and all the women who have children have gone through it. Why don't you complain to the therapist that they lied to you?"

Before my son emerged from his sanctuary, I spent the last minutes in agony and exhaustion, desperately taking the short, quick breaths of a panting dog that I had learned in the classroom of lies. I believe that a high-performing athlete wouldn't, in a year of training, expend the energy I did in my eight hours of labor. When the final contractions came, the obstetrician who had taken care of the German film director's wife made a triumphal entrance into the room.

"Well, look at this. My last day of work in this happy hospital, and they have me taking care of the German woman. So, my little German, with you I'm finishing my work in Cuba, because I'm leaving for the north. You're the last person I'm seeing here."

And with that, my son shot out of my belly like a slippery rocket. The doctor collected him, gave him the obligatory slaps on the backside, and deposited him in a basket next to me. We had decided to name him Dictys after the Greek fisherman who saved Perseus' life and gave him shelter.

It was exactly twelve noon, time for the doctor's lunch. It seemed he didn't want to miss his turn in the dining room, because he didn't take the time needed for the placenta to come out by itself. He twisted the umbilical cord around his wrist and pulled it with such force that the placenta broke. A very large portion was left inside my uterus. This mishap didn't prevent him from abandoning me to go eat lunch. He left me with a nurse's aide who knew as much about giving birth and related matters as I did about the Chinese language; that is to say, nothing. I was too drained to realize that something very serious had happened.

Another doctor, very young, who hadn't seen the previous steps and thus didn't know that the placenta hadn't completely emerged, performed the routine task of repairing the external areas before releasing me to a nurse's aide, who took me to the recovery room. Of course, this last step also took place without an anesthetic. Why use an anesthetic if I had withstood consecutive and intense pain without any kind of analgesic for eight hours?

Five hours later I was in septic shock and hanging between life and death. However, the diagnosis of "sepsis from remaining pieces of the placenta" wasn't given until three weeks later. I was found with barely perceptible vital signs. It seems that the doctor on call had fallen asleep or was indisposed; the fact is that there was no doctor at this time in the emergency room. By telephone—I found out later—they asked for instructions from the doctor who had caused the rupture of the placenta. He gave the nurse instructions to give me an antibiotic to "treat what is surely a kidney infection."

This was the first time in my life that I had received a dose of antibiotics. It had the desired effect. That is, I survived, at least, although nothing was done to fix the root problem: removing the rest of the placenta. The two days I stayed in the hospital were a challenge. No one noticed the infection that was eating me up inside. No one noticed that I had a high fever. No one noticed that I was bleeding copiously, that I was anemic. No one realized that I didn't have the strength to take care of my son.

After we arrived at our hovel on the third floor of the apartment building in El Vedado, we discovered that the water pump had burned out during my stay in the hospital and that for two days there hadn't been any water. The icing on the cake was that the gas line to our apartment had been shut off because the pipe between the wall and the kitchen was cracked. We didn't have water or gas. This was the welcome home we offered our son.

I was alone with the infant. The father of the little creature couldn't manage to get a few days off to help me solve the serious problems in the apartment. Nor did he know that I was very sick. Neither did I. For me, all this was part of the labor. Hadn't they told me that delivery wouldn't hurt? Hadn't they told me later that all this torture was normal? How, then, was I going to complain if everything was normal? I consulted my wise book about pregnancy and childbirth. The consultation left me confused, since I didn't know how to evaluate whether my state was owing to phenomena that still qualified as normal or whether it was some pathology.

Motherhood, so fervently desired, began in a truly chaotic and nerve-racking way. My new obligations with the little one demanded all the strength I had left, day and night. The baby couldn't get what he most needed: mother's milk. The search for powdered milk prescribed by the pediatrician became one of the many nightmares that still loomed on the list of calamities reserved for me. With every day that passed, I was, without realizing it, slipping closer to the grave. The baby cried, shrieked, and screamed every two hours, driving me crazy. In order to prepare the milk, the food, and do the washing and scrubbing, I had to go down to the basement and scoop pails of water from the tank, since the pump was still not repaired. I owned twenty cloth diapers; my son wet and soiled them all in less than a day.

My captain got a woman from the neighborhood to take charge of washing the clothes, especially the diapers. She had to go down to the basement from the third floor several times a day to get the water, and she soon lost the desire to earn a few pesos by washing diapers. She didn't take her leave before "disappearing" half of the diapers hung out to dry on the roof.

"*Señora*, the wind took away almost all the diapers," she informed me when I asked what happened to these important items.

"But the clothing of all the neighbors is still on the clothesline; the wind blew away only my diapers? How do you explain that?"

"Because the clothespins on yours didn't hold," she answered, trying to justify her lies.

She was angry and resentful about the unacceptable work conditions and said the lack of water and gas kept her from being able to work like she should, that she had a sick mother to take care of, and that I should find someone else who would accept these working conditions. My "help" hadn't lasted long, and, on top of that, I now had to beg for diapers, since you couldn't find them in the shops or even through the ration book: "the wind" had taken them away.

The detergent that was being distributed to the population couldn't be used to wash the few diapers that the child had left; if it was corrosive to my skin, it was going to leave the baby's backside even worse. I bought special bars of soap in the pharmacy. Within a week of receiving my ration, I requested another bar.

The pharmacist scolded me in front of all the customers, accusing me of squandering the baby's soap for my own use.

"No new-born needs so much soap. Go somewhere else!" he screamed at me, anticipating a chorus of approval from the clientele who were watching me with scorn.

Embarrassed, humiliated, and without soap, I had to return home. I cried at my son's side like Mary Magdalene, and, although it didn't solve anything, at least I felt better, and my head cleared enough to think about how to solve all the problems that had no solution.

We continued to live without water and the gas to heat it for washing diapers and cooking. Every night, my husband filled buckets and pots with water from the tank so I wouldn't have to carry them myself, and he got me a camping stove and a gallon of alcohol, with which I performed miracles.

My state of health continued to decline. After three weeks of carrying on as best I could, of trying to solve problems and fulfill my role as a mother, I couldn't do it anymore. My captain called a doctor who was a friend of the family so he could take me to a private specialist. Without asking my opinion, they admitted me to the hospital. When I woke up from the anesthesia—the first ever in my life—they told me they had tried to remove the rest of the placenta, but they weren't able to do it completely because they were afraid of rupturing the uterus.

"Girl, what did they do to you? If there had been a midwife in the delivery room, you wouldn't be in this pathetic shape," the nurse assured me. "What kind of animal of a doctor broke the placenta without taking out the rest? It's a miracle you're alive."

The doctors who tried to eliminate the damage were scandalized and wanted to accuse the person who had done it, but this didn't make any sense. For one thing, the damage had already been done; also, the doctor responsible was now in the north.

Anemic, with an infection kept in check by very strong antibiotics whose numerous side effects made me feel miserable, I tried to be a good mother. There weren't enough hours in the day. During my stay in the hospital my son had been passed from one person to another. They had all tried to do their best, but as each substitute mother had her own methods, beliefs, and remedies, the baby was in worse condition than when he was with me. On top of this, there was no more of the powdered milk that the doctor had prescribed. In order to get it, we had to go to San Antonio de los Baños, because the Havana pharmacies didn't have any powdered milk for babies, and when the can from San Antonio was empty, my son had to get used to drinking whatever milk we could find. He soon stopped being picky and selective, but he showed his discontent with a series of allergic reactions that still today haven't left him.

About a month after our son was born, a miracle happened: the Office of Supply Control, knowing that I had worked in the German chargé d'affaires office, put me on the list of foreign technicians who were eligible to receive a special quota of food. It was really my neighbors who benefited from this privileged status. For the child, for example, they gave me *malanga*, a type of yam. This strange root vegetable, slimy and dirty-gray, didn't seem the right thing to feed to a newborn. I continued consulting my book, which prescribed food that was totally unknown or nonexistent in Cuba, imported products that weren't coming into the country. The *malanga* and other delicacies, whose fantastic qualities I knew nothing about, ended up in my neighbors' cooking pots, and they didn't take the trouble to explain to me how to prepare them. Leaving me ignorant was for them a guarantee of obtaining those products that I didn't know how to appreciate properly. They knew exactly the day and time when I received the carton full of rare goods. Not five minutes would go by before they made their requests.

"Mónica, please, I need you to 'loan' me a little oil, rice, coffee, salt, butter, condensed milk, malanga, preserves ..." It was clear that "loan" meant "give."

"Mónica, I need you to give me a little *Fa*."

This syllable I only knew from music terminology. I couldn't imagine anything by the name of "Fa."

"Carmita, what are you asking for? What is it?" I inquired.

"*Fa*, to wash the clothes," she answered and took a container of detergent from the kitchen shelf, where she kept it.

"And why do you call this *Fa*?" I asked.

"Ah, it was called that before."

She was referring to the detergent brand FAB, which years later I saw in the U.S. through an ad on television, which Dictys repeated, singing like a parrot, "Oh, FAB, I'm glad they put new borax in yououou," and which was one of the first sentences in English that he learned.

As was their custom, my neighbors wanted to show their joy at the birth of our son. They visited me to bring gifts appropriate to the occasion. Each one explained the purpose of the little medals, earrings, and images of the saints they gave us. I understood nothing whatsoever. Caridad, the mother of two daughters, gave me a pin with a small ball of black glass as a substitute for jet, along with instructions about where I had to put it. Her friend, Carmita, gave me a tin badge that represented a saint and explained to me which corner of the crib I should tie it to. Their explanations would be interrupted by cries of "Ay! What a handsome boy, how beautiful!" "God bless him!" screamed Esperanza, in ecstasy. I heard "I could eat him!" but I couldn't understand why I should eat my son.

Our firstborn, instead of thanking the neighbors for their cordial welcome and the gifts, omens of good luck, offered them a concert of unbearably strident screams and cries, which made them say goodbye in a hurry, but not without repeating the instructions on the use of the pins and badges of saints, which remained in a little box where I kept trashy ornaments, rope, string, nails, screws, and other junk "just in case." I had learned not to throw anything away; when I least expected it, I might need one of those treasures. There was nothing left in the hardware stores but bare shelves and some useless pieces of junk recently imported from the U.S.S.R.

Three days before my first birthday in Cuba, at the beginning of April 1963, and six weeks after giving birth, I was again admitted to the hospital. I was still alive, thanks to the antibiotics, which were the most important part of my daily diet. This time, the doctors removed an unrecognizable ball of tissue from me. It was clear to them that a malignant tumor would soon finish me off. Luckily, a skilled pathologist identified the tumor as the remains of the placenta, which had embarked on a process of transformation. This brought on a chain of other pathological problems, which over the years required several extremely delicate surgical interventions, in the course of which large quantities of degenerated tissue and deteriorated organs were removed which were thrown into the hospital trash in three countries on two continents. The day my first son was born was also the end of my excellent state of health. Never more in my life would I know what it was to feel no discomfort, no pain, and no health problems. Never again would I know what it was to get a good night's sleep, without interruption.

I was discharged on the afternoon of my birthday. At home a tremendous surprise awaited me: the water pipe had been fixed, and my captain had found a piece of copper pipe and a fifty-pound cylinder full of liquid gas, which was installed directly in the kitchen. Of course, this was an emergency solution; it was prohibited to place a gas tank inside the house, but by now I knew that the laws and provisions concerning individual safety were enforced with quite elastic standards in Cuba. The little tank stayed there forever. What happiness it was to have water and to be able to cook! I initiated the gas, which now worked, by cooking a soup of potatoes with white beans, using a pressure cooker that my captain had brought back as a gift from one of his trips to Canada. The pressure cooker was packed in a very pretty box and came with an instruction booklet that was full of recipes.

"Before you start using the pressure cooker, do me a favor and be sure to read the instructions. This type of cooker is a marvel, but it's also very dangerous if you don't use it correctly," my husband warned me.

I began to read the instructions, which were written in English

5. *Monika holding baby Dictys in Havana*

and French. And without noticing, I got wrapped up in reading the recipes. My imagination took off, while I peeled the three scrawny potatoes and filled the cooker with the white beans and water. I closed it, put it on the burner, and went back to studying the instructions. Suddenly I heard a strange whistling. The little weight placed on the top of the lid was dancing around frenetically, letting puffs of steam escape to the rhythm of a *chachachá*. I remembered that it didn't take long to cook things, so I turned off the flame and struggled to remove the lid. The lid was stuck. *Damn pressure cooker, what good is it if I can't get it open?* I thought, giving it another strong pull that violently released the lid. The complete contents, now puréed, shot out in all directions, totally transforming the décor of our apartment. Wherever you went now, there were little pieces of potato with white beans: in the kitchen, in the bathroom, in our living room, on the furniture, and on the ceiling. Terrified, my legs like rubber, my hands trembling, and holding the lid with my right hand, I managed to protect my face from terrible burns. I had on a loose-fitting cotton housedress, which was splashed with potato and beans.

After this traumatic experience with the pressure cooker, I never used it again. I gave it to my sister-in-law who knew how to use it, and every time I saw her manipulating the monstruous pressure valve, I walked away. This fear sank into my bones and remains today.

The Germans in the chargé d'affaires office needed my services again. Their interpreter was on vacation, and to avoid paying, they hadn't hired anyone to fill in. The trade advisor visited me in person to request my help.

My son was already spending the day in childcare. For three hours a day, I tried to teach German to a group of young people and help the Germans with an engineer in Havana, who was setting up an exhibition of electrical equipment. My knowledge of physics, acquired in pre-university school, wasn't sufficient for me to serve as an interpreter in this business, so I asked the engineer to give me an introductory course and explain to me how the equipment worked. He was extremely patient, and thanks to his effort, skill, and gift for teaching, I was successful in my job, for which I had no qualifications. The work, although highly complex, was so satisfactory—of course, he wanted the work to be successful—that he took away my fear of the unknown.

However, on the innumerable occasions when I had to translate, I found very few specialists, scientists, or technicians who were capable of understanding the difficulty implicit in the work of translation. I was always surprised to discover that self-sufficiency is arrogantly demanded of an interpreter, who must translate any subject in science or art, as if translating means mechanically replacing the words of one language by another.

A few days after I finished my work in the field of electronics, I was presented with a challenge that put my ability to adapt to unusual changes to the test. The Germans called me again to tell me that the director of the Berlin State Opera was in Cuba to teach a course in choral conducting for one month to various choral conductors from around the island. The official interpreter scheduled to do the simultaneous interpretation for this course had to cancel because of an emergency. When they explained the content of the course to me, I said I was really not qualified and wouldn't dare take up the baton of interpreter, since I knew absolutely nothing about the subject. I knew how to read sheet music, but that was it. From there to serving as an interpreter for a course of this complexity was a real stretch. I didn't have the required training and didn't want to make a fool of myself or waste their time. But they told me that I would be the salvation of the course, that I had to do the work, that I couldn't leave them hanging, and that I could ask them to explain the special terminology of the program. We agreed that I would learn it the best I could and that we'd give it a try, always with the caveat that I could cancel my participation at any time if I wished.

The problem was solved quickly and in the efficient Cuban way: the course would begin on Monday morning, and on Sunday afternoon, the specialized interpreter, before leaving, would sit down with me and the director of the opera and develop a glossary of the terminology for the course. These work sessions were fascinating, and I learned how to do simultaneous translation for many aspects of choral and orchestral conducting. I learned that each movement performed by the conductor has its own vocabulary in the language of music, and that the conductor translates the score into movements. My work as an interpreter in this choral conducting class became one of the most enriching and satisfactory jobs of my life. I got to know outstanding Cuban and German musicians. The course culminated with a concert, and we bid farewell to the German professor with a no-holds-barred reception: roast pig, banana chips, mashed bananas, and delicious *chicharrones*, which are pork cracklings. I ate so much that I still remember the stomach cramps I got from my out-of-control gluttony of the rich food with masses of fat, not seen or devoured since I arrived in Cuba.

This course was the beginning of a series of interesting, stimulating, and enriching volunteer projects with the Havana Conservatory. On several occasions throughout the years, I was asked to help with texts and works in the German language. Again I was astonished by the enthusiasm, application, and tenacity with which the members of the National Chorus of Cuba and their students dedicated themselves to music. They were a welcome contrast to my pupils in the language school, who had killed my desire to teach. Furthermore, these musicians, who didn't know a word of my native language, were memorizing extremely complicated texts. I translated the content for them, sometimes phonetically transcribing the innumerable stanzas of Brahms, Schubert, and Schumann *lieder*, and even Beethoven's Choral Fantasy. Our joint efforts were rewarded with a premiere that took place in the Amadeo Roldán Theater, a beautiful auditorium in El Vedado, which burned to the ground many years later.

Our son was now three months old and sleeping six hours straight at night, which was quite a relief. I finally could also sleep and recover my strength in this crazy struggle called motherhood. From our arrival home, two days after the birth of our son, my husband and I had agreed to take turns with the baby at night, when he was waking up every two or three hours, screaming so despairingly that it drove me mad. This agreement didn't hold, because the creature's *papá* slept so soundly that he didn't hear his son crying. I didn't have enough stamina or patience to listen to those nerve-wracking screams.

One night when it was my captain's turn, I woke him up since neither cannons nor earthquakes nor the eruption of a volcano would have done so—much less the crying of a newborn. I then understood that only a mother's response would do. It seems that from the day of a baby's birth, there's an alarm and warning system installed in the mother that keeps her vigilant, even though she's dead tired. I didn't hear the noise on the street or the neighbors next door, but all it took was one whimper from my son and I was at his side to try to calm him. It was hard to believe my husband when he assured me he hadn't heard a thing—not the crying child or that I had taken his turn. I was angry; I said terrible things; I considered his apparent indifference a violation of our agreement and truly inconsiderate.

The first crisis between my husband and me came about when he, more asleep than awake, at the crack of dawn, took the last bit of milk from the refrigerator, trying to warm it up. The baby was screaming so desperately that even his father, calm and almost immune to these sounds, lost his head and didn't know what to do to silence him.

"Now you have to boil the water, let it cool, and when it's warm, throw in the powdered milk, shake the bottle so there aren't any bubbles, and only then you can give it to the baby," I instructed him, my voice breaking amid sobs.

"Okay, go back to sleep. I know how to prepare it," he answered.

I saw him fill up the bottle with water from the tap without boiling it. For me this was the last straw. On top of this, the kid was shattering our eardrums. Desperation made me lose control, and I said a lot of ugly things to my husband. I insulted him, told him off, humiliated him; I think I even called him a bad father, which made him angry, and he turned his back on me and left the room. Fortunately, these Dantean nights also came to an end. But when this happened, my ability to support stress of this kind also reached its limit. I was in a frankly deplorable state.

The child's medical attention was in the hands of an old pediatrician in a private clinic. Since the disaster with the delivery occurred in a public hospital, where I miraculously emerged still alive but paying the unforgivable price of my health, which until that date had been enviable, my husband decided to enroll our son in this clinic, where, by paying a monthly fee, he acquired the right to be seen.

When the baby was three months old, the pediatrician told me to include eggs in his diet, beginning with a piece of boiled egg. In May of 1963, the CAN (I think the initials meant Combinado Avícola Nacional, the National Poultry Industry) did not yet exist. Beginning in the seventies, it was the institution par excellence, responsible for the supply of eggs to the whole Cuban population. Miraculously, for years the CAN managed to maintain a regular and abundant supply, so that eggs became the island's most important protein, and the peas imported from the U.S.S.R. displaced the black bean. In Miramar—if I'm not mistaken, on Fifth Avenue and Tenth—a monument was erected to the egg.

In 1963, anyone with no relationship with farmers, or without a piece of back yard for raising chickens, could only get eggs in his dreams. We didn't have a yard, nor did we know any farmers from whom we could buy the articles that had disappeared from the markets. A friend gave me a gift—as if it were gold—of a small egg so I could feed it to my son. I kept it in the refrigerator for a while in order to prepare it precisely on the right day. That day arrived. I boiled the egg, removed the shell, cut it into little pieces, and gave him the smallest piece like the doctor had told me. My son didn't like it and spit it out.

"How dare you spit out this delicacy that I saved for you as if it were the most precious thing in the world? Stop being so spoiled and eat this piece of egg. Who knows when you'll see the next one?" I said to him threateningly, and I made him eat the yolk.

Suddenly I saw that he was swelling up. It looked like someone had inflated him with air. His lips, face, hands, feet, legs, arms—his entire body—had puffed up like bread dough. At first I thought I was losing my sight, but soon I realized that it was true: my son had turned into a deformed mass. Desperate, incredulous, almost crazy with terror, I grabbed him and ran out into the street with him in my arms in search of a taxi. There weren't any. I saw a bus and got on, asking the driver to stop in front of the hospital. I ran like a crazy person to the emergency room, where, luckily, they took us immediately.

"*Señora*, your son is allergic to eggs. He is in anaphylactic shock. You got here just in time; one minute more and he would have been asphyxiated, since he was as swollen inside as he was outside," the emergency doctor explained to me, as he adroitly injected the medication needed to deflate the little creature.

Surprisingly, Dictys returned to normal in less than an hour. What an atrocious nightmare. I had been about to kill my son by making him eat an egg. I don't remember how many times, but I know that there were many when I had to accept the validity of the saying "the road to hell is paved with good intentions."

CHAPTER NINE

AN ALMOST FATAL ACCIDENT

The language school wants me back. I can use motherhood as an excuse to stay home, but the students can't wait that long. At the rate we're going, they'll have already forgotten everything.

The school's director promises to find my son a place in a childcare center. In the meantime, while I'm teaching two hours of classes, Dictys, my treasure, is asleep in a baby buggy that some Venezuelan friends got me—this convenience doesn't exist in Cuba; mothers carry their babies in their arms—and he's with the secretary, under the watch of whoever happens to be in the office.

One day I'm advised that they're giving me a spot in childcare, which has opened recently in a house in El Vedado, two blocks from the school where I'm working. Fortunately, there aren't many children and there are more than enough "educators," an ideal situation that will soon be no more. So our son will have a place in a childcare center that meets, essentially, the standards established for this type of institution.

Dictys accepts his new environment from the very first day. The girls who are working there are teenagers. They still haven't received the pedagogical varnish to be able to act with "full knowledge" but intuitively do the correct thing. They are attentive to the little ones in their care; they play a lot with them and are very affectionate with the children. The principal knows nothing about education—neither the techniques to stimulate development nor nutrition—but in her forty years of life she has raised not only her own children but also the offspring of her bosses, in whose houses she worked as a domestic employee before the Revolution. She's a very pragmatic person who also knows how to take care of youngsters.

At home, when Dictys and I are alone because his father is constantly traveling, he makes my life impossible. He cries and doesn't want to eat the mash that I prepare for him with so much care and following, as far as possible, the instructions in my German child-raising manual. I begin to have a complex about being a bad mother, incapable of raising a son. I need to consult the "educators" at the childcare center to see if I can find the reason for this behavior that seems to me so abnormal. The girls reassure me:

"Your boy is one of the happiest ones here; he eats everything we offer him, sleeps well, and almost never cries."

"And how do you manage this?"

"Nothing special, he simply feels good with us. Why don't you stay here for a few hours and observe him? But he mustn't see you. Stay outside and look through the window," they advise me.

Years later, all the mothers who have a child in childcare will be required to stay with the child until the little one adapts to his new life, but at this time, being able to observe the child and the girls working with the children was an exception, a huge favor they were doing me. And sure enough, Dictys is calm. When he sees the food, he opens his mouth like a baby bird and swallows all that gray mush that looks like cement poop.

"But what's that paste that looks so ugly? What are you giving him to eat?"

"It's *puré de malanga*, mashed taro corms. Don't you see how much he likes it? It's the best thing we have for the kids."

Now I realize that Dictys detests the German purée, which explains his lack of appetite. Poor kid. With me he's hungry, at the center they give him what he likes. Also, I soon figure out why he cries so much at home: he misses and demands his rocking chair where his "aunties" in the center rock him. There's no rocking chair at home. I wouldn't even know where to find one, and if I did, I'd have to throw out some piece of furniture to make space for it. A child in Cuba without a rocking chair can't be happy. Little by little I'm learning how to raise a son.

Dictys is already three months old. He has regained an acceptable state of health. I am crazy about going to the beach again, swimming, and jumping off the diving board. Now the American football that took up so much space in my belly has become a baby, asleep in his baby buggy.

The captain continues to travel; I don't see him for months at a time. I have to struggle alone, with my son in tow, on this island that is heaven and hell at the same time, in this country that has so many secrets, so much mystery, and so much desperation reserved for me.

My language classes end at noon. Some people in the school and I decide to go to La Concha in Miramar, a lovely beach. Dictys is in childcare, and for the first time since his birth I can enjoy the best of what Cuba has to offer: the transparent, warm, clean sea, so blue that it looks like a cheap retouched photo. When I'm in the water I forget my problems, sorrows, frustrations, and the desire to return to the cold north of my ancestors. My miraculous imagination takes flight, and I'm in a world of water where I'm happy. I don't have to sweat or suffer the eternal exhaustion that overwhelms me on land. Everything, absolutely everything, in my surroundings is agreeable, and I'm in paradise. It's lucky that my friends from work barely know how to swim. They're not interested in venturing into the deep water. They stay on the shore of this gigantic frying pan, where they're being roasted, along with hundreds of people, in the implacable tropical sun. I don't have to listen to their comments about our school's achievements, their problems with the students, the results of the socialist emulation, and all those daily, repetitive, tiresome, boring subjects.

I swim back toward shore and pull myself up onto a ladder

that is attached to a huge bottle, a former ad for a liquor brand. Some daredevils are diving off the ladder into the water, and I want to show off my own diving, which in times past won the admiration of my college friends. So I climb the ladder to the very top, where there's a platform. After my first dive, which gives me the usual butterflies in the pit of my stomach as I fly through the air, I perform my favorite: an elegant somersault, which requires a minimum of water depth that unfortunately isn't there. I hit the bottom and feel pain when the impact takes place, like being struck on the head. I swallow a lot of water without realizing it and start seeing pretty colors. When I reach the surface, a crowd is shouting:

"She hit bottom. Get her out of the water!" and a young man is grabbing me by the arm to tow me to shore. I don't understand the fuss or the attempt to remove me, because I'm not aware of what happened.

"Let go, I know how to swim!" I yell at my rescuer, and I continue swimming out into the deep water. I leave the crowd behind, with faces full of horror, fright, and surprise. Astonished, they watch me swim away from shore.

I began to feel weird. My head spins; I feel dizzy, and the back of my neck is rigid. My legs aren't responding like I want. Floating gently, I come to the spot where I left my friends. They didn't notice the accident. They invite me to go with them on a rowboat, and I sit down in the boat. Gradually, the pain in my head and the back of my neck becomes so intense that I can barely move. A nausea like I never felt during my pregnancy, an unbearable dizziness, and increasing pain makes me ask my friends to take me home.

"What happened? You're so pale. Do you feel bad?"

"I think the sun got to me," was my convincing response.

They leave me at the childcare center to pick up my son. Don't ask me how I managed to get home with the little one in my arms.

I pass a tormented night. My head hurts and my neck is still stiff, making it impossible to move freely. I have to go to the doctor. In the clinic they give me an x-ray with the only machine that still works. They detect a dislocation of the second cervical vertebra and also diagnose a concussion. Equipped with a neck brace, which immobilizes me, and prescriptions for medication at the pharmacy, I leave to go home. It's hard to believe that I was the person who, with these serious injuries, walked alone, took buses, attended to my three-month-old son, and went back to work to give tedious classes. I continue to be alone with my son. His father is working outside the country.

I am more than fed up with being a single mother with the status of being married. Between giving my classes and teaching them badly; going regularly to physical therapy, which consists of hanging me to stretch my neck, already so long that I could compete perfectly with any portrait of a Modigliani woman; taking care of the little one, who notices my unhappiness and cries louder than usual, I try to find my way out of this dreadful labyrinth. Little by little I lose my desire to keep on living and struggling, Quixote-like, on this accursed island, the Garden of Eden, the Pearl of the Antilles, which up to now has given me more suffering than happiness.

My captain comes back from working abroad to go off again after spending a few days in Havana. I must accept the situation; I have no choice. Didn't I marry a captain? And *a lo hecho pecho* as the Cubans say: you've just got to bite the bullet, a saying that has validity for me.

CHAPTER TEN

MY PARENTS IN HAVANA

My parents secured approval to use a cabin on a German cargo ship to travel to Cuba. Since my departure from Germany on the *Sierra Maestra* the day after my marriage, we hadn't seen each other, and they had never seen their first grandson.

My mother didn't know how to swim and was panicked by the sea. For her, spending three weeks on a ship with no possibility of escape meant torture, but with the possibility of seeing her daughter, son-in-law, and little grandson, she subjected herself to this test of her strength. For my father, the trip was the realization of a dream. Not only was he an experienced swimmer—he had saved several kids, pulling them out of lakes and rivers—but he also liked the constant movement of the ship, the gusts of wind, and the immensity of the sea. He was never seasick, while my mother, from the moment she got on board until she left the ship, was in a deplorable state of health, which the doctor could only relieve with sleeping pills and drugs to prevent nausea.

The trip began in late November, 1963, when Germany was under a thick layer of snow and ice. Cuba was more hospitable, with sun and an agreeable heat, balm for my parents' rheumatic joints.

The day they arrived at the port of Havana there was some kind of disconnect in the port office. They didn't tell us exactly when the ship was arriving, and my parents had to find their own way to our place. My captain and I were at the movies for the first time since the birth of our son. The neighbor had the key to our apartment in case my son needed something, and she opened the door to the visitors, who found our child alone, sleeping in a playpen (which for lack of space also served as a crib). My mother, without understanding anything of what my neighbor was saying as she tried for a long time to explain to them where we were, pictured us in some hospital with serious injuries and was preparing herself mentally for a disaster.

It was a surprise when we came in the door. My parents were sitting in the living room, looking anxious and worried. We hadn't expected them yet, since according to the notice from the port office the ship was supposed to arrive on a different day.

My father took advantage of the three weeks in Cuba to take long excursions, fully utilizing the still-existent system of public transportation. In the mornings, after planning the program on the map, he would walk to the bus stop and disappear. My mother, faced with having to get on a bus without knowing where it was taking her and without understanding the people, was afraid and refused to accompany my father. She waited patiently for me every day, knitting placemats for hours, covering pillows, and creating other useful articles for the house. She only went out on weekends with us when my captain and I could be with the family. My mother had full confidence in her son-in-law, who drove our museum piece of a car with ease and skill and took us to calm, beautiful places, where there were wonderful exotic plants. This, at least, was an interest my parents shared.

One afternoon we were collecting Dictys from childcare to return home when we saw a mob of people with firearms—pistols, revolvers, and Czech submachine guns—screaming and shouting. They formed a human anthill in front of our building. There were isolated gunshots and people running about. The entrance was blocked.

"What's happening? Let us through! We live in this building," yelled my husband, trying to open a pathway.

"Careful! You can't go in now; they're chasing an official of the Revolutionary Armed Forces. The guy found his wife in bed with another man and went in shooting and then fled to the roof. They're after him. They're firing so he'll give himself up."

The neighborhood "reporters" were euphoric, and all who had seen something were willing to add their bit to the story. I was afraid that one of the over-eager gunmen might shoot. Nervousness and the prevailing tension were virtually inviting someone to pull the trigger.

My husband, cradling the child in his arms, made a way through, and when we opened the door to our apartment, my mother wasn't there. Before we could search for her, our neighbor brought her over. Mom was as pale as death. She didn't know what was happening, and from all the craziness in the last hour, she was convinced that Cuba was at war. The neighbor, hearing the screaming and the gunshots, and knowing that my mother was alone, had removed her from our apartment to hers. Trying to calm her, she began talking non-stop, which had the opposite effect, since my mother, not understanding even one syllable, produced her own story that had nothing to do with reality. This incident cured her for life of wanting to spend time with her daughter in Cuba.

From that day on—there were still two weeks before my parents went home—my mother counted the hours she would have to endure until she could flee this infernal environment. Two world wars had been enough for her. She in no way wanted to participate in another armed conflict. Every day she told me:

"I want to get out of here. I can't take this country anymore. I don't understand how you can stand it. It's driving me crazy."

On top of this, and to give her another reason why no one could live in Cuba, days before their return there were shots from anti-aircraft batteries stationed near the U.S. embassy, three blocks away. Through the cracks in the window, my father observed the direction of the projectiles and was scared and scandalized when he saw that our curious neighbors were posted on their rooftops, like spectators at a stage play.

"Just look at those crazy idiots! They've never seen war up close. Does it not occur to them that they're exposing themselves to fragments of mortar fire? They'll die having the time of their lives. Someone should do something! They can't be allowed to stay up there! Doesn't civil defense function here? Isn't there anyone who can order them to go back inside?"

My father was beside himself. This event also convinced him that Cuba wasn't a "normal" country, that it was better to return quickly to the frozen north, where reason and logic still prevailed.

We all felt relieved when we were able to take my parents to the port to see them off. My mother had lost her fear of sea voyages. She preferred seasickness and discomfort to the nightmare she experienced in Cuba. It was a true miracle when, ten years later, they would again undertake the adventure of traveling to Cuba, but by that time the situation on the island was different.

CHAPTER ELEVEN

THE EUROPEAN REFRIGERATOR

JUST FEW DAYS AFTER SAYING GOODBYE to my parents, my captain announced a significant change: He had been appointed to represent the Cuban merchant marine in Europe and Africa, and he was being transferred to their office in the Netherlands. This status implied a perpetual peregrination for him—today in France, tomorrow in Belgium, Spain, or some country in Africa, wherever a Cuban merchant marine ship would go to drop anchor. Our son, his father, and I would be living in Rotterdam; or rather, mother and son in the Netherlands, father constantly traveling.

Three months before I was able to leave for the Netherlands, my husband was already there. The Dutch waited three months to grant my son and me a residence permit. My captain had no problem getting one, but as far as his dependents were concerned, the Dutch authorities had doubts. They didn't want to admit people who might cause disorder in a country that was so clean and organized and with such crisp, clear laws that demanded full and complete compliance.

Finally, in January of 1964, my captain advised me that the visa for the two of us would be granted. We just had to go to Paris to pick it up at the Dutch embassy in France. I didn't understand this craziness of having to travel with a kid in tow, first to Czechoslovakia, the hub for all Cubans traveling on business to countries in Europe and Africa, then to France to pick up the visa and from there to the Netherlands, with the visa stamped in my Cuban passport. I decided to detour between Prague and Paris for a brief visit to my parents' home. It would be my first time in my country after living in Cuba for almost two years.

In a frenzy, overjoyed and full of expectation, thinking about nothing more than our next trip, I tackled the preparations. There wasn't really much to pack. The boy and I each had a change of winter clothing that the captain had found for us so we could endure the cold European winter.

Upon learning that we were going abroad, the girls in the childcare center and the neighbors requested some "loans" of my things that weren't available in the market. I thus contributed a bit to the happiness of all those people who carried some treasure away from my house: the iron, the playpen, the baby mattress, the plastic baby bathtub, and a few more things.

Organizing a pickup at home to go to the airport was one of the most difficult things to accomplish. Trusting a rental car to be delivered at a fixed hour was too risky. My friend Josefina and her husband, a urologist, decided to skip work in order to guarantee that we wouldn't have problems and could get to the airport at the appointed time.

At four in the morning they knocked on the door of the apartment. Dictys had been fussing for some time. He didn't want breakfast, and he left his bottle half full. I carefully collected all the rest of the food in order not to leave anything to the cockroaches and mice. Content, almost happy, I left for the airport. I say "almost happy" because since living in Cuba, I always had some vestige of distrust inside me. All too frequently I had experienced delays, displacements, and suspensions of projects.

My euphoria at going on a trip soon evaporated. The plane had been on the runway for hours, but some little lightbulb wasn't working. The technicians tried to fix it, but their attempts were unsuccessful. After five hours of waiting in the airport, Dictys was a ball of filth: the extra diapers were all dirty, and the two extra baby bottles I had prepared were already gone. Then they informed us that we should go home and come back the next day at the same time.

Once home, I began to beg for food for the two of us. The neighbors, who had benefited from my supplying them with different products, were good to us. One gave me a little milk for the baby; another, a plate of stew to be able to put something in my stomach; a third loaned me some diapers. That way I could quickly wash the ones that Dictys had soiled and have them clean and dry for another day.

The second takeoff attempt worked. Of course I also had to wait a couple of hours, but the plane didn't have anything wrong with it, and we took off for Canada. Gander, a small northern-Canadian city, welcomed us with a snowstorm. The Britannia aircraft in which we were flying pitched and yawed like a play yard swing as we approached, then, at the precise moment of landing, came down where it should. A stairway was positioned at the exit, and all the passengers had to get off the plane so it could be refueled.

What a fantastic landscape. Wherever you looked there was snow. Two years without snow and now here it was in glorious abundance.

With my son in my arms, I walked to the exit door. A blast of freezing air hit us in the face. Dictys clung to me and gave a cry of fear and pain, as if he were being tortured. His first contact with the cold was frankly unacceptable. He refused, when we were on the ground, to let me put him down. He raised his arms asking for help and cried and cried. It seemed like it would never end.

He calmed down in the terminal waiting room, but when we had to go back outside to get on the plane again, the spectacle repeated itself, and he screamed like an abused little animal.

From Gander the plane flew to Shannon, in Ireland. Icy, snowy winds embattled the plane all the way. The contraption must have been out of circulation for some time, but it was one of the few belonging to Cubana de Aviación that continued to fly come hell or high water, against ice or snow, and also against all the safety norms established for international air travel.

More than a day had already passed since the beginning of our trip. From Shannon we flew to Prague. We landed at Prague's international airport at night. Today you can travel from Havana to Prague in approximately ten hours. We took more than thirty.

Prague received us with a temperature of five degrees, icy winds, and abundant snow. The connecting flight to Berlin had taken off some hours before our arrival. I didn't know anyone in Prague, and I didn't have enough Czech currency to spend the night in a hotel. The Czech airline's transit hotel was already full. The airport personnel advised me to take the express train from Prague to Dresden to Berlin, which would leave within an hour. I gladly accepted this suggestion. We went to the train station, changed our tickets, and were able to travel in a first-class sleeping car. What a relief, to be able to lie down in a bed after almost two days of screw-ups, anxiety, and uninterrupted tension.

We got to Berlin in the morning. An equally frightful cold awaited us in Germany. Dictys didn't want anything to do with ice or snow. He cried almost the whole week we were in Germany. The child needed this time to adapt to the climate, which was, for him, inhospitable, aggressive, and frozen. He was puzzled and didn't understand the new world to which he had been relocated. I have some photos of this stay, in which I see my kid constantly crying, streams of tears running down his face. He looks like the most wretched child in the world. With a look of supplication, of unjust punishment, he managed also to make me feel guilty for something I couldn't avoid and for which there was no solution.

We spent a week in the German refrigerator and then continued on our trip to Paris. Inevitably, we had to go through Prague again. Our plane landed on the frozen runway of the Czech capital. There, too, the Ice Age was in full swing. The cold wave had wreaked havoc on almost all the hotels, whose heating systems weren't able to handle the extremely low temperatures and had burned out. The guests, disguised as Vikings, covered themselves with layers of winter clothing and slept in gloves, scarves, and wool overcoats, showing how strong they were while suffering and wishing for better times.

We learned that our flight to Paris, by the time we landed, was already on its way to the French capital. For lack of passengers, they had changed the timetable, and next flight to Paris was scheduled in a week. We were stuck in Prague, then, for seven more days.

I had reached the limit of my patience and capacity to withstand the continual hardships. The idea of spending a week with my son in Prague freezing, with no Czech money and knowing no one, was frankly intolerable.

I insulted the airline employee who was going over my documents and had given me the news that my plane had left before the scheduled time. The poor woman told me, in "Czech-Spanish," that I was right, but there was nothing she could do, she assured me time and again.

"I'm not airport boss, I don't have fault plane go Paris now and you here."

I insisted that they had to find some solution, that I wasn't going to stay an entire week in Prague without money and with this brutal cold. The girl took my documents to consult with her superior. A bit later, she returned, smiling from ear to ear. It looked like her face couldn't accommodate such a big smile.

"Your problem okay. Flight to Amsterdam half an hour. Not many passengers. Director says you and your boy space."

From this I understood that the boss had given authorization for us to take a direct flight to Amsterdam that was leaving in half an hour. I was more than content, I was happy. It took my angel-employee five minutes to change the ticket and dispatch us and our suitcases for the KLM flight to Amsterdam.

When I went up the gangway with the little one in my arms—border guards were posted on both sides with Kalashnikov rifles at the ready—I felt as if I were beginning an extraterrestrial trip. Inside the plane there was so much space you could play ball. There were passengers in the first row, the center, and at the back. Most of the seats were empty.

We had a layover in Frankfort. Two immigration officials came on board to count the passengers. It seemed they weren't satisfied with the result. They went back to counting and compared the result with a list. The time planned for the layover had now passed. The officials were still talking, and I heard one say to the other:

"There are two too many passengers. We better check the passports to see what's going on."

Those "two too many," of course, were my son and I. Just like I used to do in school when the teacher asked a question, I raised my hand to save the officials the work. I told them that we were surely the passengers who weren't on their list. After checking our passports against their list, they indeed verified that we were the ones who shouldn't be on this plane. In great detail I explained to them how I came to be on this plane without having a visa or being authorized.

The West German officials didn't care at all about my bad luck with the cold and the missed flight to Paris and the visa that was in Paris and all the crap that had happened, which they couldn't understand for not being experienced in the tricks and problems created in Cuba, the country where if anything can go wrong, it will.

"You have to get off right now and return to Prague. You can't continue on to Amsterdam with this plane. You don't have a visa."

"I'm not getting off for anything. This plane is Dutch territory, and only the police or the Dutch border guards can take me off."

"You can't continue on this plane, because in Amsterdam they won't let you into the country."

"That's my problem. I'm continuing to Amsterdam on this plane."

The German officials departed and gave permission to the captain to continue the flight.

I was on pins and needles. The Czechs had allowed me to travel on this plane; what's more, they made it possible for me to take it. Why then were the Germans saying such terrible things?

In Amsterdam, I took my place in the long line that had formed in front of the immigration counter. It was a truly special line, in a developed country. In less than a blink of an eye I arrived at the counter. I handed our passport to the official, and without seeing how it happened, suddenly there was a soldier at my side, with a gun and a fixed bayonet, who was looking at me in such a threatening manner that my hair stood on end.

"Don't move!" barked the soldier.

The soldier and the immigration official struck up a conversation that I didn't hear. I knew that it was about us, since they both kept looking from the passport to us, from us to the passport.

The line behind me was growing until it was longer than the ones that form in Havana to buy alcohol or cotton in the pharmacy. People started to protest because they couldn't accept a line that wasn't moving. The soldier ordered me to accompany him. With our passport in one hand and his gun in the other, he escorted us to a booth that was more like a cage in a zoo, only instead of a fence of barbed wire, this cage had walls of transparent glass.

The soldier remained at our side, standing at attention, with the fixed bayonet and a hostile look, as if he feared that the child and I would attack him at any moment. It was a tense, though ridiculous, situation. This soldier, who appeared to be leaden, immutable, rigid, with fiery eyes and a menacing look, made me feel like a mouse before a snake.

I put Dictys down because my arms couldn't take holding him anymore. The soldier, without blinking, stayed at my side. I sat down and dared to ask him what this show was all about. He didn't answer but kept looking at me, full of disdain, and the absurd silence continued. I didn't know why this deaf-mute soldier hated me so much.

What came to mind was a poem by Nicolás Guillén: *Soldier, why do you hate me, if we are the same, you and I?* This brief escape to the island disappeared when my brain triumphed over the fantasy that for an instant had disconnected my gray matter. Then I thought about how absurd that comparison was. The soldier next to me—I'm sure—didn't know the tropics and had never heard of a poet named Nicolás Guillén.

Some tortured minutes passed. Suddenly a man dressed in

civilian clothing entered the cell. His icy stare made me forget that we were in a heated room. He instilled fear and a chilling cold in me. In a cutting voice, metallic like a tin bucket—in my burgeoning imagination he was the prosecutor in a trial, accusing me of terrible crimes—he gave a speech full of reproach and recrimination. He called me shameless, cheeky, sassy, a violator of Dutch laws and regulations. Continuing, he began an interrogation that repeated itself at least five times, with the same questions:

"Why did you take this plane? Why did you enter without a visa?"

I explained to him over and over that the plane to Paris had left, that the visa was granted, and that it should be the same as if I got the visa in France or in the Netherlands.

My answer made the man so angry that he couldn't contain himself. He screamed at me, repeating his insults. After a while, another man came in, also dressed in civilian clothing, the one who had our passport.

What will they do with us? I thought. *Why are they being so aggressive? Is my crime really so bad, having entered the Netherlands without previously getting the visa? Can't these people understand that it was impossible to wait a week in a frozen country with a small, tired, scared little boy who can't take the cold, the snow, the strange smells, the lack of sun, and the hostile sounds?*

The one who had my passport returned. The one who had interrogated me addressed me again.

"Put it into your head once and for all that you are thinking about staying in a country that has generously given you permission to stay. This means that you must comport yourself in agreement with our regulations. You have entered without permission and have been flagrantly in violation of our laws. If this conduct continues, you will feel the rigor of the authorities and will be expelled. We are allowing you to enter, but only to take the time until morning through afternoon to get the residence permit in the office of immigration, which is situated on ..." He wrote down the address and the time the office opened. With the sermon ended and the passport in my hand, we were freed.

Meanwhile, Dictys had found a large ashtray full of half-burned matches, cigarette butts, and ashes and was using it as a toy. Because of my fear and nervousness, I had to concentrate on what the Dutch officials were saying, and I hadn't noticed that the little one, outside the reach of his mother's vigilant eyes, was performing his own special program. Crawling from one end of our momentary prison to the other, he had polished the floor with his wooly jumpsuit, changing its color from light blue to gray with touches of black, and had converted himself into a dirty mass of dirt, cigarette butts, and ash. Dictys now reeked of burned tobacco and smelled like a cheap, dirty bar. Fatigued, exhausted, with a large dose of indignation and rage in my belly that I had to hold in so as not to provoke the anger of the Dutch officials again, I picked up my belongings and the boy. I finally managed to communicate by telephone with my captain.

"I need you to come get me as soon as possible. I've had it; I can't take any more. Come quickly."

"But how do you want me to do that? Where the hell are you?"

"The boy and I are in the airport in Amsterdam."

"How is that possible? Weren't you supposed to pick up the visa in France?"

"No, I repeat, I'm in Amsterdam, on the verge of collapse and exhaustion, and your son, dirty and whining because he's hungry, is tired and driving me crazy. I'll tell you the details later. Now, please, come get us."

Thus, considered an undisciplined Cuban, rude and disrespectful, a foreigner with the stamp of a black sheep, I began a stay of one and a half years in the country where honey, cheese, and cream abounded; where there were millions of tulips and many windmills; where the people lived on land stolen from the sea; and where the streets were so clean that rolling around on them doesn't require a bath later.

At this point, suffice it to say that, as someone who learns another language relatively quicky, I learned no more Dutch than the most elemental expressions of courtesy, because I never managed to establish emotional contact with the inhabitants of the country. From the moment of my arrival in the airport in Amsterdam, I didn't feel welcome for one single instant.

Of course, I was guilty of being German. In the sixties and seventies, the Dutch continued to have a very hostile attitude toward Germans. Even without having had any part in the war—I had been born when the disaster was in full turmoil—I served as the scapegoat for the atrocities committed by the Germans during World War II. My mother tongue, in particular the Low German dialect that was spoken in the region where I grew up, was very similar to Dutch. Logically, I spoke to the Dutch in German, knowing that they understood. They were atrocious to me. When I asked the bus driver to explain the way to my office, he indicated the wrong way, which made me waste hours in an unfruitful search for the address. When I wanted to buy bread, they refused to sell it to me, pretending they didn't understand me; when I wanted to pay on the bus, they didn't have change, although they did have it for the person behind me with a bill that was ten times bigger.

In the Netherlands, I was fortunate to be able to work outside the house. I was given a job as translator, interpreter, and secretary at the trade office, which allowed me to save some money for books and to buy articles needed for our home in Cuba.

Also—this can't be left out—I suffered a spectacular accident on Dutch soil.

"I have tickets for the premiere in Rotterdam of *My Fair Lady*. I'll pick you up in the central station at six in the evening. Please don't be late, because they won't let anyone in after it starts," my captain informed me.

"At six sharp; don't worry, I'll be on time," I answered.

In order to be on time in Rotterdam, I had to take the bus at five in the afternoon near the office and the train from The Hague to Rotterdam at five thirty. At three minutes to five, I left the office to get to my bus on time. When I came to the intersection, I saw that it was already at the stop, one minute early. With my eyes fixed on the bus, I crossed the pedestrian strip and didn't see that a car was approaching at full speed, turning onto my street. The driver, a novice at the wheel, wasn't experienced enough to know he had to drive carefully when the traffic lights were out of service, which had happened just that afternoon. The right bumper hit me, and I flew up and through the air. The left bumper hit me again, propelling me violently enough to throw me into the next lane of traffic, next to the island in the middle of the avenue. For a tenth of a second, a horrible movie passed through my mind. *My son will be without a mother, because I'm sure another car will run over me now and crush me.* At the same time, my instinct took over. I got up in a flash and jumped to safety, the divider. My handbag had flown to one side, its contents scattered; I, to the other. *You saved yourself by a hair*, I thought as I checked myself. I was apparently unharmed.

I quickly recovered my things and saw that the driver of the car that had knocked me down had stopped more than fifty yards from the accident. My bus had already gone. The driver of the car wasn't about to get out. If Mohammed won't come to the mountain, I thought, then the mountain will go to Mohammed. And I walked toward the driver, who was leaning on the wheel, trembling like a leaf in a storm. With a face green with fright, he stammered something incoherent, or so I thought, because I didn't understand anything. How could I if he was speaking Dutch? This guy, more than the trembling in his voice, gave me the impression that he was telling me something in Chinese and that he was in a disastrous mental state, on the edge of collapse, so I tried to calm him down. I was clearly in shock; I wasn't able to do anything reasonable. I told him that nothing had happened to me, that he could continue on his way. I didn't realize then that he answered me in very good German, saying that he must take me to the hospital. Horrified, I answered him.

"No. Nothing happened to me. You can go on your way."

Thus, no one knew who had hit me. I could have recovered a fortune from his insurance company, but as often happened to me, I knew nothing about the possibility of benefiting from an accident. People knowledgeable about public liability insurance told me that I lost the chance of receiving the equivalent of a lottery jackpot.

I arrived late to the date with my captain. We missed the premiere. My husband was off the charts when he saw me arrive a half hour after our agreed-upon time. He was so angry that he let go with all his anger against me and closed his ears, so I didn't have any chance to explain my reason for being late. We didn't speak to each other on the way home. Meanwhile, the lesions on my skinned legs, knees, and the palms of my hands began to really hurt. I could barely sleep during the night, but stubborn as I am, I refused to go to the doctor, and, ultimately, the abrasions healed on their own. One month after the accident, the large bruises had disappeared, and my knees and palms were covered in new, pink skin.

Our time in the Netherlands passed without anything spectacular happening, in the Dutch way. My son and I—frequently alone—recovered from the obligatory Cuban diet. The boy adapted to the climate slowly but surely, without major difficulties, and he enjoyed the Dutch food, rich in protein and vitamins. When his father was in the country, we traveled through the Netherlands from one end to the other, and we satisfied our hunger to see works of art in numerous visits to some of the most spectacular museums in the country.

One week before returning to Havana, I had to undergo a frightening surgical intervention, the worst of the more than dozen that I had endured, and, again, my husband had to leave me alone. I was admitted to a hospital attended by nuns, and I began to become suicidal, because a post-surgical peritonitis was taking away my desire and strength to continue fighting. But I recovered from that , too, and three weeks later I was discharged, having lost almost five kilograms of weight. I was skinny, weak, and looked like a scarecrow.

I went on to Belgium, where Dictys awaited me, in a house of people I didn't know. When the little one saw me, he clung to me like a hermit crab in its shell and didn't let go for an instant. He held on tightly to my skirt and screamed with fear if he let go. I couldn't even go to the bathroom alone, and from then on, I had to carry him everywhere. When I laid him down to sleep, I had to stay at his side. Holding my hand, he slept, and he woke up if I dared to take my hand away from his. We were like Siamese twins. The forced separation, motivated by my stay in the hospital, had traumatized and disturbed him so deeply that he couldn't handle being alone.

We returned to Havana in the middle of summer. So long, good food. So long, life abroad, comfortable and cool. Goodbye, taciturn, rigid, and germophobic Dutch, of guttural and roaring speech, creaking like a stone-grinding machine. Farewell, tulips, windmills, fat cows with udders bursting with milk. Goodbye, Vincent van Gogh. Goodbye, cold rain and fog, thicker than anything London could cook up. Good riddance to administrative perfection and organized life, boring like the flat meadows cut with millimetric exactitude, allowing no hint of spontaneity or improvisation.

CHAPTER TWELVE
BACK IN HAVANA

WELCOME, Cuban diet of perpetual shortages and once-a-month chicken—stringy like a marathon runner, mainly bones and tendons. Welcome, black market, bartering, and shady deals. Welcome, miserly little *malangas*, bought at the price of gold. Welcome, bureaucratic chaos, disorder, and pigheaded officials. Welcome, Cuban verbosity, screaming, strident music, and sensuous dancing. Long live the sun, the delightful beaches, the heat, the mosquitos, the cockroaches, the hurricanes, the drought, the mangos, the soursops, the *mameyes*, the avocados, the limes, the oranges, the coffee, the *Machismo-Leninismo*, and the eternal and omnipresent "I have to solve a problem! Fatherland or death! We shall overcome!"

After months of not seeing each other, Dictys and I are back with my captain, the child's father, for a few days in Havana. Of course, this living together won't last, but at least we have the time needed to move from the hovel in El Vedado to a small apartment in Miramar. We've gladly lost our neighbors in the building next door, my teachers of vulgar, crude *cubano*, and exchanged them for a group of girls from the eastern provinces who've received Makarenko scholarships. Lodged in a luxurious mansion next to our building, they've managed in record time to convert the gardens and patios into a lunar landscape. They've used the branches of the *mamey*, avocado, mango, and orange trees as a source of fuel to boil clothes in large tin cans in the middle of the courtyard. With heated metal tongs (where did they come from, these instruments that were used before electricity?), they straighten their curls while observing the process of boiling their towels and sheets. Where just a few days ago there had been a beautiful hibiscus bush, there was now a hole filled with the remains of wood, ashes, and half-burned branches.

The washing machines, water heaters, electric stoves—all these modern devices—were of absolutely no use to the girls, and they were stolen and carried away, leaving the formerly magnificent house dismantled. A few weeks later, the water faucet that supplied water to our building and the one where the scholarship girls lived was broken. Since there was no water, the girls were now determined to bathe in the cistern. It served as a swimming pool, a source of water, and a sewer.

It did no good to talk to the young neighbors. They didn't understand that the cistern wasn't a public bathroom, nor the appropriate place for human waste. The "aunt" designated by the Ministry of Education to watch over the youngsters, poor thing, was a nice person but just as uneducated as the girls. Regretfully, and without being able to avoid this process of deterioration, we watched as the most beautiful houses, along with their gardens and patios, were turned into veritable slums.

As a counterpoint to the deterioration and destruction of the environment, I created some flower boxes for our balcony. I filled them with good soil and planted some tulip bulbs I'd brought back from the Netherlands, to remind myself of a time of comfort and abundance. However, all my knowledge of agriculture, planting, and the essential characteristics of different kinds of flowers and vegetables were for naught. How did I think I could grow tulips in Havana? Had I ever seen them in a Cuban garden? It's essential for tulips to go through a cold spell in the winter, sleeping and dreaming in comfort, and then in the spring to be reborn with strength and spirit, showing off their beautiful colors.

A few days after planting my pretty tulips, there were some rickety green sticks coming up in the boxes, with no trace of a bud. The ugly sticks grew quickly and soon looked like reeds. Every morning I ran to the balcony to see if, finally, buds were appearing. Nothing. When the woody stems began to turn yellow and withered completely, I was convinced that my experiment of planting tulips had been a failure. The same thing happened to them as happened to the poor penguins in the Havana aquarium: they couldn't tolerate the heat.

My son and I passed through a similar process, but unlike the tulips, we had the beach less than a hundred yards from the house. The beach was our salvation; it satisfied many needs. The beach meant freedom in its maximum expression. When I was swimming, my imagination took flight. When I needed to speak of things that were prohibited and no one should hear what my friends and I were saying, we went swimming offshore and beyond, without witnesses, changing the world, conversing until we wore ourselves out, happy and content.

The time I'd been told that the university reform would take had passed. In an interview with the Faculty of Humanities administration, I learned that I had to begin my studies from scratch. Except for Latin, they didn't recognize the subjects I had taken and passed in the German university, nor did my courses conform to the present program.

There were about twenty of us students, almost all family members of foreign diplomats in Cuba. Some of us really had the desire to study language and literature, but most wanted to take advantage of their stay in Havana to acquire a veneer of culture and, incidentally, a university diploma. In the course of time, the group shrank; the only ones who remained were those of us who were serious about studying. Fortunately, this process was accompanied by an upgrade in quality since it increased the demand for professors and the willingness of the remaining students to work harder.

Again, the Germans in the trade office remembered me. They

needed a substitute interpreter; the official one had left Cuba, and the successor still hadn't been named. Owing to our prolonged stay in the Netherlands, I had lost my place in the childcare center. The Germans had a fantastic, recently-created childcare center. I imposed the condition of getting a place for my son there in exchange for working in the trade office.

"It won't be a problem," the advisor assured me,; "there still aren't many children in the new center."

However, the following day I received a call from the director of the institution informing me that they didn't have a place. Outraged, I asked the advisor to explain the situation. I already knew the answer: they couldn't let in a child whose parents were outside the circle of official employees filtered through the security organs of the East German government, but they didn't dare say that to me clearly and directly.

I said goodbye to the Germans, in a definitive manner. I sent them to hell with their childcare center and occasional work, and I made them understand that they needn't ever count on me again. Thus I entered the archives of the East German embassy as a contentious person unworthy of their trust. I didn't renew contact with the German embassy until the mid-seventies, when it was imposed on me. I was then working with the First Lady of Cuba and was a high-level Cuban official. But that's another story.

In the Netherlands, Dictys had turned two. He spoke no German, which I tried to teach him, or Spanish, which the Spanish nanny spoke with him, or English, either, which was spoken constantly when I had visitors; nor did he speak Dutch, which he heard from the neighbors. He spoke his own language, created exclusively by and for him. I was worried, because he didn't have a single word in his vocabulary that came from or belonged to any of those languages. He spoke in fluent and well-differentiated words. He was like a little Demosthenes, affecting the pose of an important orator, accompanying his own unique language with facial expressions and gestures that were expressive enough for me to understand the subject matter without understanding the words.

Back in Havana, Dictys continued to speak his language, and there was no way that he was going to pronounce anything intelligible. I was now convinced that he had a serious problem, that he was never going to be able to speak normally, and that we would always have to read his gestures and facial expressions to be able to understand him. In Cuba, however, there weren't as many sources of linguistic confusion for a child, since we all spoke Spanish to get his ear used to one single language. Days and days went by, and Dictys continued developing and refining his own idiom. For me it was clear: the kid had a defect, a burned-out connection. There was something wrong with him, a loose wire that prevented him from speaking Spanish. I hadn't taken into account that for months, the little one hadn't seen or communicated with other children. He was almost always with adults.

One weekend, the woman who cleaned the house, the mother of two toddlers, asked permission to take my son so he could attend a birthday party and play with the children.

"Yes, he can stay with you but don't let him get on your nerves with his tantrums when he doesn't see me. Go ahead and take him," was my reaction.

At the time she took my son, I was already convinced that he would be returned quickly, but that didn't happen. At night, the woman called to tell me that Dictys was staying overnight with her and her sons, sleeping in their house, that he had behaved "divinely" and had enjoyed himself a lot, without asking for his mother. The following morning I was restless and worried because the child still hadn't come home. I phoned the woman. She assured me that everything was going perfectly, that Dictys had eaten breakfast and was now playing on the patio with her children and those of the neighbors. It was a long, anxious, and distressing Sunday.

Finally, at four in the afternoon, the woman appeared with her son and mine. Dictys, upon seeing me, ran up and threw his arms around my neck, kissing me and laughing, as if to say, *I had a lot of fun, but now I'm back with you.* The woman and her sons went home. I grabbed my son to cross Fifth Avenue and go swimming in the Patricio Lumumba Social Club—the old Miramar Yacht Club, later the Social Club of the Revolutionary Armed Forces, which was less than a block away.

Sitting in the sand, Dictys began singing *María Caracoles, Baila Mozambi-i-que* and swaying to the beat of the song. I couldn't believe what I was hearing. Those were the first words that my son had uttered clearly in Spanish. All the attempts to have him speak something intelligible had resulted in a big zero, and now, suddenly, Pello el Afrokán, whose music was in vogue and made me cringe every time I heard it, had inspired my son to such an extent that from that day on, an uninterrupted process of learning Spanish began.

Every day, Dictys spoke more and better Spanish. In a matter of weeks he had regained all the terrain he had lost in two years. I believe the Dutch environment was so hostile for him that it paralyzed the part of his brain responsible for speech, and that the tropical atmosphere stimulated it, making him as competent as the most talkative parrot in all of Cuba. He started having long conversations with our neighbors, the scholarship girls. He told them off when they spoiled his nap and encouraged them to talk to him when he was bored. Standing on a little chair set out on the balcony, he would ask them to tell him, in full detail, everything they had done during the day.

CHAPTER THIRTEEN
DICTYS THE PING-PONG BALL

SIX MONTHS AFTER RETURNING TO CUBA from the Netherlands, I took a job that required me to be there at a time when Dictys needed attention. My parents offered to take care of him for three months. This was another violent change for the baby, but it convincingly demonstrated that he had a good capacity for tolerance and adaptation. In a matter of days, he erased Spanish from his head, giving way to German, a language that became his favorite, even though he never set foot in a German school.

My parents lived in a large house, surrounded by gardens, patios, and greenhouses. They cultivated ornamental tropical plants as a business, and these plants grew abundantly even in the harshest winter. My sister, a teenager at that time, played the role of substitute mother for my son. She often took him to the neighbors' home, where a mob of kids became his playmates. Barely would breakfast have ended when Dictys would disappear to his new friends' home. He would be brought back, sometimes by force, to his grandparents' house to have lunch and take a siesta. This routine repeated itself day after day and was accompanied by the worst insults that the little one delivered to his young aunt, because she made him come home when he wanted to continue playing. So it's not surprising that his first words in German were an enormous collection of vulgar curses that he learned from his playmates, who taught him this language.

When, after three months, I went to pick up my son, he received me with a rosary of expletives. In German, he gave me to understand that I was out of my mind because I was speaking to him in Spanish, and he no longer understood it. During the train ride to Berlin he performed an act of repudiation. He cried and grabbed my hand, begging to go back to his beloved grandmother's house. In Berlin he decided to go on strike. He sat on the street and refused to walk any further. As none of the resistance maneuvers had the expected effect, he resigned himself. His sadness made me feel guilty: I was a bad mother, abusive heartless. But I couldn't leave him in Germany; his home was in Cuba, although he didn't want to accept this reality. The flight back was a nightmare, and when we finally got home he leaned against the doorframe, telling me with tears in his eyes:

"This isn't my house, I want to go home, I want to be with my grandmother."

When I served him food, he asked me for things that existed only in my parents' house. In perfect German he recited to me the list of delicacies he had been fed by his grandparents, and he refused to eat what I had. No cassava, no *malanga*, no rice, no black beans: he liked nothing, and everything made him nauseous.

Dictys was losing weight, he was as skinny as a toothpick, and his prolonged hunger strike began to cause health problems. He always had a cold, with fever and ailments of the most diverse nature. He had become a sickly, skinny, weak, sad child. Weeks passed before he finally accepted his fate. He gave me the impression that he was only doing it because he had no alternative. In the nursery school, where I got him a place after much bureaucratic struggle, he adapted somewhat better. It seemed that the children in his group, for the moment, had cured him of his "germanitis."

Dedicated to my studies at the University of Havana, I found that the months went by quickly. These were the days when Eusebio Leal, who later became, and remained for decades, Havana's official historian, made enormous efforts to restore the Palace of the Captains-General. In excavations carried out on the street, the remains of church walls and many traces of the inhabitants of that area from centuries ago had been found. With a box full of pieces of ceramics found during the excavations, the new director of the Museum of Havana appeared at the university to seek support from students for the restoration work, which were to include a search for valuable objects from the different periods of Havana's history. Motivated by the detective spirit, like crazed hounds, we joined in the collection and research, visiting the new inhabitants of old houses, almost always the former owners' service personnel who had appropriated the mansions of their patrons of yesteryear. In this way, the museum received more than one precious lamp, chair, or armoire that had been deposited in a garage or hallway because their new owners found them ugly or because they took up too much space.

My marriage had turned into a relationship of chance. In a year, my husband and I would see each other for only a few weeks. I could hardly ever count on his support, because in times of greatest need he was out of the country. His co-workers who weren't working abroad took it upon themselves to help me, but I didn't like having to ask them for favors. I couldn't demand anything of them, and the usual Cuban relaxed attitude drove me crazy more than once. I must have pushed them to the limit of their patience with my strange requests, and I developed a reputation for being picky, persistent, and headstrong.

A friend of ours was in charge of picking up our son from his nursery school. His little daughter was in the same institution, so they made the trip together every day. It wasn't surprising that Dictys also called the man "daddy" like the daughter did. He was the only daddy Dictys saw regularly during the absence of his real father.

Every now and then Dictys would have outbursts of rebellion. Traits inherited from his mother were clearly evident. On a very hot day in August, for me the most unbearable month due to the prevailing heat and humidity, the little rebel decided to put on a woolen cap and gloves, clothes that he had worn during that last cold winter in Germany. It seemed that, for an instant, the idealized memory of the enchanting months spent in his grandparents' house had entered his head.

"I'm going to the *círculo* like this," he announced, very resolute. The *círculo* was the "children's circle," the kindergarten he attended.

A shirt and shorts completed this ridiculous combination. There was no convincing him that this wasn't the time to wear a hat and gloves. We went out into the street. Before reaching the bus stop, Dictys could no longer bear the itchiness caused by the cap on his sweaty head or the gloves stuck to his fingers. With gestures of contempt he removed the extemporaneous garb and allowed me to save it for a more appropriate time.

A few weeks later, the boy had reached the limit of patience with his mother and the environment at home and simply didn't want to continue to support the current regime. With great determination, he grabbed a small briefcase and threw the most important thing into it: a white piece of cloth, his perpetual and essential companion, and a few garments. This wasn't just any piece of cloth. He had clutched it from the time he was very young. He would squeeze it and turn it rhythmically with his left hand as he sucked his right thumb. The cloth, which had to smell like soap and be ironed, served as a tranquilizer and calmed his nerves. He asked me for a penny to pay for the bus and proclaimed:

"I'm leaving home this minute—¡ahora mismo! I don't want to stay in this house. I'm going."

"Where are you going?" I asked him.

With the serious, determined face of a man, he replied:

"I'm leaving, I don't want to be with you in this house."

He grabbed his briefcase, clutched it tightly, and left. Surreptitiously, so he wouldn't see me, I followed him. He came to the bus stop and began to wait. The bus came. My heart clenched, and I wanted to yell at him:

"Come here, there's no need for you to go," but I held back.

The people in front of him got on. He let those behind him pass. The bus started up without him. He stood in the same place.

About five minutes passed (an eternity for me and probably for him, too). Little by little, the stop was filled with people again, and he stood in the middle of them, solemn and sad. I saw that someone tried to strike up a conversation with him. He wasn't interested in talking to anyone and looked up at the sky. The second bus arrived. Dictys took a step forward, but at the door of the vehicle he stopped, suddenly turned, and headed back to the house. All this time I had been watching him, and I was already home when he returned. He rang the bell. I opened the door for him and, hiding surprise, said:

"But are you back? How fast!"

I hugged him and ran my hand over his head. Grumbling, he told me that he preferred to be at home, even though he didn't like it, and that he hadn't gone with the bus because the bus couldn't find the place he wanted to go. I think I've never felt so miserable, so frustrated, like a mother unable to protect her child. Luckily, Dictys never brought up his desire to leave again, at least not during his childhood. Cuban daily life enveloped him, and it seems that he endorsed the saying "better the devil you know than the devil you don't."

CHAPTER FOURTEEN

OUR FAMILY WILL BE COMPLETE

Dictys was now three years old, and it was obvious that he needed a little brother or sister. Fortunately, the trauma of the first birth had faded, and the desire to have another child was gaining ground. We took advantage of my captain's stay in Cuba, which lasted longer than usual, to try to fulfill our wish.

For a pregnancy to occur, chance plays an important role. That I got pregnant at all was more than a coincidence; it was a miracle. The doctors had left me with no more than a piece of an ovary when I had the operation in the Netherlands. At the time, the doctors weren't sure whether I would be able to have more children, so we were extremely fortunate to see our dream come true. This time I was treated during my pregnancy by a doctor who was among the *crème de la crème* of Cuban obstetricians. But unfortunately, he was so burdened with responsibilities that my healthcare fell short. When I was six months pregnant, he was sent to teach a course in some Latin American country.

"I will be away for three months," he announced to me at the consultation.

"You promised to be present when the child was born, and now I find out you're leaving me to my fate. You know full well what a disaster it was when my first child was born, and now you plan to leave me in the hands of someone I don't know," I reproached him.

"Listen to me: I said three months; so when the little one is born I'll be with you."

"You won't be with me, because in less than three months the baby will be born."

"But you aren't even six months pregnant. I'm an obstetrician and I know what I'm talking about."

"I know exactly how far along I am. It's six months."

When my doctor examined me, taking measurements and listening to the heartbeat of the little guy in my belly, he told me:

"You're right. It seems that the only thing you have in your abdomen is the fetus. I don't know how you have any other organs in there. I have never seen such a small belly with such a big fetus inside. Anyway, I hope to be back in Havana when you give birth, and I will assist you. If by chance I'm not back, I'll leave you with my colleague. Here's his phone number; he'll take care of you."

I spent three months on tenterhooks, fearing that the doctor wouldn't be back by my due date. Added to my fears was not being able to count on my husband's presence. The date for the birth of our second child, according to the calculations, was right around December 25, Christmas day, and on precisely that date, the captain had to be out of Cuba.

At the end of 1966, there were hardly any rental cars. Taxi service was already part of the history of Cuba, and trying to find a vehicle that would work and that in addition would be available when the day and time arrived was impossible. I had no one who could take care of Dictys, my firstborn. He wasn't even four years old; I couldn't leave him home alone. Fortunately, the captain's trip was delayed for a few days, and luckily also, my doctor returned. We agreed to set the birth date for December 20. That way I wouldn't have transportation problems to the hospital; the father would stay home with his son; and I could go through my labor without having to worry.

During the last weeks of my pregnancy, the university program was in full swing. I had to take several final exams. With my fat belly I looked like a kangaroo. I was dead from lack of sleep, slouching in the wooden chair, sweating "fat drops," as the

Cuban saying has it, and forcing my brain to scribble something coherent on the paper. Dictys was by my side because I had no one to leave him with. He had a great time, taking his place in front of the blackboard, writing his "lecture," standing in the professor's chair and imitating his gestures, which should have condemned me a thousand times, because instead of watching over his students during the exam, the professor was involuntarily playing the role of baby-sitter.

On the day of Dani's birth, everything went according to schedule. My captain dropped me off at the hospital entrance. My doctor, after inducing labor, instructed the obstetric nurse to follow the progress of my labor and call him when the time for the child's birth was near. As soon as the doctor left, the nurse began to shout terrible insults against him. It seems it was a bad day for her. Since she couldn't vent all her accumulated anger against the doctor, she used me as a lightning rod.

"These little doctors who think they can throw out orders, I don't like them. Let them find someone else. Unbelievable."

With clenched jaws and sparks coming out of her eyes, she began to unleash her uncontrollable anger on me, grumbling and swearing, while she blasted my veins to infuse me with oxytocin, a drug that caused uterine contractions. The nurse had to carefully regulate the number of drops per minute, but her hand wasn't steady, and amounts of oxytocin far above those required entered my body like a mighty river, provoking a dangerous earthquake.

For the baby, who was halfway out, these excessive amounts of medication had an electroshock effect. The little one fought a life-and-death battle to escape his narrow, oxygen-starved cabin. Meanwhile, I was about to explode like a firecracker, and when the boy finally emerged from the womb, which was now an erupting volcano, he left behind a field of torn and shattered tissue. His mother was a wreck, totally exhausted, and on the verge of collapse.

Dani was taken care of by a gynecologist and a neonatologist. The little body, weighing eight pounds, was limp, with no signs of life. His color changed rapidly from pinkish to deep purple. He didn't cry, even though he received the classic spanking on his rear end. He didn't move or react to any of the maneuvers the doctors tried with him.

"You write this death down for yourself," I heard the gynecol-

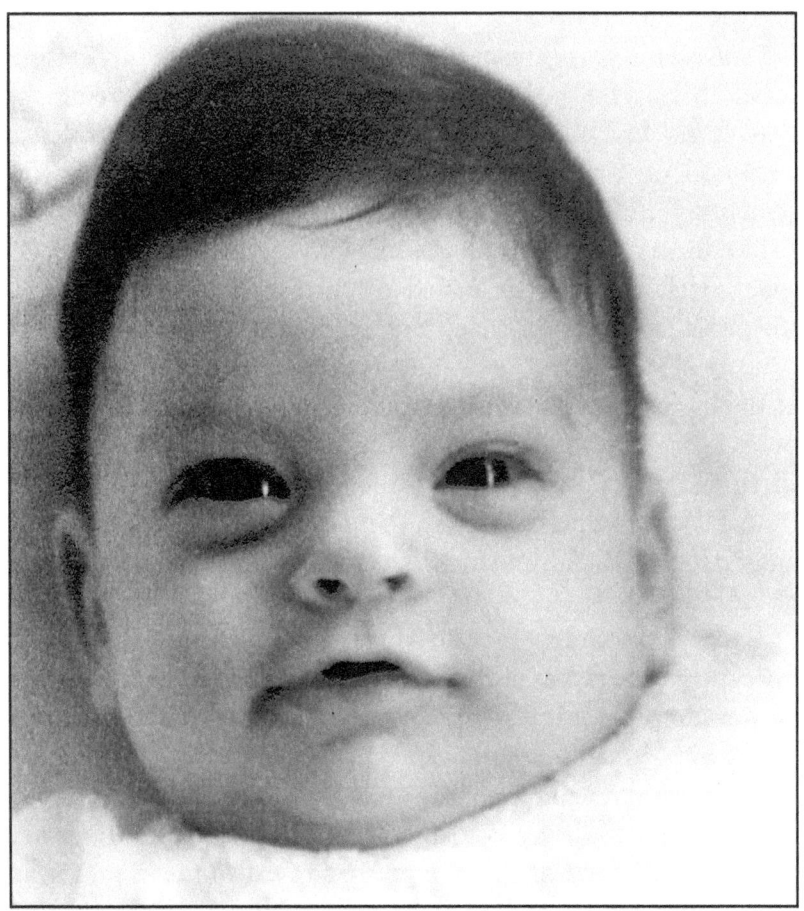

6. *Dani (Julian Daniel), three months old*

ogist say, "because I heard his vital signs while he was still inside."

"I'm not to blame; this death isn't my fault," replied the neonatologist.

I was too exhausted to fully realize the spectacle that had taken place in the room. I was thinking *It was all in vain: nine months and this horrible childbirth, this prolonged torture, and the result is a dead child.* Nobody wasted a second checking to see if I was even conscious, and I heard the doctors shouting:

"Try to revive him, give him massages, inject him with this or that thing."

"He's dead; it's over."

I was losing consciousness, but I woke up after a while, in time to see them place an injection into the umbilical cord vein, and that, at last, had the desired effect. The purple bundle contracted and suddenly screamed in horror. From then on, he didn't stop screaming until he was placed in the crib.

My doctor, oblivious to all this hullabaloo, was on duty. Naturally, the resentful nurse hadn't called him in. He only appeared when the pediatricians had revived the child, who was still giving his concert, shrieking to the joy and contentment of the specialists at having one less death under their belt. My doctor saw his promise to assist me reduced to suturing up the huge tears in my "birthing apparatus," which took over half an hour. During this time, I lost consciousness several times. I had made a fierce effort and no longer had any energy, but now I could rest, knowing that my son was alive.

Twenty-four hours after delivery, we were discharged. I called my captain, the father of the newborn, and what happened? Well, he was simply not in the office, nor did anyone know where to locate him. With my belongings in tow, the child in my arms, I tried to find a vehicle to take us home. A car from the fifties, totally dilapidated, was available. The owner offered to transport us, but not before warning me not to sit next to the left door, as the lock was broken and it could fly open. He kept the right door held shut with a length of sisal rope, undoing the knot only to let the passengers out.

I set my bag on the left and sat with the child in the center. With a roar like a rhinoceros, the car came to life and lurched forward. A black cloud emerged from behind and underneath; the exhaust pipe and muffler were missing. Looking down at where the floorboard should be, I realized that there was a huge hole. A piece of cardboard that served to cover it had shifted, revealing the street. At every stoplight, the poor creature refused to start. Its owner had to get out and push it, leaving the gearshift in second so the engine would start once the car was in motion. The journey home was an odyssey, and it was a true miracle that we arrived safe and sound.

A few hours later the baby's father appeared.

"Why didn't you wait for me? Why did you go in a rental car?" he asked, reproaching me for taking such an unsafe means of transportation.

I was outraged by the question; it made me angry, almost like he was making fun of me. He couldn't imagine how much I had wanted to get out of the torture chamber, out of that horrible hospital that I hated. He couldn't imagine how disappointed I felt when I called my husband and couldn't locate him, and on top of that, nobody in his office caring one way or another whether I did.

The birth of my second child undermined my trust in doctors. I was offended; I didn't ever want to have anything to do with them again. The only one who was exempt from this sentence was our pediatrician, a family friend, who couldn't have children of his own. He had been taking care of Dictys for a long time, and before Dani was born, seeing me with a big belly, he was already telling me:

"*Señora*, I'm going to be a god-uncle for this child. I won't let him get as sick as Dictys, and you can be assured that he'll have the food he needs. My patients in the countryside pay for my services by bringing me taro, eggs, and other produce. Don't worry, this child will be able to eat well. When it comes to food, he'll have everything he wants."

After the tremendous shock he gave us when he was born, Dani developed well. He had the great luck, unlike his older brother, to be able to have the best food—breast milk—so he never had allergy problems like his brother, or the diseases that affected the older boy's health. At three months I began to give him orange juice and solid food: boiled *malanga* with onion (if we had any) and meat (if there was any). A fabulous machine that ground everything thrown into it, a real Osterizer, a gift from my captain, pulverized all this stew, turning it into an ugly but substantial porridge.

I will never forget the day Dani tried it for the first time. The little boy announced his hunger with a huge concert. He was screaming so loud that the neighbors became concerned, thinking that I was torturing him. The porridge, diluted with a little water, was ready for the test. I brushed the nipple over Dani's lips to allow the baby food to come out of the bottle easily. Like a wild animal he clamped down on the nipple and sucked in a large mouthful of porridge. But then he suddenly spat out the nipple, sprayed out everything that had entered his mouth, took a great breath of air, and gave a cry of rage, despair, hunger, and outrage that was truly frightening. I repeated the operation several times. He kept grabbing the bottle, dropping it and spitting out everything left and right. He definitely didn't want the porridge, but he was hungry, and I offered him nothing else, so with big tears streaming down his cheeks and sighing deeply after each sucked mouthful, he ended up taking the entire portion. Exhausted by his efforts, he surrendered, and from then on he ate Cuban food as a substitute for mother's milk.

The first month of his brother's existence was a huge challenge for Dictys. He couldn't bear the fact that I had to take care of the baby so often. When I gave Dani milk, Dictys demanded food. He would stand in front of us, tugging at my robe and making gestures like his brother, moving his arms like the baby did when he started to scream, and imitating the sounds he made when he was happy, a gagagaga, grgrgrgrgr, blowing bubbles of saliva. He insisted that he wanted a bottle, too.

One day I came upon him dressed in baby clothes. He had emptied the closet and, in a fit of jealousy, had taken off his own clothes and put on his brother's. I took him into the bathroom so he could look at himself in the mirror and realize how ridiculous he looked in the too-tight little shirts. He didn't care, as long as he was wearing new clothes. Fortunately, this jealousy gradually abated. It wasn't easy to give both of them the attention they needed, or craved. Obviously, the newborn required more time. I had to find a way to give the older one the simultaneous attention that made him feel important.

Long before the Cuban motto *no es fácil*—it's not easy—came into being, expressing the massive number of calamities and problems that occur every day, the expression was part of my Cuban philosophy. It doesn't solve anything, but it's soothing.

CHAPTER FIFTEEN
IN NEW YORK

ANOTHER ABRUPT AND WELCOME CHANGE occurred in mid-1967 when my captain was appointed representative to the United Nations. He would be working at the Economic Commission for a year and a half. I was able to finish the semester at the university on a high note, but not before having a terrible time with several women, whom I paid a good salary to stay with Dani during the four to five hours a day of my absence.

In 1967, not much could be done with Cuban pesos. It was almost impossible to find a responsible person willing to care for a child. Dani didn't resist, but he flew into a rage if they didn't give him his baby food and bottle at the time he decided he wanted it. I left everything ready for the caretakers—bottles with the milk already measured, orange juice, boiled water in the refrigerator, and peeled *malanga* ready to boil. It didn't take a genius to prepare what the child needed, but I had the problem of the century with all these con artists, because instead of taking care of the child, they went to sleep (one had the audacity to bring her boyfriend into my house while the baby was screaming in his crib) or chatted on the phone, and not even the baby's most heartbreaking cries could wake them up or interrupt them.

I was forced to fire one after the other, but I went from the frying pan into the fire. The last one, recommended by someone who wanted to play a joke on us (at least that's how I interpreted it when she was "working" for me) was the last straw. This person couldn't read or write, which should have put me on alert, because where was she during the literacy campaign? But being naive, silly, not to say idiotic, I believed them all when they assured me that they wanted to take care of the boy.

Paula, the last one, though illiterate, knew the numbers up to ten and used the phone almost uninterruptedly to talk for hours with her boyfriend. My dear neighbor downstairs alerted me every day when I returned home from university that Dani had screamed for hours, and that Paula's telephone orgy could be heard throughout the building. Paula shouted her declarations of love as if she had to overcome the distance to the loved one, increasing the volume of her voice like an actress without a microphone in a large theater.

On the fourth day of Paula's employment, I dismissed her and gave her five minutes to pick up her things and disappear from my sight forever. I had returned from the university earlier than planned. Already in the hallway of our building I could smell something burning and see a black cloud coming out of the living room window. *There's a fire in my house; the child is inside, and Paula . . . What is Paula doing?*

Desperate, in a panic, horrified, already imagining the worst, I managed to open the door. The black cloud hit me in the face. Paula was on the phone. She looked like she was welded to the apparatus and couldn't get away. I ran to the kitchen to put out the flames. The casserole, with what was left of the *malanga* intended for the baby, was jet black; its contents, charred. There was black smoke everywhere in the room. The boy, locked in his room (so as not to disturb Paula during her endless love talks), lay face down, so exhausted from screaming that only sobs escaped him. His clothes were soaked in sweat and tears, and his diaper, the sheet, the mattress, soaked in urine.

Now certain that Dani wasn't in danger, although his desolate state could have softened a heart of stone, I was consumed by rage.

I was like a maddened lioness, and I pounced on Paula. She was still talking sweet-talk, with the phone in her hand, oblivious to anything happening around her. Almost blind with fury, I tore the phone out of her hand, and it was hard to keep from hitting her. I rained down curses on her and called her everything I could think of, from "soulless, scoundrel, and brute" to "irresponsible, abusive, and potential murderer." Paula raised her arms, as if I were pointing a gun at her, and with eyes that seemed to be popping out of their sockets, stammered:

"But *señora*, I was only talking on the phone. I couldn't hang up on my boyfriend, and the *malanga*—I didn't know that *malanga* burns so fast."

I don't remember what I did to control myself and not beat her up. I wanted to throw her out of the house with my fists. While Paula was packing her suitcase, I set about changing the baby and calming him with a bottle of juice. The neighbor gave me a tiny *malanga* root. Fortunately, she had a supply through relatives in the countryside.

I had no need to look for a replacement for Paula, because shortly after this episode we learned that we were leaving for New York. The prospect of change, of taking a plane, of having an adventure, had a stimulating effect on Dictys. His brother, being too small, had no opinion.

It was unbearably hot. We had to be at the airport at seven in the morning. A friend of ours offered to take us in his car, a vehicle worthy of exhibition in a museum. We had reached Avenida de Los Boyeros, passing the Ciudad Deportiva, when we heard a strange noise, as if we were dragging something under the car.

"Shit, we have a flat and I don't have a jack. Not that I need it, since I don't have a spare tire," was our friend's laconic comment.

We got out. The men pushed the car to park it out of the way of the traffic and walked away to see if they could find a phone. They found several, but none worked. It was the long-awaited stage of real communism when public telephones were used without having to pay and when people made indiscriminate and abusive use of the equipment until it broke down. An hour after we'd been stranded in the street, the guys managed to call my husband's work from a nearby hospital to request help. There was no car available, but they said they'd do everything possible to help us out. Indeed, they did, but when we got to the airport, we saw our plane taking off in the direction of Mexico.

It was the same soup as the trip to the Netherlands with other ingredients. Dictys presented us with a high-profile act of repudiation. He threw himself on the floor and yelled at us:

"Liars, you told me that we're going to take a plane. I'm not going home; I want to fly."

During the return, he cried, screamed, and grumbled, outraged at everyone. We had "liquidated" our food supply, and I had to go through the embarrassment of asking the neighbors for milk, food, and other things. We no longer had our ration book, and without it you couldn't buy even a pinch of salt. We had to wait a week for the next flight to New York, via Mexico City.

Dictys took advantage of this time to burn himself with the iron. It was carelessness on my part: I had left it within the child's reach. He'd been fascinated by the iron since he was a toddler. The fact that an object heated up when it was connected to something invisible was magic to him, a true mystery, and he was dying to experiment with it. He found a small table to serve as an ironing board. He put the iron in a plastic bucket, plugged it in, and when he saw that the bucket was turning into a misshapen mass like an amoeba and giving off a foul, hideous smell, he panicked. He knocked the smelly mixture off the table and burned himself. It wasn't anything serious, but the scare cured him of wanting to know anything else about the miracles of the electric iron. The iron ended up in the trash can, of course, since there was no way to separate it from its deadly embrace with the melted plastic bucket.

During the week of waiting to resume our pilgrimage, I took the children to the social club, the beloved beach that was close to the house. No toys were needed there. All I would take were some diapers and shorts. For the children we didn't need anything else, and I would use a terrycloth towel as a beach dress over a swimsuit. Dani had been bathing in the sea since he was two months old. There was a comforting peace at the beach, and even Dictys forgot his tantrums and erased from his mind the disappointment suffered the day of the missed flight. His burned leg was healing, and the salty water and sun helped a new layer of skin cover the injured area.

The week of waiting passed quickly. This time on the way to the airport, we didn't get stranded on the road and arrived on time. We landed in Mexico City around ten in the morning. From then until noon, we weren't allowed to leave the plane, which was parked five hundred yards from the air terminal building. Several times an official came on board and argued with the captain. It seemed that we were carrying the continental revolution on board, a terribly polluting and extremely dangerous thing, since they would remove the ladder and close the door after each visit by a Mexican authority. Dictys was already beginning his protest song:

"Mommy, why are we sitting here if we've arrived? I don't want to be in here. I'm hungry; I want to go."

Dani expressed solidarity with his brother with a concert that meant:

"If they don't give me a big bottle right now, I'm going to burst their eardrums."

The human contingent of the Cubana de Aviación equipment was convincingly demonstrating a behavior acquired by Cubans in eight years of intensive daily training during the Revolution: their capacity for endurance, patience, and stoicism, which seemed to have no limits. People were simply waiting as if they were in a line at the *bodega*. No one but my children protested. Everyone else knew we weren't going to be left on the tarmac until Judgment Day. So we all passed the test of meekness imposed by the Mexican authorities with great success, and at last the ladder was brought back to the exit door and we were given permission to deplane. The passengers of Cubana de Aviación were the only ones in the entire Mexico City airport who had to walk all the way to the terminal building; all the others were collected in buses.

Customs officials continued this outrageous procedure. The passengers ahead of us had their luggage checked and their pockets searched, from top to bottom. It looked as if the customs officers were analyzing the chemical and physical composition of each molecule.

"You'll see, things will be different when they get to us," my captain whispered in my ear.

Indeed, while receiving a box of Cohiba cigars from my husband, the officer we got closed our suitcase without even glancing at it. Instead of barking, he began to flatter us, eager to savor the delicious tobacco. I had heard that Mexican police and security officials were the most corrupt in the western hemisphere, which I couldn't imagine, but I had just witnessed a small demonstration of this reality. Years later, during longer stays in Mexico, I was able to corroborate, more than once, the widespread corruption in Mexican institutions.

We had to stay in a seedy hotel. It was dirty and smelled of mildew and stale food. In the airport, I had given Dani the last reserve bottle, so empty that not even a drop came out. Now he was screaming so desperately that it was clear he'd brook no delay. I urgently needed milk for the baby and some food for his brother. They were both hungry, as more than half a day had passed since we'd left Havana. I called room service for what we needed, shouting over the sound of Dani's police-siren screaming. Half an hour passed and nothing. I called again. I had to shout to be understood because Dani's screams made any conversation impossible.

"*Señora*, I have to find a *tarro* to boil the milk. I'll bring it to you right away," the employee replied with her enviable Mexican accent.

"I don't need a *tarro*; I need boiled milk," I replied, annoyed. I didn't know that *tarro* meant exactly that: a little pot to boil milk in.

Half an hour later, the hotel's cook-cleaning-girl-message-taker-telephone-operator-illiterate-secretary appeared, with something in her hand.

"Here's the milk, *señora*!"

And she set it on the dresser for me. The little pot was so dirty, so incredibly disgusting that I could hardly bear to touch it. The handle was encrusted with remnants of food—different kinds of food, to make matters worse. The interior surface was covered by a layer of grime that was at least a quarter of an inch thick. But at least the milk was boiled, I said to myself. Turning a blind eye, trying to convince myself that the dirt wasn't there and that the milk was in good condition, I filled the bottle and gave it to my son to drink. The siren was instantly silent, and the desperate sucking of a starving kid could be heard all the way across the room.

After filling the little boy's belly, I went down to the kitchen to return the pot and ask them to prepare the meals for the rest of the day and night in clean cooking equipment. I was intending to inform them of the baby's feeding schedule for the next few days, but I gave up on that idea the moment I set foot in the kitchen. There was no way this was going to work: the kitchen was a pigsty.

"We're going to find a market, right now," I told my husband. "I have to buy a camping stove, a pot, and ready-to-eat baby food. We can't use anything from the hotel kitchen."

My captain accepted my demands without question, which meant totally unexpected expenses were going to decimate the tiny amount of money we had received to be able to pay the expenses of our week of transit through Mexico. We asked the multi-profession employee to bring a crib up to the room for us, since Dani had no place to sleep. The room had only a double bed and a sofa. In addition to those essential items I mentioned, we bought disposable diapers, detergent, soap, toothpaste, toothbrushes, and shampoo. It was a luxury to be able to get such wonderful things. I felt like a child at a birthday party in the distant past, when Cuban stores were still shops and not just four walls with empty shelves.

When we returned to the hotel, in the middle of the room sat a cradle of indefinite color, dirty and dusty. Its original color was visible only in the places where the fingerprints of the employee who had deposited it in the room had been left. I don't know why in situations like this my imagination produces absurd comparisons. Instead of the cradle I saw *The Harp*, by Gustavo Adolfo Bécquer: "In a dark corner or the room / Perhaps forgotten by its owner / Silent and dim with dust / I saw the harp." Like the cradle, the harp was forgotten in a corner, covered in dust, waiting for someone to take it out and say to it, like Lazarus, get up and walk. No one said to the crib "get up and walk" or "get clean so the child will accept you and can sleep peacefully." The poor multi-tasked woman, the only employee of our seedy compulsory hotel, had carried it up by herself from the basement to our room, and she must have thought a thousand times, *These damn Cubans are ruining my life with their demands*. I had the satisfaction not only of feeling like the queen of the world with my purchases, but also of being able to turn dirty things into sublime objects with my imagination.

After cleaning the crib, it was like new, ready to be used. We were all so tired of this long day full of surprises that we went to bed with the chickens, and we surrendered to sleep. Early the next day, my husband had to take care of our entry permit to the U.S. The Americans had promised to give it to us for the weekend, since it had expired on the day of the trip, when we missed the flight due to the punctured tire. The week of waiting in Mexico was the punishment that the U.S. authorities imposed on us for not having complied with the original itinerary. They could have given us the visas without a problem because what difference did it make if we arrived on Monday or Friday, but it seemed that the "welcoming committee," the officials of the U.S. security services who were in charge of monitoring the new Cuban officer's every step, and that of his whole tribe, needed a break after having suffered the great disappointment of not seeing us arrive on the scheduled day. For me, this was the second time I had collided with the stubbornness and selfishness of a powerful country's representatives, so even before we arrived to begin life in New York, I had decided I wasn't going to like it.

The day before we were to leave Mexico City for New York, the two children were ill. The burn on Dictys' leg was quite inflamed. After being almost healed on the beach in Havana, it seems that the new layer of skin was very thin, which allowed the entry of pathogens. He had a fever, the glands in his groin were swollen, and his leg hurt. He was limping and in a bad mood.

Dani, in turn, had a red, swollen face. His cheeks were covered with tiny blisters, an ugly dermatitis. He had a high fever and was in obvious discomfort. He went on a hunger strike—the first in his life. There was no way he was going to take the bottle, and he flatly rejected the baby food that had cost us an arm and a leg. He whimpered almost non-stop. We didn't have health insurance, and we didn't know of any doctor who would take care of the children without charging us a fortune that we didn't have. The kids' father asked the Cuban embassy for help. A Cuban doctor came to see the children. He diagnosed them both with a dermatitis caused by contact with the sheets, which were apparently so dirty they were contaminated with virulent microorganisms. The consultation cost us nothing, but the medicine—a potent antibiotic—again depleted our monetary reserves.

The run-down, filthy pigsty in which we were forced to stay because it was cheap turned out to be very expensive in the long run. Even being outside of Cuba, we had been forced to apply the absurd policy widespread in the Cuban economy: buy low and pay high. We arrived in New York on a hot, suffocating summer day, and the first thing we had to do was consult a doctor, because the children still had high fevers, and their health worried us more than the precarious state of our finances. Fortunately, the remedies the doctor prescribed soon had the desired effect. Within days, the two little ones were in perfect health.

In New York, our co-workers hadn't bothered to find us an apartment. They thought it would be enough for us to stay in the hundred-square-foot studio that had been vacated by our

7. Dictys and Dani celebrating Dani's first birthday, New York, December 1967

predecessor. He was now back in Havana after being wounded when a package bomb sent to him by an anti-Castro terrorist organization exploded in his hands. He had lived in this studio alone, without a family. There were four of us, and we couldn't live in this hovel infested with cockroaches and totally unsuitable for our family. With all due respect, I wasn't going to tolerate this ironclad policy of saving money anymore. In Mexico City we had gone from the sublime to the ridiculous, and I wasn't willing to continue on that road.

For the next few days, my main task was to find an acceptable apartment. I didn't need luxury. I just wanted a clean house, equipped with at least one bed for each member of the family. I won't give the details of our pilgrimage through New York. I'll relate these stories, of which there are many, in another book. Suffice it to say that almost two years in the city helped me not only to learn English, but also to be a magician in managing the scarce financial resources at my disposal. I got to know the mentality of New Yorkers and found true friends among them; I also lived among fellow Cubans whose pettiness, hypocrisy, and unfounded arrogance drove me crazy. Other Cubans became dear friends, and to them I still owe gratitude.

My captain and I took advantage of the cultural wealth of New York City, spending our last pennies on concerts and visits to museums. I bought books, more books, and records, true treasures that helped keep at bay the thoughts that often attacked me in this great city and left me feeling depressed and miserable. I definitely didn't like New York. There were too many troubles, scares, and problems that we endured there, from a bomb planted by anti-Castro terrorists in front of our apartment to accidents that Dani and I suffered, which not only affected our physical well-being but also—and above all—our budget, which was so tight and insufficient that I had to perform miracles to lead an acceptable life.

While still in New York, my faith in the Cuban Revolution received a huge blow when the news reached us of the death of one of our friends. Paco informed us of the details: Braulio, a member of our friends' circle, who was a staunch defender of the Revolution, had become a dissident. It seems that he was involved in some clandestine activity and was arrested. Because he was diabetic, he was transferred from the Principe prison to a military hospital. No family members were allowed to visit him to bring him the insulin and food he needed to keep his diabetes under control, and the authorities gave him absolutely nothing. They left him to die miserably, denying him the most elementary medical care. This happened in my beloved socialist Cuba.

My husband was also affected by the death of this friend, but he muffled his doubts and mistrust in the system with the justification, which from then on we would hear often: *The Revolution is made by human beings. Human beings make mistakes. There is no absolute justice.* I was left wondering where tolerance for mistakes finally ends. To what degree are they justified? Are we caught in a vicious circle? I wasn't able, at that time, to take these thoughts to their ultimate conclusions, perhaps because of the fear of seeing my illusions disappear, and yet reality was showing us an increasingly great distance between discourse and practice. However, by repeating the proclamations over and over, we accepted them as indisputable. With the magical thinking of small children who cover their faces and believe they're invisible, we acted as if the eternal and always repeated blah-blah-blah, by the simple act of repetition, was the immutable truth.

From my current German perspective, more than thirty years after these events, I ask myself time and again: How is it possible that we accepted and supported this system? Didn't we have eyes and ears to perceive? Were our gray cells frozen? So many years of school, university, and life experiences had served to make us like tamed animals in the circus. People have always said that no one is as blind as the person who will not see, and no one more deaf than the person who will not hear.

It took two more decades for the castle of dreams, delusions, and wishful thinking to collapse, for us to become aware that we had spent our energies, intelligence, and strength—had sacrificed our lives—in a futile effort to construct a society based on dreams, ideals, and infantile desires, exempt from realistic, objective, and rational considerations.

CHAPTER SIXTEEN
DANI IS BROUGHT BACK TO LIFE

Back in Havana, after a year and a half in New York, a hard period of readjustment began. The kids, especially, felt the rigors of their environment. The scarcity, the lack of order in the daily routine; the constant "I don't know, my little one, if we can" and "Let's see if we can find it"; the omnipresent noise; the disorderly, but above all noisy, life of our neighbors; the boarding girls occupying the adjacent house, who never slept or let anyone else sleep before midnight—it all constituted real torture for the children, whose rhythm of life was suddenly disrupted.

My captain's superiors gave us a week off in Varadero. Four people in a room is not exactly a luxury. The constant lack of water and the abundance of cockroaches and mosquitoes reminded us at every moment that we were back in Cuba. But the lovely, almost deserted beach (international tourism wasn't yet happening), the crystal-clear water, and the immensity of the sea made us forget all the other discomforts. In March, the tropical sun and warm water were heavenly.

The children couldn't get enough of swimming, something they hadn't been able to do in New York. They soon took on the color of mulattos, and their hunger for uninterrupted exercise in the open air made them forget the monotonous food: rice and beans, beans and rice, *arroz congri* (rice and beans cooked together), rice with egg, rice with banana, and every other permutation. They ate mechanically so they could immediately return to the beach.

Dani, due to his Nordic appearance—green eyes, blonde hair—drew attention. He was also sociable, and with his Anglo-Cuban jargon he amused people. He always had someone by his side—almost always adults—who talked and played with him. I hadn't paid attention to that man who picked him up and threw him into the air as if Dani were a ball. When I noticed, it was too late to intervene.

Obviously, Dani didn't like this game, and when he made a face of horror and supplication to be released, the stranger suddenly threw him at my husband, who was totally oblivious to what was happening. He just felt something land on top of him and instinctively threw out his right arm, giving Dani a sharp slap with his wristwatch on the glottis. With the other hand, he grabbed the boy out of the air.

Dani couldn't even utter a cry. He threw his head back, and only a strangled, guttural rasp was heard. His head turned forward and back until it was definitely hanging, with wide eyes, staring at nothing. My husband, incredulous and totally confused, looked at his son in his arms, a puppet without strings whose color changed from white to purple, and he shouted in terror:

"What happened to him? Who threw him at me?" as if this question were important, but in situations like this, we sometimes say things that are neither intelligent nor coherent.

"We have to revive him; he's not breathing; he has no pulse," I managed to stammer.

I took the child and placed him on the ground. I shook him, pinched him, and blew air into his mouth. I don't remember what else I did. A circle of people had formed around us, voyeurs, scared but unable to do anything but comment on the show, while I kept trying to breathe life into our son. In those moments of horror, panic, and despair, a movie passed through my mind: I saw Dani in a white box, his last resting place, and we, his parents and brother, were walking along a path in the cemetery, toward a grave, to bury him.

With this in mind I kept trying to resuscitate him. Suddenly, I saw Dictys strike a pose in front of the onlookers and say, in a slow and serene voice, like a professional announcer:

"I think my little brother just died."

The onlookers continued to watch. Someone said:

"*Señores*, isn't there a doctor here?"

Nobody answered. From afar, as if I were miles away, I heard comments like:

"Did you see what happened? Where's the man who threw him? How can he be dead if he didn't fall and hit his head?"

It must have been at least three minutes—for me three hours—when Dani began to move his head, followed by a tremor throughout his body. His eyes moved so slowly that I felt like I was watching a movie in slow motion. He tried to blink but his eyes closed again. Every slow movement he made seemed to cause him an unbearable effort. But he was moving. His color changed from purple to white. I tried to hold him up, but his legs weren't working, and he collapsed like a torn, empty sack. He wasn't dead, but he wasn't alive either.

Little by little, Dani regained energy, like a battery that was being charged. I managed to get him up, but his legs faltered, like a valiant stalk of sugar cane in a windstorm. He spread his legs to keep his balance, and a little time passed. He fixed his eyes on a horizon, where I couldn't distinguish anything important. With a penetrating gaze, as if observing something extremely interesting, he explored its horizontal line. His eyes didn't move; only his head traced this ghostly line, turning back and forth like a fan at reduced speed due to lack of electricity. He didn't react to my words or his surroundings.

I began to ask the questions that the doctor had taught me in order to evaluate Dani's physical functions after an accident (this was the fourth and most dramatic time I had to do this):

"Dani, where are your feet?"

He took his eyes off the horizon to focus on my face. A brief frown, and the index finger of his right hand pointed to his feet. Not the slightest sound came from his mouth. *The child is speechless* was my logical conclusion. He wouldn't be the first human being to have such a thing happen.

"Dani, show me where your brother is," was my next diagnostic order.

He raised his right arm, showing his brother with his index finger, while his face expressed surprise at the silly order his mother was giving him. With these moves it was already clear that he hadn't suffered any considerable brain damage, although his apparent inability to speak had me scared and unsure. I wanted to consult a neurologist, but this kind of specialist wasn't within reach at Varadero Beach. Meanwhile, Dani was gradually moving his joints, starting with his arms, shoulders, torso, and he finally took his first steps, like a wind-up doll. He staggered like a drunk, but only for a little while, holding my hand, and then sped up little by little. Five minutes later he let go of my hand and ran off, his usual mischievous self.

My husband and I were tired and exhausted. The panic, despair, and horror of what we'd experienced were still reflected in our bodies. We sat down in the cafeteria of the Hotel Internacional to have a drink and calmly assimilate what had happened. We waited a long time to get the soft drinks we ordered.

We couldn't take our eyes off Dani, who was sitting next to his brother on a bench. Dictys, now with his mind cleared of what happened, talked with us, and Dani began to annoy his brother. He took away his silverware, his glass, and shoved and elbowed him. Dictys complained, which only encouraged Dani to continue his teasing. I couldn't manage to do anything other than admire the abnormal metamorphosis of my son.

Suddenly, Dani jumped on the table, knocked over glasses and silverware, and let out a laugh and shouts of euphoria, uttering a torrent of words. It was then clear to me: The child isn't dead or mute, but he's definitely crazy. Despair took hold of me again, and my exaggerated imagination contributed to my disastrous mood.

I don't want to recite the nightmares—day and night—that,

for years, this accident and Dani's subsequent behavior caused me, although the child quickly returned to normal. I understood the meaning of what my mother told me one day, I don't remember why or when it was:

"When you're an adult, I hope you have a child who has your character, who takes after you, so that you know what it means to make a mother suffer."

Fortunately, we had to return to Havana and could leave Varadero, which I stopped liking for a long time. Every time I was lucky enough to be on this beautiful beach again, I was reminded of the terrible, agonizing moments with Dani.

Important tasks awaited us in Havana. We had to find a place in a kindergarten for Dani. I had to negotiate with the administration of the university faculty I was studying in to finish my degree, and Dictys had to go back to school after the summer vacation. He had begun first grade in New York at the U.N. school, and his life as a schoolboy had to proceed without interruption.

CHAPTER SEVENTEEN

VACATION WITH THE GERMAN GRANDPARENTS

I ASKED THE NATIONAL BANK OF CUBA for permission to buy tickets in Cuban pesos to travel to Germany and spend the holidays at my parents' house. I wanted to take my children, as the grandparents still hadn't met their grandson Dani. It was a tedious process of filling out request forms and more request forms. There was a lack of paper in the country; however, for these purposes it was in abundance. Filling out the forms was one thing; enduring extensive questioning was another. Why had I been in the country for so many years and never before requested the exchange of national currency to buy a plane ticket? I was told that the national situation didn't allow for payment of airline tickets for foreign travel. Didn't I have someone abroad who could pay for my ticket? Of course we had the right to visit our relatives, but we had to make sacrifices to save. I had to provide certificates of good conduct from the university and seek the support of an important official to recommend the approval of my application to the presidency of the bank. *He—or in this case, she—who has a friend, has everything.* The truth of this Cuban saying was tested and proved thanks to my husband's friendships. We were lucky, and we were finally given the right to buy the tickets.

Then another important obstacle had to be overcome: obtaining passports, which must be provided with photos of the children, and obtaining the passports in a short time. We got the photos with—naturally—the intervention of a friend. This type of aid was already called a *palanca* at that time: using pull, or leverage. Without pull, the photos wouldn't have been possible, since the institution that did that sort of work—I called it the House of the Monsters—had neither film nor the chemicals needed to develop the photos. Original Wolfen (ORWO) photography products from East Germany were not yet entering the country, but *sociolismo*, friends helping friends—the only system that worked in *socialismo*, socialism—once again proved its effectiveness. In Cuba, the word *socio*, usually meaning "business associate" or "business partner," had been extended, in colloquial speech, to refer to any friend or acquaintance. It seems socialism had turned the entire country into one enormous mega-enterprise.

On the day scheduled for our flight we found ourselves in an old Britannia airplane that took its last gasp flying us to Prague and from there to Berlin. A short time later it was withdrawn from circulation, replaced by an Ilyushin. When we landed in Berlin, we had a huge scare. The immigration officers didn't want us to enter the country.

"You're German. How dare you travel with a foreign passport? You're not getting in. You have to return on the same plane you arrived on. In two hours it will be in the air again, heading to Havana. And don't ever come back without East German documents. You won't be able to enter. You must learn that law and order are respected here!"

Luckily for us, the then-Cuban ambassador to East Germany, my husband's old comrade in the struggle, was waiting for us. As a diplomat, he had the right to enter the receiving room. And so it was that for the second time in my life (the first was when I got married and left for Cuba), the Cuban side intervened to free me from East German domination. The next day, the ambassador personally asked the Ministry of Foreign Affairs for authorization for me and the children to stay in East Germany for three weeks without having to change our documents. Was this, perhaps, the first confrontation between Cuba and East Germany on citizenship issues of Germans married to Cubans? For me, personally, I took it for granted that I was on the list of black sheep. I had decided that I would never again work with any East German institution in Cuba, following the refusal of the East German trade office in Havana to place Dictys in the German kindergarten.

At my parents' house we quickly forgot the incident. We had a splendid summer, with sun and warmth, as in a Cuban winter. We spent the days on the shores of the Baltic Sea and in the lush forests that are a five-minute walk from my German home, where I was born. Seeing the Baltic Sea for the first time, Dictys gave a cry of horror and disappointment:

"Mommy, how disgusting, a gigantic sewer!"

Indeed, the shore was covered with a thick layer of algae in a state of putrefaction. It seems that the prolonged heat had caused an algae bloom, a sort of maritime cancer. There were people bathing in this stinking broth! We went to another beach, less protected from the wind and, marvelously, it was clean. I knew that the water was useless for swimming, not because it was dirty, but because it was too cold for those used to the deliciously warm water of the Caribbean. The children ran in, but they ran out faster than they had entered. The beach, although not good for swimming, was good for running, playing, rowing in boats, and having fun. There were always a lot of children that our sons could play and frolic with, so holidays with the German grandparents were unforgettable events for Dictys and Dani.

The most striking thing for them, however, was the German food. In my parents' house, thanks to a number of greenhouses and fruit orchards, there were all the vegetables and fruits you could imagine: apples, blackberries, plums, pears, cherries, strawberries, and even grapes. The house was full of guests; in addition to the three of us, an uncle, aunt, and almost always the occasional cousin, niece, and nephew would be visiting for the summer. A huge table would be set up for meals. The dishes would be prepared—in honor and for the pleasure of my children— according to their wishes, because "poor little ones, in Cuba they can't eat what they like."

My mother went so far as to look up the words for different foods in a German-Spanish dictionary, to be able to understand Dani and prepare the delicacies he requested. Dani refused to learn German, and he bombarded my parents and everyone else with his verbiage in Spanish, correcting his grandmother's Spanish pronunciation and laughing at her if she couldn't say the words correctly.

Iron discipline always reigned at the table in my house. Talking or laughing was forbidden. My father was the supreme authority. A glance from him was enough to call us to order if we had dared to reach the limit of his tolerance. My children managed to destroy all the established norms, though. Dictys loved *bratkartoffel*, German-style fried potatoes, and during the holidays they were never missing for dinner. My mother always prepared such a huge quantity of this dish that anyone else would have thought she was feeding a battalion. If before it was the adults who were served food and then the children, with mine at the table the order was changed. Seeing the huge platter full of steaming potatoes, smelling like heaven, Dictys wouldn't be able to contain himself, and once he embraced it as if it were a treasure, exclaiming ecstatically, in faulty German: "This is all mine, mine!"

A laugh from everyone at the table was the response to this manifestation of gluttony. Dani, of course, wasn't going to be left behind. Four years younger than his brother, he didn't expect to eat many potatoes, but the huge clay jar full of pickled cucumbers in the center of the table had an attraction for him that was impossible to suppress. Dani jumped on the table like a cat. He put his arm in the jar to the bottom, wetting his shirt up to the shoulder, and took out a beautiful pickle, which disappeared entirely in his mouth, passing from there to his stomach almost without having been chewed. My children continually contributed to the family's entertainment.

Cheerful, spontaneous, speaking and singing non-stop in a mixture of English, Spanish, and a pinch of newly-learned German, they were the sensation and attraction of the neighborhood as well. My parents and guests loved to see my children eating like barbarians in ancient times. It was a pleasure to cook for them and give them tasty bites. They ate it all, without anyone having to ask them, quite the opposite of their female cousins, who were fussy, made faces, and left more than half on their plates. They should have been sent to Cuba for a time so they could learn what it means to be hungry and have nothing to eat but rice and beans, and sometimes not even that.

The three weeks passed quickly. The day before we were to leave, my father surprised us with an extraordinary gift. At my father's request, a butcher friend of the family had cured two exquisite hams in his smokehouse. With these items packed in my carry-on bag, we hoped to get through Cuban customs, but the smell of the hams was so strong that we were betrayed. Everyone, passengers and customs officials alike, was salivating. The hams were removed in less than the blink of an eye, and we were lucky not to have to pay a fine, as it was strictly forbidden to bring in food from outside. I am sure that the hams ended up in the belly of the officials and not, as directed and prescribed by law, being burned as contraband. The soothing effect of our vacation disappeared with this reception at the Havana airport.

CHAPTER EIGHTTEEN
DICTYS TRAINS TO SWIM AND DANI ALMOST DROWNS

There was a short break in Havana before classes were to start. I was in the university, and Dictys was in elementary school, but he still had to take a special test. All the children who went to a school on the Ana Betancourt Plan had to undergo a diagnostic test to determine their aptitude to be in such an institution.

A resolute psychologist, recently graduated, with a head full of knowledge but no life experience bombarded Dictys with questions.

"What is a *quilo*?" (a Cuban penny) the specialist wanted to know.

Dictys looked at her, looked at me, shrugged his shoulders as if to express that the person in front of him was stupid and answered the question with another question. He obviously didn't know what a *quilo* was. The young woman showed him a penny.

"Ah, this . . . This is a penny."

"What is he saying? He's impossible to understand," complained the psychologist.

Dictys began to be bothered by the repeated "the child doesn't know how to express himself; he can't communicate; he's confused." At the end of the exam, the psychologist showed him a series of cards with colored pictures, and the boy, already wanting to go home, gave her his interpretation so quickly and hastily, using his polyglot vocabulary, that the young girl was dizzy, frustrated, and outraged.

"If you want to prevent the little one from going crazy, you shouldn't speak to him in any other language than Spanish," she told me. "At least eight years must pass before he can start with another language. He has to consolidate his Spanish."

This young specialist hadn't seen anything like this before. She felt sorry for the "unfortunate" child, whose parents had exposed him to such abuse. Dictys, recently returned from Germany, where he refreshed his German language skills a little, had reached a level similar to when he was younger, when he spoke his own language. This time, however, it wasn't an invented language, but an Anglo-German-Spanish mix, and with this mixture he had tried to communicate with his inquisitor, who, knowing absolutely no foreign language, couldn't imagine that the boy would feel happy and content with this state of things.

"You have traumatized this poor boy. He doesn't know how to express his feelings, his thoughts. He lacks vocabulary. This is awful. This is criminal," the young woman scolded me.

"The child has no trouble expressing his feelings and thoughts," I replied. "He's just doing it in three languages. When he doesn't know a word in Spanish, he substitutes the corresponding one in English or German."

"That's precisely the problem: nobody understands it," the psychologist returned to the charge.

"A child of his age learns a language in a short time, so I have no doubt that in a few weeks, his Spanish will be up to par."

I gave my opinion to the stubborn woman; this was a tedious waste of time.

Dictys had told us quite categorically, when the continuation of his life as an elementary school student was under discussion, that he wouldn't go to any school that didn't have a swimming pool. The only Cuban school that met this condition was the Camilo Cienfuegos swimming school. We explained to our son that it was a boarding school located in Guanabo, a seaside village seventeen miles east of Havana, where the kids slept in collective rooms from Sunday evening until Saturday morning, having just one and a half days off at home with the family.

8. *Dani, Dictys, and two classmates at* Ciudad Deportiva, *the pick-up point for the Camilo Cienfuegos swimming school*

The school followed strict discipline, and swimming wasn't just a hobby but a daily, mandatory routine. It was an institution famous for preparing the future swimming champions of Cuba, which meant that book-learning and swimming had the same priority. The school had dormitories, classrooms, a dining room, and, of course, swimming pools (yes, plural). We knew that Dictys was too young to be able to evaluate the possibilities and realize the consequences of his demand. All our attempts to put the idea of learning to read and write in a swimming pool out of his head were for naught. Dictys wanted to go; it was this school or no school.

Dictys took the entrance exams. Each child had to fully

demonstrate his abilities as a potential swimmer. Trained specialists, experts in the stages of swimming development, made the selection of future champions. Many children were accompanied by their parents, who were experiencing a thousand and one unbearable anxieties, wanting to see their treasures be, against all odds, among those selected. The kids would throw themselves into the water, fighting against the element like Don Quixote against windmills.

Dictys was one of those selected. There were a few days left before he moved to the school, and we took advantage of the time to refine his breaststroke, because he knew that his kick was far from perfect (I myself had actively practiced this sport and knew the correct movements well), although this drawback hadn't kept him from being admitted to the swimming school.

Living less than a block from the coast, in Miramar, it was the most natural thing in the world for the children to spend most of the day in the water. I took Dictys into the deep water, while Dani sat on the wall of the Patricio Lumumba beach. Beside him he had a bowl of sand, a bucket, and a little shovel to play with. As a precautionary measure, I had attached a belt with a small plastic buoy around his waist that would serve as a life preserver should he accidentally fall off the wall into the water. Dictys and I swam about forty feet out from the wall to practice arm and leg movements. Every now and then, I would glance back at Dani, who was watching us from the wall.

It seems that Dani had a fit of jealousy at not being the center of attention. I saw him undo his belt and throw it over the wall, with a gesture of contempt and hatred. Then he got close to the edge with his toes sticking out over the wall; he raised his arms, and, like a trampoline master, jumped into the water.

I was horrified and frightened. What a bold, fearless, headstrong child. This was far beyond any crazy thing I'd done in my childhood. There was no time to think about anything but getting to the place where Dani had gone in. He still couldn't swim, so I had to get him out as soon as possible. Dictys was scared because he'd seen his brother disappear into the water. I had to leave him alone to save his brother. I was afraid that Dictys would get nervous and swallow too much water, but Dani needed more air than he did because he had been underwater for a while, unable to breathe.

Never, even in my best days, had I swum so fast. There were swells that made it difficult to see clearly. I dived down and found the boy about four feet deep. I lifted him up, towed him up the ladder, and put him on the wall. I had to empty him upside down like a bucket. He spat out a barbarous amount of water and went limp, white as wax, ready to receive—for the fifth time in his now two and a half years of life—the indispensable help of his mother, who had already become a specialist in applying various resuscitation techniques to her son.

When normalcy was restored, I sat down with Dani on the wall. I spoke to him at length, calming him down, thinking that the little boy must be more scared than we were. Dani looked at me with hatred and didn't answer me. I gave him the shovel and the bucket. He threw them into the water. I put the lifebelt back on. I walked with him on the wall for a while, showing him the little fish that could be seen from there. Dani was angry, or still so scared that he wouldn't talk to me.

Fortunately, Dictys managed to get out of the water without help, but he was frightened. He couldn't understand why his brother had thrown himself into the water with no life belt and not knowing how to swim. Obviously Dani wanted to attract attention; he felt abandoned, but taking off his life jacket and throwing himself in the water was crazy.

I was convinced that Dani would never learn to swim, that this unpleasant experience of swallowing so much water and feeling drowned would make him an eternal enemy of the water, and that he would be afraid, as might have happened to a child who accidentally fell in. But my fears were not realized; what's more, on the same day, just a few minutes after nearly drowning, Dani presented us with yet another demonstration of an abandoned child screaming for attention.

Certain that from now on it would take a thousand tricks to get Dani to go into the water voluntarily, I went out swimming again with Dictys to continue our swimming lesson. We were about fifteen feet away from the wall when Dani took off his lifebelt again, and though I desperately yelled at him not to, he jumped into the deep water with the same expression of contempt and hatred.

"Dictys, stay here; I have to get your brother out."

I repeated the entire procedure of a few minutes earlier, which included emptying the child of swallowed water, resuscitating him—although this time he recovered much faster than the previous time—and giving him a psychotherapy session. I then refastened his lifebelt and took the boy into the water with Dictys. Dani was happy there, and he paid attention to see if he could imitate the arm and leg movements his brother was practicing.

From then on, Dani swam regularly in deep water. He learned to swim in less than a week and delighted in jumping from all the diving boards within reach, reliably demonstrating that he was a champion at holding his breath. After each springboard jump, he would dive for at least twenty feet before coming up for air. It was clear that the experience of almost dying six times had served as practice. He was trained to be able to stay alive, without breathing, for at least two minutes, which is a good record for a child under three years of age.

PART THREE
THE SEVENTIES

CHAPTER NINETEEN
THE BOYS ARE GROWING

At the swimming school he had been so determined to attend, Dictys learned quickly that real life is different from dreams. We had to drop him off at the pickup point, the Ciudad Deportiva, on Sundays at five in the afternoon, from where students were taken in prehistoric buses to the school in Guanabo. They came home on Saturday afternoon—in other words, they lived with their families only one day a week. The other days were spent in boarding school, under a regime similar to that of military schools.

We, too, soon realized that the child's adaptation to this new life wasn't as quick and easy as we'd have liked. Dictys started to suck his thumb again, after having stopped, years ago, using his therapeutic cloth and thumb, a substitute for affection. This reversion was a sign more than sufficient for us to realize that he was missing the warmth of home, its protective environment and love.

On Saturdays when he arrived at the pickup point in the bus and see us waiting for him, his eyes would light up, but during the car ride home, he would curl up in the back seat and suck his thumb. It seems that from the moment of his arrival home he was already preparing for the farewell the next day. Hours before having to go to the Ciudad Deportiva on Sundays, he would sit in a corner. He seemed to be meditating. Quiet, looking sad, absorbed, and uninterested in what was going on around him, he would be preparing himself for the moment of departure. On the way to the bus, he wouldn't speak; he would suck his thumb again, making us feel guilty for condemning him to a punishment he'd done nothing to deserve.

When the bus to Guanabo started up, all the children began a terrible concert of crying and screaming, sticking their hands out the windows, begging to be allowed to return home. All the parents were left behind, sad, some with nervous laughter, with difficulty digesting that tragicomic spectacle repeated every Sunday. Fortunately, within two months of starting the course, most of the children began to accept the boarding-school regime, and their emotion subsided. Dictys, aided by his faithful and ever-present thumb, which he used to fall asleep and for car trips, also adapted. He didn't suck it in the presence of anyone but his family; he knew that this "weakness" (a perfectly normal coping mechanism, of course) could lead his little companions to make fun of him.

* * *

By the end of 1969 in Cuba, toys could be bought only for Three Kings Day on January 6. Later, when for ideological reasons Three Kings Day was canceled, July 26 was declared Children's Day, and children could receive their gifts in the month of July. Each child had the right to receive one basic toy and two additional toys. For that day and that day only, the toys were imported almost exclusively from China, and when relations with the *narras*, the Chinese, devolved to the level of insults, the toys would be brought in from the Soviet Union and East Germany.

But there were never enough toys. For every thousand children there would be one bicycle, one pair of skates, or one stroller. Days before the sale of toys began, the treasures would be displayed in the windows of the stores selected to sell the toys (all the stores were state-owned). Swarms of children with their parents, grandparents, uncles, aunts, and other relatives would press their noses against the windows, fantasizing about the basic toy of their dreams, the one that was most worth having, because the extras were of little importance: rubber balls, bags of marbles, or plastic maracas that broke the third time they were used.

Given the small number of better toys and the tremendous demand, systems had to be devised to distribute them. Lottery gambling was forbidden, but the sale of these highly coveted items turned out to be a diabolical, and well disguised, lottery. One year the government tried to organize the distribution by following the numerical order of the ration books; another year the toys were sold on a "first come, first served" basis, so people lined up for days and nights in a row. It was impossible to satisfy the population; there was no way to achieve an even superficially fair and balanced distribution; such an attempt was totally irrational. Nor, certainly, did they have the help of Jesus, who had been able to multiply a few loaves and fishes to feed the masses. The few imported toys were not multiplied—not by magic, and not by Fidel's speeches.

The distribution system by phone was the last straw. I don't remember whether it was in 1969 or 1970, the Year of the Ten Million; the date doesn't matter. But this brilliant idea, the spawn of the distribution system, should be inscribed in Cuban history books. The Minister of Light Industry, a man named Serafín, was responsible for organizing the toys' distribution, and he had come up with the idea of selling the toys by appointments that could be reserved by phone, almost paralyzing the national telephone system. The day after the toys were sold, there was no public telephone in all of Cuba that worked. The mistreatment of the phones, their indiscriminate use without any cost to the users, the inability of the toy stores' staffs to answer thousands and thousands of calls to coordinate the appointments, destroyed the already aging, anachronistic equipment, which had by now endured many insults in the first decade of the Revolution. The Japanese telephones that replaced these ancient American devices years later didn't even remotely withstand the mistreatment suffered by those from the North. As for the ingenious minister, the mastermind of distributing toys by phone appointment, the incident cost him his position, and the poor man had to put up with the nickname "Serafín-ring-ring."

Nor were there children's books for sale to help a child read and write. In order to make reading palatable to my son, to awaken his curiosity about the use of compound letters, I decided to create a primer using the stories of the Brothers Grimm that I vividly remembered from my own time of learning the ABCs. His teacher informed me of my son's progress every weekend, telling me what letters they had learned during the week. And to reinforce the teacher's work, I used the new letters that the children had learned in each weekly story.

A school notebook, some colored pencils saved since our return from New York, and the illustrations from an encyclopedia served as my tools. From the encyclopedia I would trace the animals, the main figures in the stories, so that the child would recognize, without having to guess, when the story was about a goat, a wolf, bunnies, dogs, geese, chickens, or other animals. Having no skill as an artist, I couldn't draw the required figures on my own. In my creations, a horse would look like a mouse and vice versa. The booklet helped us a lot, not only to gradually increase Dictys' Spanish vocabulary, but also to help him learn to read with interest and, from the beginning, to consider reading a vital need. Every time he came home to spend the well-deserved weekend with us, he asked me for the notebook to read the new story I had written for him. Then he told his brother about it and, at school, his classmates. In this way, he infected his brother with the desire to read and with a love of fantastic stories.

The effects of the intensive training in the swimming school were felt quickly, and Dictys' efforts were rewarded with winning the odd competition. He acquired the body of a true athlete, and his skin turned tan from the intense tropical sun. He no longer got sick as frequently as in previous years. They shaved the heads of all the boys *a la malanguita*, down to the skin except for the little speck of hair in the front, much like the Chinese dogs that

I had seen with horror and amazement on the day of my arrival in Cuba. In his days as a swimmer, Dictys looked a lot like his father when he was a cadet at the Naval Academy and wore an identical haircut, an exact copy of the skull ornaments of the U.S. Marines, also part of the mandatory uniform of Cuban cadets.

After using a lot of pull, we got a place in kindergarten for Dani. It was a time when qualified personnel were scarce. The "educators" would come to work sporadically at best, and any difficulty would make them forget their obligation. The day I was going to leave my son in the kindergarten for the first time, I was filled with terror. The educator, in the midst of a pile of at least forty children around two years of age, sat quietly as if playing the role of scarecrow rather than educating. She wasn't bothered by the yelling or the smell of diapers full of urine and poop. Thick yellow mucus hung from their nostrils, and nothing inspired her to get her butt out of the chair. I called her name several times until she finally listened to me.

"But what did you expect, *compañera*, I can't do anything. Can't you see I'm alone with all these children? The other *compañeras* are sick, or they have to resolve some problem, or their bus broke down, or they have some other difficulty. The kids have a lot of toys here; if they don't want to play with them, it's not my problem," she shouted, showing me a mound of already half-disjointed dolls, several tin submachine guns, and little cars made of the same metal, all from the Three Kings Day quotas that had been distributed to Cuban children as basic toys. Among them, I didn't see one that could be used for educational purposes for the little ones.

I was frankly horrified and extremely concerned. I had to leave my son in this institution to be able to finish my studies and work, but the desolation in which the children found themselves there, the staff's lack of any sense of responsibility, the unhygienic conditions, and the disorder provoked anger, impotence, and indignation in me. At the same time, I was aware that I could do absolutely nothing. Again I was filled with guilt. The conflict between wanting to combine professional life with motherhood was sapping my emotional and physical energy, and Dani made me see clearly that I couldn't count on him, that he wasn't like his brother, meek, obedient, and content with his destiny of being a student in a boarding school.

No, Dani developed an efficient system of resistance and protest. After having received, on his first day of kindergarten, a huge bite on his arm from an aggressive classmate, he refused to participate in the group's activities. He was ostentatiously placed in a corner and didn't move from there. At mealtimes he refused to eat anything. He didn't touch his tray, provoking the teacher's anger and despair. Every morning, when he woke up and prepared to go to kindergarten, the same drama would begin: The glass of milk would be turned over on the table, flooding the tablecloth with the precious liquid. Neither scolding nor threats of punishment changed this state of affairs. When I finally told him, "Dani, come on, we have to go," it occurred to him that he had to go to the bathroom. "Dani, are you ready?" I asked him.

"Not yet, mommy, wait, I'm finishing."

And he delayed and delayed until finally I had to get him out of the bathroom, kicking me and grabbing my leg to prevent me from leaving. Other times he would crawl under the table, and when I would try to get him out of there, he would hug one of the table legs and shout so loud that the whole neighborhood could hear.

In those days, you couldn't pick up your child before five in the afternoon. The rule said, "entry until eight in the morning, pickup from five in the afternoon." And if you were late in the morning, you weren't allowed in. The time of entry became an effective weapon for the child, because with his tricks to delay leaving, he knew perfectly well that he was saving himself the punishment of having to spend the day in the kindergarten. I refused to accept that my son dictated the law, so, suppressing my feelings, I forced him to drink milk for breakfast, leave the bathroom on time, and continue with me on the way to the kindergarten, so he was inspired to change tactics.

From that moment on, he became ill with an unusual frequency, which was striking since, before the "preschoolitis," and contrary to his brother, he had enjoyed enviable health. And this tactic was successful because he was continually suspended from the kindergarten. The problem was called "parasitic infection," and Dani ensured it by eating dirt. I don't know how he knew that the rich Cuban soil not only serves to feed plants, but also to provide shelter for parasites of the most varied species. And curing him of one of those parasites sometimes took weeks. Then he would spend a week in kindergarten at the most, before having to stay home for another long period. This was a real disaster for me; for

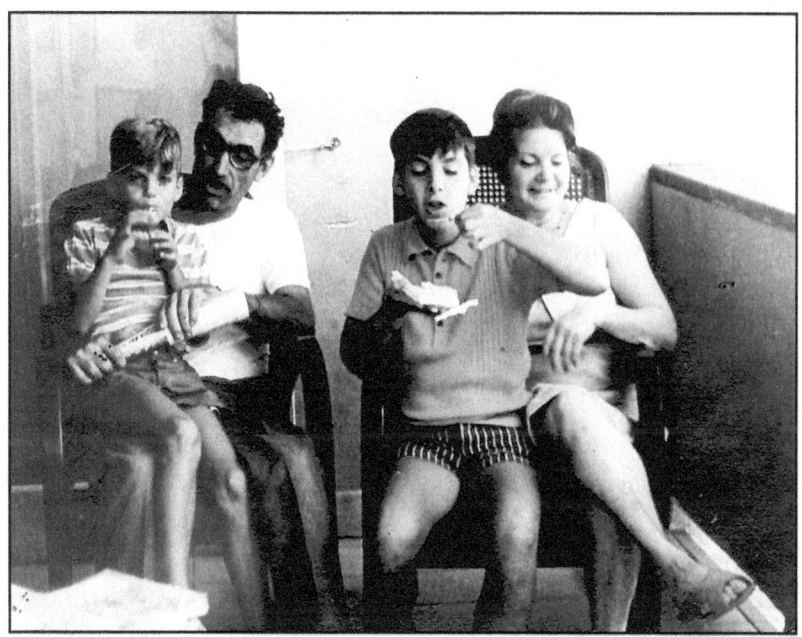

9. *Dani and Dictys with Uncle Gonzalo and Aunt Pilar*

him, it was the solution to his problem.

Every time he was suspended from the kindergarten, he would be cared for by his aunt Pilar, his father's sister. A monument should be erected to Pilar: she became my son's surrogate mother. She adored him, called him *vida mía* (my life) spoiled him, told him stories, and treated him as if he were her own son. This solution was made possible thanks to Pilar and Gonzalo's move to an apartment one block from us, just a few steps from the beach. That was the only way Pilar could take charge of picking Dani up from kindergarten and staying with him until I returned from work or university. She also took care of him at home by getting rid of the parasites that Dani collected in that miserable school. Every day, Pilar told me in great detail how she picked up Dani, her "treasure," from the kindergarten, which, according to her, turned the kids into eternal, miserable crybabies.

"Look, Mónica, this child is going to die of sadness and illness if you keep putting him in daycare. No child can feel good there. All the kids have snotty faces and wet, dirty diapers; they're crying and screaming, biting each other. There's no way this can go on. I'll take care of him for you. I don't want *vida mía* to suffer, and that kindergarten is punishment. There's no education there. My poor little nephew!"

It took a long time, but I finally became convinced that my sister-in-law was right. Her arguments were also joined by those of Dr. Valladares, our pediatrician and Dani's godfather, who advised me to leave him in his aunt's care and not continue exposing him to diseases that were not only affecting him physically but also psychologically. Pilar had lost her only child during the Spanish Civil War, and she had sworn never again to take care of a child after her niece in Madrid left home to study abroad. The charming little girl had been raised by Pilar with love, patience, and care from the diaper stage to the first acne breakouts of puberty. But Pilar put aside her firm resolve and took over for Dani. He felt so enormously good with this solution that his behavior, his once-again excellent health, his many efforts to think up creative activities, and his adoration for his aunt soon made Pilar forget her past sorrows.

On a Saturday free from kindergarten and work, I was going through my rigorous housecleaning routine. I assumed that Dani was playing in his room, where I had left him with a pile of wood blocks to build, ordering him not to move from there. Suddenly I heard our neighbor Ela talking to Dani. Her voice was filled with anxiety and terror.

"Dani, get down from there right now. Listen, boy, you're going to kill yourself!" This was followed by a strident shout: "Mónica, get your son down; he wants to jump!"

I ran to the balcony and saw Dani perched on the wall, ready to jump. I grabbed him by the arm and lowered him to the floor. My legs trembled, my vision clouded, and my stomach turned over until I felt the boy was on safe ground. Dani started screaming hysterically:

"Let me climb the wall. I'm Mighty Mouse!"

Mighty Mouse was a powerful little mouse, the protagonist of American TV, who helped all creatures in distress. He would jump off skyscrapers, break walls, fly straight up into the sky, performing all these feats with the help of a magic cape that protected him from injury. Dani was convinced that an old diaper hung around his shoulders—his magic cape—had turned him into Mighty Mouse.

"Don't you remember the mighty little mouse that is a friend of all children and helps them and frees them and nothing happens to him when he falls down? Nothing is going to happen to me, Mommy, you see, nothing is going to happen to me. Have you ever seen Mighty Mouse break a bone when jumping off a building? Never, right? And I'm Mighty Mouse! Can't you see my magic cape?"

"Dani, your magic cape is not the one that Mighty Mouse wears. The one you wear doesn't protect you."

"That's not true! It's the same one, and nothing's going to happen to me!"

"Well, Dani, if you think nothing is going to happen to you, get up on the chair and jump off of it and land on your knees. If it doesn't hurt, then it's true that you're Mighty Mouse."

Dani scrambled onto the chair and dropped to the floor like a sack full of stones. Of course it hurt; it hurt a lot. And he felt betrayed by his idol, Mighty Mouse. He wept like a creature who has lost something valuable. It took me a lot of work to console him and make him forget his friend, who was no longer a "mighty" mouse.

Dictys and Dani spent most of their free time on the beach, swimming, jumping off the wall into the Gulf of Mexico, diving, and expending so much energy that they would come home exhausted; yet when they were at home, their creativity was still amazing. One day it occurred to them to build a rocket. They cut off the heads of some matchsticks, then added a bit of gunpowder taken from pistol cartridges, obtained god-knows-where. They prepared a device containing all this mixture of explosive material and set fire to it. The "rocket" exploded with a tremendous bang, and sparks flew everywhere. A rain of fire came down on our neighbor's clothesline full of clothes. The clothes—all made of synthetic fabric—turned to ash in a matter of seconds, giving off a foul odor. Ela was left without underwear and Ela's husband without shirts. The father of the arsonists had to pay for the damage, buying replacements for the burned garments on one of his trips abroad, spending the little savings we had set aside for more useful things.

On weekends and during holidays, the two boys would ask their mother to exercise her own inventive genius. They wanted to hear stories, and always more stories. Most of the time, I would read them stories from children's books. After hearing a story once, Dani would somehow know exactly where each paragraph was. I would try to shorten the reading by skipping half a page, but Dani would immediately interrupt me:

"Mommy, that's not it," he would indignantly shout. "A piece is missing! Mommy, read it again, but in full, you hear me?" he would order.

When there was a little poem in the story, he would make me invent a melody for it. The spoken verse wasn't enough for him; he wanted it sung. This was the easiest thing in the world, but days after having invented a melody, Dani would want me to repeat it to him exactly as I had sung it the first time, and he would scold me when I couldn't perfectly reproduce it. It wasn't easy to satisfy my children's need for entertainment; they were insatiable.

Luckily, my parents sent us complete editions of the short

stories by the Brothers Grimm, Wilhelm Hauff, and Hans Christian Andersen, wonderful books, with illustrations that made the boys' imaginations take wing. I had to translate the stories for them, of course. With one of the books of enormous size and weight on his lap, Dani would ensure the accuracy of my translation. He would be guided by the illustrations and his fantastic memory, since from the first time he listened to a story he would know it by heart, and he would not forgive even the slightest deviation. But the time came when the boys were no longer satisfied with the stories in the books. They insisted that I make up stories. Each one had to give a contribution to finish a story that I had begun, but the initial idea was up to me. At story time, I would try to impose discipline, which in my opinion was necessary. I was doing my duty to invent, sing, and read at the request of the children; in return, we agreed that they would go to bed after the story.

Dani permanently sabotaged the deal. From being a sleepyhead, he turned into a night owl. At the age of two he stopped napping, and at night he had a hard time falling asleep before midnight. As an adolescent, he had the habit of going to bed at dawn, and in the morning he woke up with a hell-of-a-bad temper. Only by noon was his affable, good-natured character back to normal. Dictys and I would already be exhausted when Dani was still bouncing around like a top on the bed. Neither scolding nor threats could change him. For me, this stage became an intensive, systematic training exercise in the accumulation of patience, and it lasted a few years, until Dani replaced the sessions of stories read or invented by me with his own reading, which became food for his brain, as important as food for his body. With a clear head, free of major worries—knowing that Dictys was gradually adapting to the regime in swimming school and becoming a top athlete and that Dani was enjoying his childhood thanks to the careful, loving attention of his Aunt Pilar—I was able to dedicate myself to my final exams, and I got A's in all but one.

CHAPTER TWENTY
I COMPLETE MY STUDIES

THE CONTINUATION OF MY STUDIES was guaranteed, but not before I'd had some controversial discussions with the directors of my school. They had changed the whole program, so they didn't know how or where to place me. They wanted me to start over, as if that were the most natural thing in the world, and even though I needed only a few exams to finish. I took the solution to this problem into my own hands and proposed that I take two seminars, one in the morning and another in the afternoon, and that I complete my studies in less than a year.

So it happened that I was put in with a group of Chinese students, in the middle of the maddening process of the Cultural Revolution. Fortunately, this situation didn't last long, as the Chinese students disappeared one day, all of a sudden, without prior notice. The last weeks of their presence were tedious and fraught with tension due to the ambiguous and often absurd orders they were receiving from their government through the embassy in Havana. They had been banned from taking part in lectures on literature, history, philosophy, sociology, and art. They were only allowed to attend language, grammar, phonetics, and syntax classes. The teachers were so restricted that the classes didn't deserve to be considered university studies.

In the writing and composition classes it wasn't possible to speak, write, or debate the classics of Spanish literature or of any other country. The professors no longer knew what content to bring to their work, as the Chinese authorities continually threatened them with prohibitions and the withdrawal of students from the University of Havana, which eventually happened.

A day of classes with the Chinese was an entertaining spectacle. Before the professors began teaching, the students would recite passages from *The Quotations of Mao Tse-Tung* as if they needed to warm up, massage their gray cells, and thus be able to endure the class sessions. At each recess they continued to quote from the Little Red Book, swaying to the beat of their monotonous litanies and rolling their eyes with ecstatic gestures. We five non-Chinese students were invisible to them, as if we didn't exist. The writing and composition teacher was on the brink of collapse and couldn't handle the limitations imposed on him.

"These students have been in the country for four years, and when I want them to read their compositions, I don't know what language they're using, but it isn't Spanish," he desperately exclaimed.

When these students had been selected to study Hispanic language and literature in Havana, the Chinese authorities hadn't taken into consideration any standards of talent or aptitude; the important thing was to fulfill the plan: X number of students had to follow this course of study. The duty of those assigned was to attend classes with discipline, finish their studies in the scheduled time, and then be sent "where the Revolution needed them." This same phrase was constantly used in Cuba. Hadn't my German-language students gone through an almost identical selection process?

Our professors decided to deal with the presence of the Chinese students by ignoring them, just as the students ignored the professors' lectures. They only asked that the Chinese not interrupt or disturb the classes, that they read their pamphlets as was their duty, even during lectures, but to do so, please, in silence. The professors then could concentrate their efforts on us five non-Chinese who were eager to advance in our studies. The day we found the classroom without our Chinese colleagues, we were all relieved. Normal life was restored, and in no time we were up to date with our study program.

The Chinese were replaced by Vietnamese, young people who were highly disciplined and applied themselves. But their, and our, experience was very similar to that of the Chinese. It was extremely difficult for them to learn Spanish, or at least spoken Spanish. Even after years of studying, they couldn't assimilate the phonetics; it seemed impossible for them to grasp and, therefore, to imitate the sounds of the Spanish language.

The literature teacher asked me for help. We were analyzing El Romancero Español, a collection of epic poems from medieval Spain, and our Vietnamese companions recited the poems with true revolutionary fervor, turning them into something totally unintelligible and comical at the same time, provoking in us a chorus of laughter. Our laughs irritated them. They didn't understand why we were amused. During a break, the teacher said to me:

"Mónica, could you practice reading the poems with the Vietnamese? You have teaching skills and a lot of patience. I can't take this torture any longer; first the Chinese; now the Vietnamese. Look, they're not speaking Spanish, they pronounce it as if it were their own language. They sing it, and instead of 'erre' an 'ele' comes out. I don't know what to do to correct these problems. Please help me."

With great enthusiasm, I began my classes. Hadn't I succeeded in teaching German to my Cuban students, even though at first it seemed that they would never learn it?

"*Mo-lo de la mo-le-l-ia,*" they sang.

"No, it's *Moro de la Morería*. Repeat: *Moro de la Morería.*"

Again they sang "*Mo-lo de la mo-le-lia,*" separating each syllable as if they were cutting it with a knife. I tried to find a reading that was less complicated and not loaded with the letter "r." I presented them with anecdotes from Samuel Feijóo, who wrote true jewels of Cuban folklore. There were, for example, these sentences: ¡*No me jeringues más!* Stop annoying me! Or ¡*Qué jeringa!* What a bother! Literally, the word *jeringa* means "syringe," but in Cuban Spanish, we call a syringe a *jeringuilla*.

But this presented another difficulty. They didn't understand the vocabulary of the Cuban peasants. I had to explain the meaning of each story to them and translate it into the Spanish they knew, thereby initiating endless discussions about why the use of a word completely changed the original meaning, which clashed with the logic of my Vietnamese colleagues. They couldn't understand that a single word could express different situations or things, and they wanted to know what the rule was, so they could figure out when a word meant one thing and when another. I gave them a short class on language development, association, comparison, similarity—all the resources that play an important role in the development of a living language. They didn't have a clue. I imagined they had something similar in their own language, but since I don't know Vietnamese, I had no way to compare.

"*Compañela* Mónica, the *je-lin-ga* is an object that is used for in-yec-ti-on. What then does the *je-lin-ga* have to do with ann-o-yan-ce? When does it mean *je-lin-ga, je-lin-ga* and when does it mean bo-th-el?"

You have to know that these questions and other similar ones were repeated over and over again and always required an enormous amount of time to be asked, as the Vietnamese students had to search for words from their Spanish vocabulary, which were sparse and interspersed with a lot of garbage. They forced me to marshal my last reserves of patience, and my usual capacity for endurance soon reached its limit.

"ALWAYS," I replied, "AND NO MORE *JERINGA*. THIS CLASS IS AN ETERNAL *JERINGA*!"

I left them in the lurch. I hadn't even made it to the fifth phonetic exercise class when I threw in the towel. I asked two Vietnamese alumni, exceptional students, who had almost no problems with Spanish phonetics, to take charge of the phonetics exercises, believing them to be the most appropriate teachers because they knew the Vietnamese language thoroughly and would know how to help their companions to open their ears to the sounds of Spanish.

* * *

One of the happiest periods in Cuba was now beginning for me: preparing my thesis for my degree. Once again, I met frequently with Paco, who—for a few months—held the position of Director of the National Library, where he was surrounded by the cream of the crop of Cuban arts and letters.

My professors had allowed me to propose the subject of my master's thesis myself. While other students were trying to reinvent the wheel, racking their brains, and complicating their existence with a search for something original, I dedicated myself to doing work that would really serve language students, that could be used as a working instrument in the translation of complex texts, and that did not so far exist: a collection of German sayings, proverbs, and adages, with their counterparts in Cuban Spanish. There were monolingual dictionaries in several languages, grouping thousands of sayings and proverbs, but the equivalences of those sayings and proverbs didn't appear in the other languages, only their translations—or, rather, transliterations.

The search for the "lid for each pot" was not easy, and in the end I had to eliminate a large quantity from my collection of several thousand, for which I couldn't find the equivalent in Spanish. In this intensive process of searching for Cuban Spanish sayings and proverbs, I met—through Paco's mediation—many Cuban writers, poets, and folklorists. Everyone was willing to contribute to the collection.

Paco took me to Eliseo Diego's house, where the whole family got involved: Blanca from the kitchen, Fefita, and her siblings. While they were running around the house, they would sometimes divert their attention from their tasks to help me. It was like a game. I would translate my German saying or proverb into Spanish for them, and they would have a contest to come up with the counterpart in Spanish.

"The apple doesn't fall far from the tree," I would tell them.

"*De tal palo, tal astilla*—a chip off the old block," they replied.

And so, little by little, with contributions mainly from the families of Eliseo, Paco, and even Samuel Feijóo from Santa Clara—by correspondence—we completed the puzzle, which, in the end, was made up of more than 600 German sayings, proverbs, and adages with their counterparts in Cuban Spanish. I was truly astonished to learn, throughout this work, how many similarities existed between the two languages, but I also observed, for the first time consciously, that many proverbs have counter-sayings that express the completely opposite "truth." For example, there's the universal saying that praises people who get up early, while the opposite message says, "no matter how early you get up, the sun rises early." We found innumerable examples that confirm the existence of proverbs for all types of philosophy, situation, ethics, morality, and the need to advise or teach, in accordance with the popular Cuban saying: *aquí hay de todo, como en botica*—here there is everything, as in a pharmacy.

The task of typing the thesis and making the required number of copies for the jury and the university library was extremely difficult. There was no paper. I requested "gifts" from all the friends and acquaintances who could divert some sheets of paper, carbon paper, and copy paper from their work centers, since these materials couldn't be bought in any commercial establishment. Like a little squirrel collecting food to store for the winter, I spent weeks on end accumulating the necessary quantities.

Fortunately, I knew how to type, so I typed and bound the thesis myself. I wouldn't have found anyone able and/or willing to type a bilingual work, especially considering that typewriters in Cuba were not equipped with a German keyboard, which has a series of letters that don't exist in Spanish. Now when I work on my computer, I often remember the madness and the infinite problems that I had to solve in order to deliver the required copies on time. My old portable typewriter, which wasn't built to handle as many copies as I had to make in one go, was about to deny me its services. My fingers had to exert so much force and pressure that they cramped, and the many smudges that this inevitably produced disfigured my work. Fortunately, the jury wasn't interested in my book being pretty: their curiosity was stimulated by the content.

For the defense, the university had sought out a philologist knowledgeable in the German language who had read my thesis carefully and well in advance, so that before starting the final discussion—a quite rigorous interrogation—I knew that she had found no errors in the German text and no wrong interpretations when providing each saying with its counterpart. I already knew this, but it seems that the jury found it necessary to demonstrate that they had applied, with all the rigors of the law, the standards for the scientific quality of a diploma.

The members of the jury, other professors, and I debated at length, and very enjoyably, I must say, about sayings, proverbs, and adages, from their origins to the present, dedicating the appropriate recognition and respect to the Bible, Cervantes, Goethe, and, of course, the world's popular wisdom. Thus, the final debate of my master's thesis was really more like a chat session in a social club.

I finished my time as a student at the University of Havana with a flourish, and my regular professional life began. Already, for weeks before, I had been working at the request of different institutions. Almost always this involved translation and interpretation, and I worked with delegations of the most diverse kind. There wasn't a political or scientific congress that took place in which I didn't perform these duties.

CHAPTER TWENTY-ONE
THE YEAR OF THE TEN MILLION

IN 1970, CUBA WENT THROUGH the "Year of the Ten Million," and the entire country saw a steady deterioration in services. I remember that this was the year in which the last rudimentary conveniences still in existence went completely under. All men with two good hands—from hairdressers to eminent surgeons—were sent to the fields to cut cane. They joined the army of *macheteros* who were struggling to harvest enough sugarcane to produce the proposed record of ten million tons of sugar. The barber shops, the shoe-repair shops, the tailors' workshops, the few Chinese laundries that had survived until then: everything was closed.

I had to cut Dani's hair. Dictys, luckily, had his "bald" haircut from the swimming school, and I still had my practical short haircut from childhood. This was fortunate for me at this "everything's closed down" period, as I also had to cut and fix my hair myself. There was no shampoo, no soap, no toothpaste, and no toothbrushes. There were no shoes, not even the ones guaranteed by the ration book. I never fully understood the distribution system for clothing, fabric, and footwear. It happened that every time our family's letter was eligible to buy clothing, there was nothing left, or nothing in my size.

The children wore orthopedic shoes. They could get two pairs per year, theoretically. With insteps incompatible with the standard Cuban shoe tree, there was no way to get them the necessary shoes even if we had to buy them. My parents bailed us out more than once, getting us the articles that in Cuba were in the ration book but not on the shelves. Dictys managed to keep his orthopedic shoes wearable for three years in a row; he wore them until his feet hurt because the shoes were too small and his squeezed toes couldn't grow. By spending more time in the water than walking on land, this calamity, fortunately, did not affect his skeleton. For Dani, a pair lasted two or three months, tops. He used them to play soccer, but instead of a soccer ball, which couldn't be found, he used rocks.

There was not, and is not, a shoe that could withstand these shocks. For months, Dani wore the sad, shredded remains of his orthopedic shoes. The tips were completely missing, and his toes stuck out of huge holes. Footwear so soon beaten up couldn't possibly correct fallen arches, but at least it served to protect the soles of his feet from cuts or other injuries.

Every Saturday, waiting at the pick-up point for the swimming school students, the parents would meet to pass the time by discussing the most recent events. The permanent subject of our conversations was the ten-million-ton harvest. "It's happening; it's happening! The ten million is happening!" we heard every day—morning, noon, and night—on radio and television. We read about it in *Granma*, in *Bohemia*, in *Mujeres*, and in whatever other publication was produced in Cuba at that time.

Nobody believed the story of the ten million, at least no one who had an ounce of common sense, or who had worked in key positions of the national economy and had access to regular reports on the progress, or rather delays in progress, of the harvest. Few believed the eternal and constantly repeated claim of victory. However, no one dared to publicly express doubts or a lack of optimism. Comments would be heard that so and so had been suspended from his position, that this person or that had been imprisoned or had been assigned a new home in the Guanahacabibes peninsula, the infernal regions, the uninhabited and inhospitable national territory that was reserved, for many years, for high-level officials who had committed serious "misconduct."

During this Year of the Ten Million, we also tightened our belts even more, since the situation of distribution for food, meat, or meat products had become so dire that Cubans' well-known spirit of inventiveness was crippled. Nothing more could be invented now. Our quota of beef—if we could find it—consisted of minced skin and tendons, with more than half mixed with frozen water. To this "meat" we would add ground-up bread, making a paste with one part meat and four parts bread. We would add onion—if there was any—garlic—if we could find it—salt and pepper—if possible, and we would put this mixture in a small bag made of a piece of old sheet, turning the product into a magnificent sausage, then cook it in the pressure cooker, with which it was possible to soften the hardest skin in the world. This also protected our teeth from considerable damage.

The sausage had to last as long as possible until we had the next ration of "meat." To the children, this hideous invention tasted like heaven. They didn't question the composition or the origin of this "delicacy," and they didn't miss more nutritious ingredients. They simply ate it with gusto, just as they had come to accept having to fill their bellies with the new Cuban national food: rice with split peas and vice versa.

The historic Year of the Ten Million culminated in Fidel's equally historic speech. The first hour of his presentation was full of *mea culpa*. And, miracle of miracles, Fidel rescued— although only for this speech—the "I" that had long been banned, usually replaced by the "we." This time Fidel took responsibility for the failure, speaking in the first person singular, saying: "I am responsible!"

In a dramatic, tragic, serious voice, as if he had to announce a day of national mourning, he told "the truth" to the Cuban people: the ten million tons were not ten but barely seven. However, in reality, the entire nation had to bear the consequence of the loss, and the officials and specialists imprisoned or exiled to Guanahacabibes were not absolved.

Fidel's speech gave us another motto, a Fidelian Valium that from then on would serve as a magic formula to console us, reassure us, and give us new hope: "We shall turn setback into victory." On billboards, banners, posters, on radio programs, on television, in newspapers and magazines, no opportunity was missed to turn setback into victory. To this day "setback" and "victory" are synonymous in Cuba.

CHAPTER TWENTY-TWO
A PERMANENT POSITION

My first official job after graduating from the university was given to me by my husband's friends at the Cuban Institute of Friendship with the Peoples (ICAP). Previously, I had served as an interpreter and translator countless times, in the process learning about things that I'd never even heard of until then. Many times I was asked, or just expected, to translate topics that I didn't understand at all, and the specialists whose speeches were to be interpreted were seldom able to muster the minimum of consideration and understanding required to help the interpreter translate correctly. Almost all of them spoke at such ferocious speed that there was no time to convert the verbiage into something intelligible in another language.

It was also a real catastrophe when I had to translate texts that were read aloud without my having access to them, and then having to listen to complaints about the "stupid translators" who didn't know how to translate verbatim. They didn't spend a minute trying to put themselves in the shoes of the unfortunate interpreter, for whom listening, understanding, translating, and immediately finding the corresponding words from another language meant a simultaneous process that required truly herculean mental effort. Sometimes, when the subject was boring, monotonous, or tedious, I would find myself translating mechanically, without the speech touching my gray cells. I hate this kind of translation that makes me feel like a machine, an automaton without a brain.

Agility, speed, a good memory, ability to summarize, and, of course, a thorough knowledge of both languages are the essential requirements of a good interpreter. With these criteria in mind, I therefore began my work at ICAP, after the management approved my proposal to develop a training program for translator/interpreters of the German language.

The first days passed, then weeks, and it seemed that no one was really interested in "my" training program. I should by now have assimilated the well-known Cuban way of saying "yes" while meaning a resounding "no," but being stubborn, rebellious, and imbued with German-ness, I wasn't satisfied with the situation. I don't readily accept pretexts and evasive explanations. We had agreed to embark on a certain program, and I insisted on doing just that. That, after all, was the reason the institution had hired me.

A series of interviews with the president of ICAP, who assured me that the program would be implemented, strung me along and kept me hoping. I didn't see any movement, however, that would indicate that installation of the laboratories and other preparations had begun. To kill time they gave me silly tasks, such as writing a monograph that had already been written or checking translations whose correct content had already been verified.

"If you want me to invent something that's already been invented, to translate texts that have already been translated and interest no one, go find someone else. Don't expect me to waste time on nonsense, and don't tell me that the Revolution needs me for that. I won't accept it."

I knew they didn't like it, that my stubbornness bothered them, but I wasn't going to stop demanding, constantly, that they had to do what we'd agreed on. One fine day they announced to me that the course on translation and interpretation would begin without further delay.

"Tomorrow we'll introduce you to your future students. It took us a lot of work to find suitable candidates, but your insistence forced us to get down to business," they informed me.

Happy, enthusiastic, satisfied, and full of optimism, on the appointed day I went to work, ready to start my new job without further delay. The management had summoned a group of young people selected to form the future team of German-language interpreters and translators. I greeted them and started speaking to them in German. Only one understood me and responded correctly; the others looked at me in amazement, keeping their mouths shut. They resembled sheep in a meadow, watching children flying kites. The poor students didn't understand even one word, because they had never taken a German course or heard the language: a selection similar to the Chinese students.

"In my program, it's clearly stated that the students selected must have at least passed the advanced German course. Only one of them knows German. How do you think the training should be done, if the most important thing, the foundation, doesn't exist? The desire to be an interpreter is not enough. What were you thinking? You're making fun of me and the kids."

I had definitely reached the limit of my tolerance. I was outraged.

"Don't count on me anymore. This is the last straw. You can save your breath. I'm not staying here: I quit!"

They were stunned. They weren't used to someone giving up a secure job for a matter of "so little importance." Normally, you would be removed, but to willingly resign was inconceivable. They described me as immature, impatient, not understanding the difficulties of the Revolution, etc., etc., blah-blah-blah. I only managed to think, *This Revolution, can it accommodate all the flaws, irresponsibility, deficiencies, and unfounded arrogance that are continually thrown at it?*

From the very beginning of my maddening work at ICAP, I had arguments with my captain concerning my doubts that the many promises would be fulfilled, and when I announced that I had just quit, I had his unqualified support. The truth of "she who has a friend, has everything" was verified once again, because through friends of his I received several job offers: to teach German classes ("no, thank you"), to translate brochures on pedagogical theories ("no, thanks"). But the offer from *la Presidenta*, the president of the Federation of Cuban Women (FMC), who was looking for a polyglot person to support the work of the organization's Department of International Relations, seemed attractive enough to accept.

As early as 1970, the FMC had maintained relationships with women's organizations on all continents. My new coworkers welcomed me warmly. My knowledge of German, French, English, and Spanish served me wonderfully, and my skills were used on a daily basis. Little by little, I progressed from interpreter and translator to being responsible for the focus on women's organizations in different geographical areas. This daily work was frequently interrupted by my being asked to assist foreign delegations invited to Cuba by the country's most diverse political, scientific, and economic institutions. Thus, thanks to my job at the FMC, not only did I become familiar with the evolution of the women's movement throughout the world, but I was also exposed to the diverse processes of world political, economic, social, cultural, and scientific events, which opened horizons for me that were not available to just anyone.

CHAPTER TWENTY-THREE
ALLENDE'S CHILE

WHEN SALVADOR ALLENDE WON the 1970 elections in Chile, my husband took part in the inauguration ceremony. We were happy when we learned that he had been appointed to work as an economist (his second career) in this Andean country. This meant moving to Santiago de Chile and interrupting our regular work, but I loved it and was filled with anticipation. I was curious, full of optimism, eager to learn about a revolutionary process that had begun as a result of official, democratic elections and without bloodshed.

In early 1971, we left for Chile while Dictys and Dani stayed behind with Pilar and Gonzalo in Havana to finish their respective school years. They would join us in July.

In Chile, we witnessed the evolution of this process: from excitement, euphoria, and enthusiasm for the new government to contradictions, attempts to solve thousands of problems, and, finally, chaos and failure.

Fortunately, not everything was work, tension, or fear of the increasingly aggressive and violent opposition which characterized our stay there. We took the time to get to know the beauty of Chile. Usually there was a curfew or a state of emergency on Sundays, which meant that we had to be home before a specific time, or it was forbidden to go out at all. With or without permission, though, map in hand, we would go out to explore the mountains.

We could never get our Cuban co-workers to join us on our excursions. They preferred to stay at home in front of the television, or, if they went somewhere, it was to the beach, where they scorched their skin without enjoying a refreshing swim in the water. The highest temperature of the Pacific in this region, even in the hottest summer, wasn't even 65 degrees, too cold for Caribbean-born swimmers. The bravest of them would get their feet wet, and even then they would have terrible, persistent cramps from the "frigid" water.

My husband and I, alone with a basket of bread, sausages, and soft drinks in the trunk, would drive up into the Andes, stopping only when the road was so narrow that we couldn't continue by vehicle. We would be alone in this divine world of mountains, accompanied by only the majestic music produced by the wind, the splash or roar of the occasional waterfall, and the murmur of melted snow flowing into streams. The smell of the meadows, the alpine flowers, the tireless activities of the bees collecting nectar, the snowy peaks, the stones carved and polished for thousands of years by the force of the water—every detail transformed me and filled me with energy and joy. Not a Sunday went by in the mountains without my returning with a collection of stones, including some fossils of incalculable value to me, a stupid burden for my husband, who finally refused to help me carry "the rocks" that were "filling our house up."

We had earned a week's vacation after Fidel's tumultuous trip to Chile, during which we had to work uninterruptedly morning, noon, and night, always in a state of alert, ready to undertake whatever task was assigned to us. Fidel's state visit lasted more than three weeks. He traveled the country from north to south on his own initiative and with his own agenda, which made Salvador Allende uncomfortable. In his endless speeches, Fidel continually expressed opinions about Chilean internal matters, exacerbating the revolutionary fervor of his audiences. This was seen as a blatant intrusion into Chile's internal affairs by a foreign power, and the Chilean right-wing exploited it to discredit the Unidad Popular government.

We decided—two colleagues, my husband and I—to travel to the extreme south, which could be reached by car. We had reserved rooms in a motel in a place called Pucón, located on the shores of a deep lake whose true depth was unknown, formed when the crater of the volcano of the same name filled with water. Guided by directions that friends who knew about the places worth seeing had provided us, we made a stopover in several provinces before arriving in Pucón. On one of the breaks to stretch our legs and have a snack, we stopped the car near a field full of blackberries. Never in my life have I seen shrubs of this species so enormously tall and full and with so many huge blackberries. Crazy with happiness, I ran to one of the bushes and started eating them. One of our colleagues, who was a great connoisseur of the flora and fauna of South America, was scared and yelled at me:

"Mónica, you're going to be poisoned. Those black balls can't be eaten, you're crazy. Stop eating them! You don't know what you're doing. We don't know anyone here; we don't have a doctor on hand who can save you!"

"Look, *muchacha*, they're delicious. Try them: they're blackberries, typical fruits of cold countries. I know them very well, and I assure you that they're not poisonous. If you're afraid, wait a while. If I don't die, you can eat them."

I had only begun to taste the berries, which she distrusted and feared, when my husband gladly put them in his mouth, without vomiting or having a seizure. Later he had several opportunities to eat the "poisonous black balls," because in this region, where they grew so abundantly, they were used to make jam, marmalade, and cake fillings, and they appeared at breakfast for bread, at lunch for dessert, and as cake decoration for afternoon coffee.

Near Pucón was the Villarrica volcano, which had erupted a few days before we arrived in the area. You could easily recognize where the lava had completely changed the original landscape. There were bridges over rivers that no longer existed, channels without a drop of water but full of stones that were worn and polished from the now departed water that had flowed over them for millennia, and we found new rivers that still lacked the necessary bridges to be able to cross them.

We four adventurers hiked through areas covered in cooled lava, feeling as if we were walking on the moon. We were treading totally new, virgin landscapes. There were trees burned to ash that kept their shape thanks to a thin layer of lava. With your finger you could pierce the bark of a tree, seeing behind the hard lava bark how the ash, turned into fine black sandlike powder, fell to the bottom of the trunk.

The residents of the area told us we were crazy and alerted us.

"The volcano is going to start spewing out lava at any moment. Get to safe territory. Do you want to die burned or buried by lava? Last week it wiped out an entire town. No one was left alive, and the houses were destroyed. Get away!"

Seeing that we ignored them, they abandoned us, but not without first expressing their disapproval and condemnation of our irrational behavior.

We took a rowboat around Lake Pucón. During this ride I was in heaven and at the same time terrified, almost crazy with panic but happy, feeling like a follower of the great explorer Alexander von Humboldt. My imagination produced crazy images that made my hair stand on end. I had a terrible fear of the incalculable depth of the lake. The water was clean, and yet it was jet black; I thought this must be the entrance to hell. But my irresistible desire to be in the middle of the lake, floating above a crater miles deep filled with water, overshadowed my terror before the mystery and majesty of this phenomenon of nature. I absolutely needed to be in the center, but once we got there, as if fearing that a magnetic force could swallow the boat at any moment, I rowed desperately with my husband, gathering all my strength, fleeing, driven by an animal instinct, with the sole desire to reach the shore safe again.

We moored the boat and tested the water. It was warm and delicious, inviting a swim. I climbed up on a rock and dove headfirst into deep water. My heart beat so fast and so hard that

I felt it was going to come out of my mouth. The water was ice cold. All my muscles cramped. I screamed like a madwoman, not so much swimming as slapping the water to get out of there as quickly as possible. When I got to shore, I looked like a heated shrimp. I was flushed, covered in goose bumps, but happy and satisfied with myself.

My captain was shocked when he heard my crazy screams and saw me hitting the water as if I were trying to scare away a ghost. When he learned that my reaction was due to the intense cold of the water, he wanted to show his courage and jumped in also. The same thing happened to him, only he controlled himself and didn't scream. But his hurried strokes and the snorts of an animal in distress were a sure sign that the cold had given him the same shock as it had me.

Finally, in July 1971, the boys also came to Chile. In South America, it was winter. The children made the trip alone, with Dictys taking care of his little brother. The day of their arrival in Santiago de Chile, a few hours before the plane landed, snow had fallen. It didn't remain in the city itself, but the airport was covered with a thin layer of ice. Dictys and Dani got off the plane wearing shorts, short-sleeved shirts, and canvas shoes. When they'd left Havana, the thermometer stood at 90 degrees F; in Santiago, it was just above freezing.

We were not allowed to pick the boys up from the runway. They had to walk the long stretch to the terminal building without any shelter. When we were finally able to hug our kids, they were purple, like two popsicles just out of the freezer. Dani's teeth were chattering uncontrollably. The terrible pain in his feet and hands, caused by the intense cold, had him on the verge of losing his temper. Dictys clenched his teeth to keep from crying; he was shivering from the top of his head down to his toes. At home, I put the boys in the bathtub with hot water to defrost them, and we put on the heat to create a humanly acceptable environment as quickly as possible.

Days later, we bought them winter clothes, shoes, and various school supplies. They were happy with their outfits, their briefcases, and their shiny leather shoes, without holes and with enough room for their toes. Their new treasures seemed to them the magical work of an unknown angel who loved children. Dictys and Dani liked the house, a kind of Swiss chalet, with balconies and a garden. They were fascinated by the fireplace that we lit every night. Their predisposition to pyromania received enormous stimuli. Naturally, we had to keep an eye on them when the fireplace was producing a sea of flames. Sitting around the fire, reviewing the events of the day, inventing stories, huddled together and singing, we spent many happy nights in Santiago de Chile.

So that Dictys wouldn't lose his status as a top athlete, we immediately looked for the possibility of continuing his intensive training. There were several sports clubs that were dedicated to swimming. The Club Manquéhue was recommended to us, and, indeed, we hit the nail on the head, because the children in Dictys' group were lucky to have a coach who knew how to motivate his students and who treated them with love and dedication. And best of all: Dictys was able to sleep at home and not have to be caged in an institution.

I drove him to his swimming lessons, accompanied by his brother. Dani mingled with the chorus of family members who shouted when it was their athlete's turn to beat the record. Dictys took part in many competitions. He often won first, second, or third place, feeling himself king when he found his name among the results of the competitions in *El Mercurio*, Chile's most important newspaper.

One day, the coach informed me that Dictys had been selected to take part in an international competition in Argentina. I had to request permission from our ambassador to authorize his departure. The coach assured me that he would take responsibility for the child's safety.

"*Señora*, I am going to take care of him and watch him like my own son. We will only be in Argentina for three days. Dictys is one of the best in our club, and we need him in this competition," he told me.

The ambassador almost had a fit when I spoke to him about the matter:

"Mónica, how do you think you can send the child to Argentina? It's impossible. What if they find out that he's Cuban and kidnap him? What if they make him disappear? I cannot authorize this exit. I'm sorry. It's a sensitive political issue. I know what it means for the boy not to be able to go, but I trust your mother's ability to get this out of his head." Period.

Naturally, Dictys didn't understand why he wasn't allowed to travel with his friends. Neither did the coach. The boy cried and was desperate. For him it was a matter of honor, which the old fools who forbade him to leave didn't understand. With a look on his face expressing contempt and hatred, he punished us for days, and it was the coach who finally managed to appease his anger and motivate him to continue swimming fast to help maintain the outstanding level of his team.

In order to ensure reasonable care for the children during the holidays, we decided to apply for places for them at the East German embassy school. At various diplomatic activities I had personally met the ambassador. He seemed less orthodox to me than his colleague in Havana, who years ago had vetoed Dictys' attendance of the embassy's kindergarten, which had led to the breakdown of my relations with the East German embassy in Cuba. But that was water under the bridge now. On the part of the embassy, there were no obstacles, and the children adapted quickly to their new environment. Along the way, they both re-learned a little German. Dani, because he wasn't yet the minimum age for admission to the school, was placed in the pre-school, with the obligation to take a nap—an insult to our night-owl. This was the only thing he disliked about the place.

Every morning, we dropped them off at their school, and in the afternoons Maria, our household employee, who had become the beloved and esteemed partner-accomplice of my children, would pick them up. Maria was unable to deny the boys the fulfillment of their wildest wishes. I had strictly forbidden them to buy street ice—frozen water mixed with garishly-colored chemical junk—a dangerous product because it was handled under catastrophic hygienic conditions and therefore reputed to frequently cause infectious gastrointestinal diseases. They ate tons of this delicious slush. Maria accompanied them to buy it and eat it.

Every time I came home at an unexpected time, I discovered new violations of the agreed-upon rules. They always involved the collusion of Maria, who seemed like one more kid. Before the mandatory bath, the boys, sweaty, dirty, still dressed in street clothes, would be sprawled on the bed, watching a hideously cheesy television show, poorly done, boasting of mystery and violence. Of course I had forbidden them to watch this rubbish. Yet there they were, the three of them, with their hair standing on end, screaming and shrieking at seeing the monsters and ghosts, which blinded their minds so much that they didn't notice that I had been witnessing the scene for a long time.

Another day I grabbed them when they were giving rein to their pyromania, lighting matches and more matches, not in the fireplace—no, on the windowsill, with the highly flammable synthetic curtains a few inches away from the flames. I saw them, in my excited imagination, turn into little charred heaps. Each time, my sermons would be followed by promises not to do things like this ever again, and then they would continue on the same path. Frankly, they were happy.

One day, the Cuban ambassador summoned me to his office to reproach me for having placed our children in the East German embassy school. He called this decision a selfish and unacceptable act.

"You didn't care about the other Cuban children. You only thought of yours," he told me.

"And what did you do to find them a suitable school? Isn't education a state affair? Aren't you, the representative of the Cuban state here in Chile, responsible for that? The Cuban embassy hasn't told me anything. My children are learning German and experiencing the disciplined regime of a German school. No Cuban has wanted to accept these conditions. They found it logical for my children to enroll in this school, but they don't want to have their own children go there."

The diplomatic approach gained ground, and the reproach turned into a request for help:

"Mónica, you know about educational matters. Could you please investigate and propose a Chilean school that meets the essential conditions, that meets our requirements?" the ambassador asked.

"Of course I can. I'll keep you posted on my inquiries."

I wasted no time searching. We knew enough people who could give us the information the ambassador had requested. We found a modest school whose pedagogical principles convinced us. With the ambassador's approval, we enrolled the boys in their new school. The program corresponded to the second semester, because from September to November, the beginning of the summer in the southern hemisphere, there were just four months of work left to finish the school year that in Cuba was going to begin on the first of September. The children missed the first semester. The teachers at the school made an effort to review, in record time, the subjects that the Cuban students were missing and, at the same time, to continue with the normal program. They organized work sessions after school hours, and the children managed, little by little, to catch up.

Dani found himself suddenly, with the change from kindergarten to school, finishing first grade without having started it. The children in his classroom already knew how to read and write. His teacher set a goal to teach him in one month what the other children had learned in one semester.

"If we can reach the goal without the child feeling overstressed, if he adjusts to this intensive process, we'll have won. If it's too difficult for him, he'll have to start first grade again next year. I think it won't hurt the child if we try to leave him in the group he's in. He's very sociable; he already has many friends and participates in all the activities. Of course, without your help we won't be able to carry out the plan. I'll give you a list of materials to buy for him. The most important thing for the moment is the Latin

American Syllabus. Buy it today. Tomorrow I'll explain in detail how you can work with this material to help your child learn to read. What I can't do during class—because I have to take care of everyone—you will have to do with him every day afterward at home. I'm sure that we'll make a good team. And of course, it goes without saying that I'll be at your disposal at any time."

And sure enough, the plan succeeded. New, richly illustrated books, some with familiar tales, others with stories entirely new to Dani, improved his curiosity. Knowing how to read was the most important thing, a matter of pride, of honor. He was making incredible progress and was trying to decipher the newspaper headlines. When we drove around town, he would spell out the store signs, feeling happiest when he unraveled their meaning.

"Mommy, look, it says CO-CA-CO-LA there. Damn, there are Coca Cola ads everywhere. Fa-Fa-Fan-ta. Mommy, they make Fanta there! Mommy, don't go so fast. I couldn't read the sign; now I don't know what it says," he would scold me.

When the car would stop at a red light, Dani would have time to decipher a sign. Once he deciphered the name of a textile factory: "Singal."

"Look what it's called. Si-Sin-Singa-Sin-gal!" With each syllable his voice grew louder, laughing and slapping his thighs. "Mommy, have you seen what it says there? How shocking, have you seen it?"

"But Dani! That's the name of the factory. The factory is named 'Singal.' Don't you see the picture of the coat painted below the name? It's a factory that makes clothing," I said, trying to distract him from his discovery.

"No, Mommy, it's not the name of the factory. It's a bad word. It says 'singal' there and that's not the name of any factory. Daddy, you saw what it said there, right? Tell mommy that's a bad word, and with such big letters!"

"Look, Dani, Mommy told you that's the name ..."

Dani didn't let him finish the sentence, because having already endured the tactics of his parents to divert his attention from an issue that was important to him, he decided to chat with his brother:

"Hey, Dictys, did you see the sign?"

"Ay, Dani, be quiet, didn't you hear what Mommy said?"

"Of course I heard it, but what Mommy says isn't true. She feels embarrassed about it because it's a bad word. Do you know what 'singal' is? When the man puts his willy in a hole that the woman has between her legs, that's called 'singal', and that's how children are made, with the willy in the hole, you hear me? SINGAL! And on that sign it said it clearly."

Dani was beside himself with happiness, feeling like a king: the little brother who knew more than his big brother and who knew how to give a lesson to his parents, who had behaved like old prudes. And I wondered where this little demon knew the word *singar*, the Cuban term for sexual intercourse.

* * *

Never, before being in Chile, had I been in an earthquake. In Chile I was given the opportunity more than once. The first tremor took me by surprise on the top floor of an apartment building at bath time. I was brushing my teeth when the building started to shake. The doors slid open and slammed shut, over and over. I looked at myself three times in the same mirror and was off balance, like I was drunk. When I ran into the living room to call my husband, the ghostly spectacle had already passed. When the news came on, they reported the phenomenon, its intensity, and the damage it caused.

The second time we were sitting in the courtyard of a large house, under an apricot tree, drinking coffee and eating *pastelitos*. Suddenly, as if lightning had carved a furrow, the ground opened, lifting the flagstones. Nothing could be heard, and a deafening silence spread—like a movie without a soundtrack—only what we saw wasn't a movie; it was real. Then the tree began to shake, dancing wildly, dumping its load of ripe apricots onto the ground, releasing a delicious perfume. It looked like it was raining fruit.

The table bounced; the chairs, with their human load on them, jumped. My chair had become a merry-go-round, and I, pressing my bottom against the seat and clutching the back like a snail in its shell, kept my eyes wide open and glued on the chaotic spectacle. The coffee pot, the cups, and the pieces of pastry gave each other a fatal embrace; the result was spilled coffee, mixed with pastry and bits of broken porcelain, which were only good for being dumped in the trash. The tiles on the floor under the table and chairs cracked; some jumped out of their place as if they wanted to ascend.

I was fascinated by this frenzied movement of inanimate objects. I had seen terrible tree dances in Cuba, when the force of a hurricane displaced them, imposing an infernal rhythm, but there was no wind here, not even a little breeze. The impulse came from below the ground, without our being able to see anything, smell anything, or hear anything, and without anyone knowing how long it would last or how much damage it would cause.

Other times I noticed the occasional earthquake in the middle of the night, while sleeping. I would feel the bed bounce, hear the tinkling sound of a rock-crystal teardrop chandelier dangling from the ceiling. *If it comes down, it's going to fall right on my head*, I managed to think. *Get up and wake the boys! They have to get under the door frame!* But the dream didn't allow me to have full access to consciousness. The movements of the bed, the tinkling of the lamp, the creaking of the wooden floor only shook my deep sleep a little. More asleep than awake, I went on weaving my web: I was on a boat in the middle of the Atlantic, and the movement of the bed, its jumps, were due to the movement of the boat; the noises I heard were the typical sounds of a cabin at sea. Whenever an earthquake of short duration and moderate intensity occurred at night, I dreamed the same dream. It seems that I have in my brain a broken record in which, when the needle is on "earthquake," the same song is repeated, repeated, and repeated: the one about my boat trip from Germany to Cuba.

The situation in Chile became more complicated every day. One political crisis ended only to give rise to a more serious one.

The markets remained empty of food. Given the state's inability to guarantee the distribution of the products required for daily life, bartering was emerging. Gas stations refused to sell fuel. Just when it was needed the most for heating, there was no way to acquire heating oil.

Discontent spread, and opposition protest demonstrations multiplied, among which were the protests of the housewives of Barrio Alto, who marched in the streets banging on their pots and pans to demand food for their kitchens. The confrontations took on a tinge of violence. Patria y Libertad, a right-wing group, was collecting weapons to attack groups of communist and socialist youth, some of which were armed as well. Almost daily we saw on TV newscasts how pitched battles had taken place between political opponents. We had to send the children back to Cuba. The tension, the insecurity, and the eternal state of emergency didn't allow them to continue living with us.

Before the Pinochet coup and the fall of the Allende government, we had returned to Havana. I arrived with a terrible case of pneumonia: a "gift" received three days before returning. I was in the center of Santiago, where I had to deliver some documents. I couldn't find a place to park and had to park two blocks away. It was cold, and I wasn't wearing a heavy coat or a raincoat. There was a crowd near the building where I had to leave the papers. I ran there, ran in, climbed the stairs, and looked for the office. I finally found it, handed over the documents, and ran out. When I reached the street again, someone closed the door of the building behind me.

You could no longer walk on the street. A *guanaco*, an armed vehicle used by riot police, was spraying icy water left and right. Hundreds of young communists and socialists, on one side, and Patria y Libertad, on the other, were fighting—a real battle being fought in the street. There was shouting, cursing, cold water, tear gas, gunfire, people reeling, others ducking, trying to escape. In a word, war.

I wanted to go back into the building. I was soaked, shivering with cold and fear. We had been warned over and over again not to get into situations like this. No one would believe that I was in this scene of war by pure chance. The door remained closed. No one heard or wanted to hear me banging on the door. I had no choice but to try to duck and run to reach the street where my car was parked. The cold water from the *guanaco* hit me two more times. The tear gas was choking me. I had almost reached my street, when a young man, maybe fifteen years of age, collapsed next to me. He couldn't stand, and a group of friends picked him up and dragged him away like a wet sack. A trickle of blood came from behind his ear.

When I turned on the television that night to watch the news, it reported that in the violent demonstration earlier that afternoon the young man who had collapsed next to me was killed. The cameras were focusing on him when he was on the ground and when his friends took him away.

I arrived in Mexico City to continue my trip a few days later, heading for Havana, burning with fever and my lungs in terrible condition. Instead of visiting museums and art galleries, I had to go to bed; instead of delicious food, I had to fill my belly with capsules of super-potent antibiotics that killed my appetite, made me dizzy, and caused me to vomit. Finally, thin, weak, tired, sad, and worried about the fate of our friends back in Chile, where the fatal end had been imminent for a long time, I arrived in Havana.

General Pinochet's coup did not surprise us. What did surprise us was the violence, the brutality with which the military coup leaders attacked those who were ousted. We learned of the murder of several of our colleagues, with whom we had shared our last months in Chile. We learned the fate of others much later. Some were able to flee via different embassies or go into exile. Others were imprisoned in the national stadium and then put into concentration camps. We never found out what happened to some of our friends.

With the coup in Chile, I buried many illusions and dreams. They necessarily implied failure.

CHAPTER TWENTY-FOUR
A BITTER EXPERIENCE WITH CUBAN HOMOPHOBIA

After Cuba received hundreds of Chilean refugees, countless activities of solidarity with Chile were organized in Cuba and abroad. As an officer of the Federation of Cuban Women, my job was, mainly, accompanying delegations, acting as interpreter, and translating, parrotlike, politicians' speeches in German, English, French, and Spanish.

I had lost contact with Paco and his friends. I didn't even know if he was still meeting with them, regularly devoting a minute of hatred to those who had become their enemies.

"Paco and Chomin are prisoners in Villa Marista, the prison of State Security, accused of being involved in counterrevolutionary activities," one of the members of Paco's circle informed us.

The informant was devastated, desperate, and terrified that he might also be taken to that terrible place. For weeks we had no more news about Paco and Chomin.

From the time I'd known him, Paco had enjoyed badmouthing people who, in his opinion, deserved to be banned. He wouldn't have given a second thought to "putting them in irons," and he also spoke with contempt about personalities in the "stratosphere." There must have been more than one snitch among those who heard him.

But Chomin, a state security official, a professional guerrilla, a more consistent revolutionary than Fidel himself, who had spent his life defending the Revolution against enemies within and without, who had never missed a mobilization, who always dressed in olive green, with a Czech submachine gun as an integral part of his anatomy; Chomin who, much later, when the Czech weapon was exchanged for an authentic Walther P38, which was what he had most wanted in the world, took off the weapon and his uniform only to lie down on the beach or go to bed; Chomin, who called me a "revisionist German of petite-bourgeoisie mentality" when I told him he was immature for having left his university studies to perform tasks for the Revolution: this same Chomin, in prison for counterrevolutionary activities? Impossible, absurd. It simply couldn't be.

But it was true. He was a prisoner. They had taken both him and Paco to that dark, dreadful place which even the strongest and most courageous people were terrified of. And later, we learned the reason: the two were a couple.

I couldn't believe it. It was the craziest thing I'd ever heard. Chomin, the father of three children, a womanizer, the incarnation of macho, a superman, strong and athletic, someone who never hesitated, who never let any occasion go by to say horrible things about the "faggots," "sissies," "fairies," and "queers," as if they were a plague that contaminated the Revolution. Chomin, who punched his son when the little boy, skinny and timid, cried after being hit or freaked out about something that would frighten any child, screaming at him, "Don't be a coward, don't be a fairy, I'm going to kill you!" It couldn't be possible that this same person was homosexual. It simply was ridiculous. Chomin was anything but that, I thought.

That Paco was homosexual was no big surprise to me. Now I understood why his relationships didn't last very long, why the girls who got involved with him quickly disappeared from the scene, why his repeated attempts to get married went up in smoke without rhyme or reason. But Chomin: I couldn't even imagine it. This was a truly schizophrenic situation. But finally, I had to believe the story, because I learned from a reliable source that it was true.

At that time, I didn't know anything about the "homosexual problem" nor was I interested. I had no reason to focus on the matter. I didn't know anyone around me who had "problems" of that sort. I didn't know about the existence of UMAP, the Military Units to Aid Production, a macabre euphemism for concentration camps established to lock up anyone considered "anti-social" or "counter-revolutionary," mainly religious and gay men. I wasn't aware of the First Congress of Education and Culture and the nefarious resolution it passed in 1971, defining homosexuality as a condition incompatible with being a revolutionary, a militant, a trustworthy person.

At the moment that Paco and Chomin were in prison, I repeat, I still wasn't in the right frame of mind, free of prejudice and knowing all the facts. I reacted like everyone else around me. I felt deceived, disappointed because our friends had committed such appalling misdeeds. It didn't occur to me then to think that they must have had a reason to hide their relationship, that there must be motives for intelligent people, of proven bravery, to have a dual personality. Paco was a leader of the July 26 Movement, and he had more than once risked his life, evading the pursuit of no less than Ventura, the henchman of henchmen. And Chomin had a respectable history of underground struggle; he was known to be a combatant whose bravery and audacity had been demonstrated countless times in the Revolution.

I knew that Paco idolized Lezama Lima, that he knew entire paragraphs by heart of his *Paradiso*, which dealt with homosexuality and which he quoted to us with enthusiasm. Paco constantly walked around with the book under his arm as if to say to everyone, "I share the maestro's exceptional condition of belonging to a repudiated minority."

But no, I didn't notice anything. I didn't know how to interpret the many signals that Paco gave. Only many years later, when for professional reasons I had acquired the needed knowledge and radically changed my indifferent, intolerant, prejudiced attitude—only then could I imagine what a burden it must have been for Paco and Chomin to have been forced to deceive family and friends, to not have any possibility of living a normal life, to have been deprived of a basic human right: the right to love anyone they chose as a partner, without outside interference.

We condemned them. And the saddest thing of all was that they condemned themselves and felt themselves to be despicable. We didn't waste any brain power, energy, or time trying to avoid destroying their reputation, and with that, the lives of our friends. Physically they continued living, but psychically they were devastated. We dropped them like rotten tomatoes; we were incapable of overcoming the limitations imposed on us by a traditionally intolerant society with respect to sexual orientation.

A profound sadness, a terrible disappointment, and also, I have to confess, rage overlay my feelings of appreciation for Paco, this friend who was charming, affectionate, gentlemanly, who had accepted me as a sister, and who had introduced me to the world of Cuban arts and letters.

In later years, the driving force of my efforts—deployed in my professional endeavors day by day, in my work as a teacher, through the media, clandestinely, covertly, risking my reputation and also my job against almost insurmountable barriers that existed in minds clouded by prejudice and anachronistic, totalitarian structures, against the ignorance and intolerance that made and continue to make Cuban society one of the most homophobic in the world—was fueled, by, among other things, the sad, terrible story of Paco and Chomin. With my work in Cuba in the field of sexual education, I also tried to make my contribution, however small, to sensitize and humanize society, to repair the injustice committed against the many Pacos and Chomins, against the many Elviras and Olgas, and against so many others whose names I don't know, who were victims of their aggressive and intolerant environment.

CHAPTER TWENTY-FIVE
THE FEDERATION OF CUBAN WOMEN

I WAS ESTABLISHED as a recognized officer at the National Directorate of the Federation of Cuban Women (FMC), a person who knew about women's transformation in Cuba as well as in the countries that maintained relations with the FMC. I took part in countless national and international activities.

The results of socialist emulation and balance assemblies, and the analysis of accomplishments and problems in municipalities, provinces, and at the national level were debated every year in plenary sessions attended by representatives from every province on the island.

The incorporation of women into the workforce, the state of education and childcare, problems with infant day-care centers, with boarding schools, with health—specifically the reproductive health of women—and with cultural development: these were subjects of permanent importance that were an integral part of our work. Across Cuba, it was clear that women's cultural and political standing was attaining theretofore unheard-of heights. Women who had once been illiterate were discussing problems in agriculture, production, their position in society, equality, and the conflicts that arose in trying to solve them.

Naturally, there were still enormous cultural obstacles, and it wasn't possible, and still isn't, to talk about equality in real life, although—according to the Constitution itself—men and women are guaranteed a development based on equality. The results of centuries of lack of education and inaccessibility to culture and art for the masses can't be eliminated in a few years.

Nevertheless, there were substantial changes in awareness and position for thousands of women who had previously been disadvantaged. For many others, however, the Revolution meant nothing. They weren't even aware that Cuba had experienced a Revolution. I had the good fortune to know about and take a direct part in of this process of training women for the most diverse tasks in society.

The National Directorate regularly received information about the work the Federation was doing across Cuba, and officials traveled regularly and periodically throughout the provinces to monitor, assess, and assist. A truly efficient feedback mechanism was established that allowed us to be constantly on top of what was happening in every municipality and province. The seriousness and standardization of the analysis would be interrupted from time to time, however, with events that I'm convinced could only happen in Cuba.

Within the framework of the cultural program, one municipality had prepared a meeting with poet and writer Félix Pita Rodríguez, who was in vogue and considered by the leaders an appropriate person to stimulate the cultural education of the masses. The local FMC leaders in charge of preparing the venue had painted an enormous banner and hung it over the entrance to the courtyard: "WELCOME FELIPITA!" You can imagine the women's surprise when instead of the poetess Felipita, an old man appeared, Félix Pita, presenting himself as the guest of honor for the cultural activity.

In one of the eastern provinces, high in the mountains, the educational drive for the "culinary arts" caused problems. It was part of the cultural work plan and would win important points for the socialist emulation if it were fully implemented. The difficulty was in not knowing categorically what the women should do to win the competition in the area of the "culinary arts," for none of them knew what "culinary" meant. Of course they did know that *culo* means "ass" in Spanish. The days of measuring the quality of a woman based on her dimensions and anatomical proportions had passed, but the program said clearly, "Select the best *compañeras*."

The mountain women told the central-level representative, who was supposed to monitor and evaluate the competition:

"So, as far as the competition in the culinary arts, okay, that is, well, we don't know if what we did is correct. We asked the teacher, the *compañera* directress of the childcare center, but no one could tell us what this means exactly, what we should do to meet the requirements. And to tell the truth, really, your instructions aren't exactly clear. In order to not fail, you know, just in case, and so you don't say later that we didn't do it, well, look, we selected the women who seem to us to have the most appropriate dimensions to win the competition. And, please, you have to help us choose the best candidate from this preselected group."

And they presented to the central evaluation committee the *mulatas* with the most monumental asses in the region.

But not only in the scope of the work with women did we encounter amusing surprises that broke the daily monotony. In my work with the different levels of the health sector I also saw things that were funny.

An analysis of the situation of infant mortality—one of the health system's most important jobs—was carried out regularly, with rigor on all levels, and in that analysis administrators from department heads to vice-ministers took part. The Minister of Health himself, in fact, was preparing to go on national television to talk about the project, so everyone involved buckled down to ensure the activity's success. There was an atmosphere of excitement and enthusiasm. The officials were proud of the results: infant mortality had been recorded at levels that might well be among the lowest in the world. In front of the provincial hospital, the setting where the solemn presentation of the results was to take place, a platform had been erected, and from one end to the other a banner of white cloth was hung, with enormous red letters containing the slogan for the event: "LONG LIVE INFANT MORTALITY!"

No comment needed.

Every year without fail, the FMC held a plenary session that was attended by representatives from all the provinces. Its purpose was to analyze and discuss the fulfillment of the organization's work plans.

In one of these plenaries, we received a visit from a member of the Politburo of one of our sister socialist countries. I was asked to be her interpreter; that is, the umbilical cord for this distinguished visitor, who didn't speak one word of Spanish.

The plenaries were truly folkloric activities. Mixed in among serious speeches, heated debates, and analyses of the socialist emulation were singing and spontaneous dancing, the women from the eastern provinces always the highlight of the event with their rhythms and the originality of their lyrics. Those who didn't seem cut out for that sort of spontaneous celebration were invariably from Pinar del Río and Matanzas, hot on the heels of those from Havana and Sancti Spíritus.

It was very difficult to translate the debates of the *federadas*, the FMC women. A person accustomed to the procedural rigidity in her own country's assemblies could be overwhelmed at seeing and listening to the multitude of women who were talking, discussing, intervening, and—horror!—interrupting without recognizing any internal order, without any established discipline that regulated how the activity was run. Many times I felt incapable of translating the *federadas'* specialized jargon, and when I was asked to translate the song lyrics, I felt like telling the person asking to go to hell.

Fidel was joining us for the long afternoon break and was already in the amphitheater to observe the session and offer his inevitable contribution. He never lost a chance to participate in the central activities of the FMC; he was *federado número uno*. Normally, the entertainers were picked by the leadership, but the combo they originally requested wasn't available, so they had to settle for another one, hoping to "create an atmosphere" with the most prestigious music the *federadas* could produce. We were all seated in the large amphitheater waiting for the cultural program to begin. In the first row were Fidel and Vilma Espín, Raúl Castro's wife, *la Presidenta* of the FMC. At Fidel's side was the guest, with me next to her, and members of the hierarchy in order of importance.

The combo didn't waste any time. The members came in dressed as circus acrobats, armed with trumpets, trombones, and a lot of sound amplification equipment. There were also tumblers. They began to produce a racket so loud and so dreadful that we had to plug our ears. We prayed to the heavens that there would be a power outage, but it didn't happen. The loudspeakers worked perfectly. The "musicians" were jumping, screaming, shouting; in all, they put on a horrifying performance. It was a nightmare.

10. *Monika, left of Castro, translating for a high-ranking official from East Germany, with Vilma Espín, president of the Cuban Women's Federation*

I couldn't stop looking at Fidel. The *Máximo Líder*, with his eyes half-closed, was twisting the hair in his beard—a well-known sign that he was displeased. *La Presidenta* of the FMC was shaking her head in disapproval, and the distinguished guest, seated at my side, rigid and frowning, gave me a withering look, as if I were the one producing this infernal noise. She screamed in my ear:

"Mónica, translate what they're singing!"

"This can't be translated," I replied.

"Well, which is it, do you know Spanish or not? Translate what they're singing!"

There was no way out; I had to tell the truth, and the truth was that the combo was repeating over and over until exhaustion the same phrase: "Who's going to sharpen the pencil? Who, tell me, tell me, oh yes tell me, is going to sharpen the pencil? Who, who, who is going to sharpen the pencil, let me know, the tip of the pencil?"

They contorted themselves, shouted their heads off, and blew their lungs out on the trumpets and trombones; it seemed like they were going to raise the dead at any moment. The guest didn't want to believe what I had translated. It seemed absolutely inconceivable to her that in a political activity they were singing something that didn't refer to the event.

"There's nothing in these songs about struggle, combat, or reflecting on the hard work of the masses. Why?"

At least I don't think she grasped that "sharpening the pencil" had a double meaning.

For me it was the most ridiculous cultural program I'd ever seen. The person responsible, the one who had contracted the "artists," had to endure our jibes and jokes about the show for a long time.

I began a period during which I often attended national and international congresses, held in the U.S.S.R., Yemen, Poland, Czechoslovakia, Albania, Rumania, Hungary, and several countries in Latin America, training myself in the art of listening and metabolizing; that is, translating interminable speeches into another language, hour upon hour, day after day, without falling asleep, although the lack thereof was killing me. The fierce competition among the delegates of every continent was repeated in every event: who could manage to speak the longest or the fastest, often employing a thoroughly indigestible rhetoric. Many participants considered their speeches the most important of that particular congress. And since no one would give in, the sessions would go on until dawn. Each congress for me meant exhausting my brain cells. I was, I think, almost burned out.

But however torturing my work was, I learned a lot, principally in the corridors, between sessions, talking to men and women from different countries who represented, presented, and defended their ideologies and philosophies. My horizons were expanding, little by little, without my noticing it. My closed island of thought began to open, allowing other ideas, other concepts and analyses to enter. Flexibility and tolerance began to displace the rigidity of my conviction that I possessed the "absolute truth," which had been instilled in me, reinforced permanently by the media and the political activities in which I necessarily had to take part, and, of course, in my professional life.

Gradually, I had erected a system of internal protection, defense, and impermeability. In this schizophrenic environment there could be no normal development of personality. Although it's true that no subject was out of bounds, that all subjects could be discussed, analyzed, evaluated, and criticized, it all had to lead to a position of unrestricted support for the *Máximo Líder*. Disagreements and divergent opinions were not allowed. Self-volition, the power of individual analysis, was repressed, and so it atrophied.

I had a dual personality. The change was not premeditated, or something I did on purpose. No, I wasn't even aware of having one (or two, that is). It's a phenomenon that develops little by little, formed by circumstances and environment—or, better said, deformed ("molded" is perhaps the best word to describe this process of metamorphosis)—until one fine day you realize *Damn! What's happening? Am I really a person who says, does, approves, raises my hand, doesn't dare protest, and submits to "our" collective?*

At work I functioned like a puppet, in accordance with the official program imposed and engraved on my brain. Correctly and earnestly, even—though it seems absurd—with loyalty, I performed my role as an official at the National Directorate of the Federation of Cuban Women.

After an exhaustive investigation of my past, I went through the process of admission to the Communist Party of Cuba without a hitch. I think I was the only German woman who, with the red identity card as a passport, became part of the exclusive, select circle of the Party. The only obstacle to making this step official was my German citizenship. Soon enough, however, this barrier was also eliminated, and with the presentation, in a solemn act, of the citizenship certificate I became a Cuban citizen.

I was now *aplatanada*, a native. I felt Cuban, with all the responsibilities, duties, and obligations that were implicit in this condition. At the same time, I didn't renounce my German citizenship. The officials of the East German embassy insistently requested my letter of renunciation. I ignored them. Every time they called me to give me another deadline to settle this matter, I stalled, telling them some story and, finally, asking them to lock my file in some drawer, where it wouldn't bother anyone, because I wasn't going to voluntarily give up being German.

In my unofficial life, I nourished my neurons in order to give the other side of my repressed personality some needed attention. I would sink up to my neck in the warm waters of the Gulf of Mexico, just a block from our apartment in Miramar, and would swim out to sea where there were no witnesses. There, combining physical exercise with the spiritual, I would give free rein to my need to unload, to speak, to communicate with the people in whom I could confide, who also found themselves in a situation of metamorphosis and permanent ambivalence. If the Gulf of Mexico had listening and recording devices installed, it could have heard my story—full of contradictions, conflicts, doubts, desperation, hope, fear, but also daring and confrontation.

CHAPTER TWENTY-SIX
SEX EDUCATION BEGINS

The second congress of the Federation of Cuban Women (FMC) was held at the end of 1974, twelve years after the First Congress. I took an active part in the preparation of the documents that would serve as the basis for the debates in the municipal and provincial assemblies, which took place months before the National Congress began.

For the first time, the FMC Congress was going to discuss issues related to sex education. I was taking my first steps in this field of work, virgin terrain for me that a few years later would be my profession, my vocation, and the occupation to which I would dedicate myself with all my soul.

Throughout the country, in both the provinces and the big cities, there was a gradual and evident progression of indifference and lack of responsibility, especially on the part of young people, teachers, and—it must be said—many parents, in the face of a problem that had grown intolerable: sexual libertinism, misnamed "free love," accompanied by the consequences. It was logical, but no less disastrous, that this attitude had engendered a vertiginous increase in rates of early pregnancy, the rise of girl-mothers, and abortion, to which schoolgirls resorted more and more frequently. Of course these problems had further consequences: school dropouts, an increase in the number of single mothers, marriage at a very early age, and the divorce of too many marriages that shouldn't have been entered into in the first place, because the couple was immature and lacked a sense of responsibility.

Without exaggeration, this was a social problem completely incompatible with the formation of the New Man that the Revolution aspired to. From all corners of the country we received requests to provide family education, to stop the social decay, and to prepare the new generations for stable and responsible relationships. Few dared say "sexual" or "sexuality" without blushing; these terms were still avoided. The taboo attached to these words exerted a paralyzing power. The more I dealt with the subject, the more I realized that the contradictions, the hundreds of thousands of ideas of what love is, what sexuality is, what is desirable, what should be developed and what should be rejected were going to make the appropriate working documents enormously difficult to prepare.

Among the small group of "experts" responsible for preparing the documents, I was commissioned by *la Presidenta* of the FMC to study the numerous books and brochures in the FMC library, which had not thus far been reviewed. They were written in different languages and on subjects ranging from women's reproductive health to sex education and sexual orientation. I wrote up summaries of this material and prepared proposals for programs and working strategies. We had almost endless debates, in which the most diverse philosophical and ideological positions were expressed, as well as a good number of beliefs and myths, all supposedly possessing absolute truth, and all cloaked in the terminology of Marxism-Leninism, which, if you dug down a little, showed that we were all slaves of our past, of traditions, of beliefs full of deficient knowledge, fraught with errors, prejudices, and anachronisms.

Reaching a consensus in the group of experts, even on the most elementary questions of principle, had to be, therefore, the beginning and the essential condition of our commitment. We worked very hard. The result of our work was some documents that could be considered—if they had been freed from the mandatory verbiage and bombastic embellishments typical of official language—the backbone of our future action. More importantly, these documents, once approved by the National Congress, would constitute a mandatory work program. The ministries of Education (MINED) and Public Health (MINSAP) and the mass media committed themselves to implementing the sex education program approved by the Second Congress of the FMC.

11. *Monika and Dora Carcaño, a senior FMC executive, at a discussion panel preparatory to the II Congress of the Federation of Cuban Women, 1974.*

In 1971, the Cuban government institutionalized a system of boarding schools throughout the country. More than half of all Cuban teenagers—girls and boys in secondary and pre-university education, that is, between the ages of twelve and eighteen—were being educated in schools in the countryside. They would stay at their boarding schools all week, then return home on Saturday and go back to school on Sunday. In the more remote schools, like those built on the Isle of Youth (formerly the Isle of Pines), the students would be given passes only every six weeks.

The boarding-school concept was nothing new. It was based on the elitist school system in which brothers Fidel and Raúl Castro had been educated. By copying and generalizing the Jesuit system, the MINED officials who came up with the "new" schools missed some details of essential importance. In Fidel and Raúl's school, the teachers, wonderfully trained and educated, were priests whose life's mission was to educate the students in their care. They practiced their profession with absolute dedication. They watched over their students, kept them under control, and promoted activities that kept them in check. They didn't expose them—as happened in the new schools—to permanent temptation. They didn't create conditions that would stimulate sexuality. They didn't mix, as they did in the new school, dynamite and fire (teenage girls and boys), since there were only male students on the Jesuit campuses.

The Basic Secondary Schools in the Countryside and the Pre-University Institutes in the Countryside grew, multiplied, and sprouted like mushrooms after a good rain. They were in the middle of nowhere, far from civilization, with no existing infrastructure, and conflict and catastrophe were programmed into them from the start. The system was based on conditions, criteria, and convictions that could only end in failure. MINED accepted no criticism of any kind; much less did the mastermind of this system, *El Comandante en Jefe*. Cuba's educational system was the "best in the world." Because he said so, it was the unquestionable truth.

An entire generation of young people was brought up not knowing how to wash underwear or cook a plate of rice, let alone knowing where beans and rice came from. They didn't know where to get a sheet of paper or how to make their own decisions. Plain and simple, they were part of a gigantic machine, each one a small cog in the gears. Everything was programmed and planned in obedience to instructions received from the higher authorities.

The training of the teachers required for the new schools went slowly, and it was totally insufficient. Most of the teachers were very young, hacked into the shape of pedagogues by a machete blow; they had little training, and what training they did receive wasn't intended to make them substitutes for parents of teenagers in boarding schools. Many married teachers couldn't bear the permanent separation from their families, especially if they were working in hard-to-reach areas that made it impossible for them to return home each day. Never before had there been so many teachers in Cuba with mental health problems.

The students and teachers were largely ignorant when it came to sexuality. There were no books, magazines, or film material available to them, nothing that could serve as an objective source of information or a guide for their behavior. Their heads were filled with confusion, half-truths, myths, and prejudices. The teachers weren't adequately trained to think about their own sexuality, let alone that of their students. Boys were asked by their fathers to demonstrate their masculinity, in true *machismo* tradition. The boy who at fourteen years of age couldn't report to his father his experiences, conquests, and successful sexual performance with girls—the more, the better—was considered weak, a sissy.

The prohibitions imposed by the authorities to control the complex, contradictory, and often truly catastrophic situations that were unfolding in the boarding schools were of no use. It was strictly forbidden to have sex in schools, and being caught in the act meant immediate expulsion. Girls who became pregnant were also expelled, but the boy who was jointly responsible for the pregnancy went unpunished, an example of *machismo* and blatantly unequal treatment.

To believe in the efficacy of the prohibitions posted on school walls or laid on administrators' desks was tantamount to believing that a gigantic cake placed in the schoolyard with a sign saying "forbidden to eat" was going to stop the students from devouring the delicacy. Many—too many—students were disgraced by eating the forbidden cake and receiving the punishment—undeserved but announced and known—for violating the regulations.

Everyone knew that the boarding-school students escaped to the citrus groves to unleash their impulses, to experiment, and to vent their uncontrollable desires, which were exacerbated by their raging hormones. What adult, not to mention teenager, is capable of putting on the brakes when there is fantastic warm weather, a breeze with the perfume of orange blossoms, and a full moon as a silent witness illuminating the peaceful beauty of the landscape? Yet when I asked a boarding school director what the most frequent sexual problems of her students were, her answer showed how out of touch with reality she was:

"*Compañera*, this is a school; sexuality has no place here."

None so blind as those who will not see.

When the guidelines, rules, and regulations were ineffective, the blame wasn't laid on the higher authority, or on the blind director, no: the black sheep were, invariably, the kids and their parents. Parents were the last to have any influence over their children, however. They weren't allowed to visit the kids at school, with very few exceptions; for example, when they were called to receive a brainwashing about transgressions committed by a child. They wouldn't see them for days, weeks. The few moments they shared with their children were limited to eating together on Saturday evening, and the kids, after filling their bellies, would vanish from their homes to meet their friends, let off steam, have fun, and try to have a good time without the constant pressure from teachers and parents.

In my opinion, the new school was the perfect way to destroy the family, to aggravate the already existing problems of teenage pregnancy, school dropouts, and sexual excesses of students among themselves, teachers among themselves, and between the teachers and students.

The health care system had to absorb the disaster, especially the steep rise in teenage pregnancies and abortions. Despite the odds, it managed to keep infant mortality rates low. Those rates, which were among the lowest in the world, were not achieved by magic or because a special Cuban formula had been found. They were the result of systematic effort, dedication, and sacrifice on the part of healthcare professionals. Cuba had good reason to be proud, as it could boast figures that other countries with more resources and opportunities looked at with envy and suspicion.

The results of Cuba's work in public health were regularly reported to the World Health Organization, which, along with other specialized organizations of the United Nations, maintained a series of development programs with Cuba that not only meant substantial material assistance, but also required from the Cuban officials in charge of carrying out the programs absolute seriousness and rigor in carrying out the work. The control exercised by the u.n.'s specialized organizations, along with the coordinators on the Cuban side, over the implementation of the sponsored projects could be considered reliable. During the last years of my stay in Cuba, I directed one of the u.n. Population Fund's programs; our goal was to lower the high rates of teenage pregnancy.

The FMC was in charge of preparing the Cuban delegation that was going to attend the u.n. World Conference of the International Women's Year, which took place in the summer of 1975 in Mexico City. We had already received the documents for the Global Plan of Action, which reflected the vision of a world in which men and women would enjoy the same rights and have the same duties, guaranteeing equality.

This Global Plan of Action became my beacon, the guiding light for my work. It was only necessary to specify tasks and detail particular aspects, but the document itself, also approved by Cuba at the World Conference held in Mexico City, could be considered a concise working instrument and would be our backbone. Being able to participate directly in the World Conference was an event of distinction for me.

I was an official member of the Cuban delegation and felt elated as I debated issues with delegates from around the world. I felt fulfilled and took all debates and discussions very seriously. I noted—as never before—the disagreements, the enormous contradictions, and the conflicts that representatives of the different countries had with the Global Plan of Action. Real struggles were fought to modify, remove, or amend one and another paragraph. For weeks we worked with representatives from around the world to achieve an action plan worthy of being approved and carried out. It should be borne in mind that the approval of the plan meant for each signatory country the commitment and the obligation—at least in theory—to put the plan into practice.

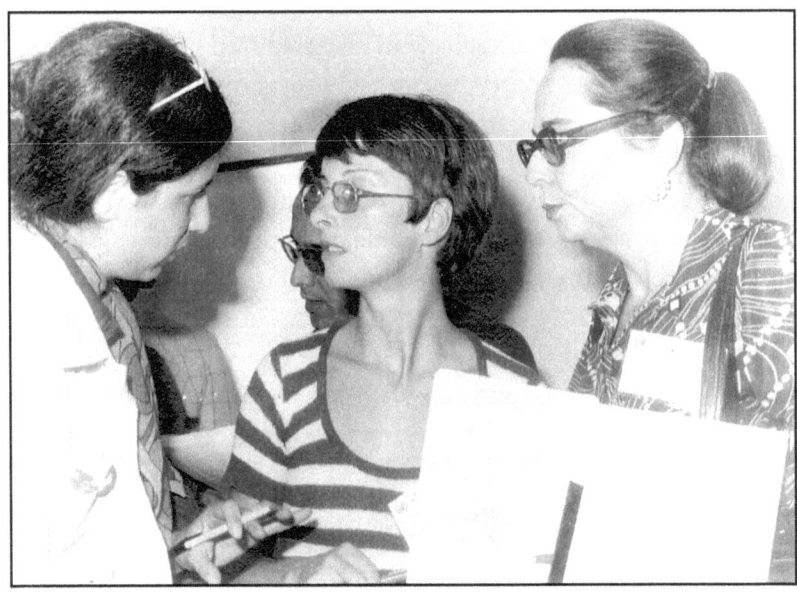

12. *Monika and Vilma Espín, President of the Cuban Women's Federation, at the UN World Women's Conference, Mexico City, 1975, International Year of Women*

In salute to March 8, International Women's Day, of the year 1975, the Family Code was approved (and is still in effect in the twenty-first century), after the project had been studied and debated throughout Cuba, from the Punta de Maisí to Cabo de San Antonio. I believe that never before or after has the draft of a code been debated in Cuba with the participation of so many people. Thousands and thousands of letters with suggestions, proposals, and statements of agreement or disagreement were received by the preparatory commission. The most open disagreements were in regard to equality in the family, when the Code stated that men and women should assume joint responsibility for caring for children and performing household chores.

Equality in matters of access to training and equal pay for equal work was accepted, not unanimously but by the majority of those who had opinions on the matter, but family equality was another matter. Who had ever seen a man in an apron, cooking, scrubbing, cleaning, and changing his child's dirty diapers or wiping away his child's snot? No, a man who would agree to this was no longer a man. Another aspect that generated a great number of contradictory opinions was related to the minimum age of marriageable girls and boys. The majority of the participants in the public discussion were of the opinion that the age for a girl to marry should be twelve years, based on the widely held opinion, but one with fatal consequences, that after the first occurrence of menstruation, a girl is ready to get married. In the end, this demand wasn't accepted. It was decided that "females and males over eighteen years of age are authorized to formalize marriage. Consequently, minors under eighteen years of age are not authorized to formalize marriage" (Article 3 of the Family Code). However, a door was left open for those situations that I called "concessions to the past, to tradition": girls were allowed to marry at fourteen, and boys at sixteen, if they had the permission of their parents or the courts. This license became the rule rather than the exception.

Thousands upon thousands of girls dropped out of school, got married, or were forced to marry to "save the honor of the family," only to "go out of marriage" a few weeks later. They didn't meet the slightest conditions for such an undertaking; they were disgraced by life before it began, and they joined the gigantic army of child-mothers, who, to their own misery and that of their children, had to get by without the material and spiritual support of their parents. Many others had to leave their children in the care of grandparents, meaning that the girl-mothers were suddenly in the role of sisters to their own children.

This situation was becoming widespread throughout the country, in both the countryside and the cities. For several years in a row, far more sixteen-year-old mothers were giving birth than twenty-six-year-old mothers, and it was not unusual for thirteen-year-old girls to have children. There were pregnant twelve-year-old girls every year, although their number did not reach "statistical significance," but the simple fact that this phenomenon existed required effective measures, because this state of affairs was intolerable, although many—too many—high-level officials didn't think it important and took the issue off the agenda with the comment that "This has always been the case; it's a characteristic of the tropics. Girls mature very early; it's logical that they have children."

I was convinced that only a concerted effort of education—not just instruction, which doesn't automatically change behaviors—could substantially modify the prevailing situation, the deep-rooted *machismo*.

CHAPTER TWENTY-SEVEN
MY CAPTAIN DISAPPEARS AND THE HOUSE FLOODS

MY CAPTAIN HAD DISAPPEARED from the scene, although this time he had not been given a chance even to say goodbye. He had been sent on an "internationalist mission" in Angola, and he was one of the first Cubans to embark for that distant African country. He was picked up from work one night without prior notice, given an olive-green uniform and a black plastic bag to put all his belongings in, handed a set of dog tags, put on a bus, and taken to the port, where the ship that would take him to Angola was ready to lift anchor.

Being a ship captain himself, he was sent to Angola in the ship's hold, in one of the large holds converted into accommodations for hundreds of combatants. Only at night were the men and women in the hold allowed to come up on deck for some fresh air. Arriving in Angola, he served as an explorer, making maps of the areas occupied by South African troops. Later he served as a gunner, a warlike trade for which he had never been trained, but after observing the handling of a cannon for the fourth time, he was considered fit to fulfill this role.

Meanwhile, the First Congress of the Communist Party of Cuba (PCC), held at the end of 1975, took me away from my usual tasks. I worked as an interpreter throughout the Congress, morning, noon, and night, becoming a real machine, a robot that transformed a speech in Spanish into German. With both their parents absent, the boys moved in with Pilar and Gonzalo, their beloved aunt and uncle.

The PCC Congress was in full swing, with almost endless sessions (and almost endless speeches) that lasted until past midnight, when a gigantic catastrophe occurred in my house: an illegal neighbor who had installed himself on the roof of our building had for months been dumping tons of waste into the pipes, causing a blockage that produced a disastrous flood in our apartment. Rivers of mud, fecal matter, garbage, and all kinds of filth from the entire building flowed through the pipes and duct openings into our bathroom.

Returning home at three in the morning, after having completed my day as an interpreter in the Congress, I found the apartment turned into a gigantic cesspool. The foul smell made me sick, and I wanted to vomit. I had never experienced such a quantity of filth, such a concentration of foul smells. I was frankly scared, desperate, powerless in the face of a phenomenon that I couldn't stop. Each time the upstairs neighbor flushed her toilet, the contents would arrive seconds later in my tub, sink, and toilet, overflowing across the floor. Almost insane, I went out in search of Uncle Gonzalo, our eternal savior.

As usual, I couldn't count on my captain: he was fighting in a surreal Caribbean war in Africa. Gonzalo's tools weren't sufficient to disconnect the pipe from the roof and from our home. We had to wait a whole day before professional help arrived; until the Congress was over, I couldn't commit to anything other than translating, nor could I locate a real plumber. Everything revolved around the Congress.

From his place of work, Gonzalo got in touch with specialists who knew how to unplug pipes like ours. What a crazy world! Fidel was speaking, speaking, speaking, with me mechanically repeating the same verbiage in German, thinking all the while about the filth that had turned our apartment into a literal shithouse. There was quite a contradiction between Fidel's world and mine.

There are no words to describe what the plumbers pulled out of the clogged pipes. We could have used the stinking mass as compost on at least a hundred acres of cane field. Armed with industrial quantities of detergent, bleach, sulfide, and I don't know how many other substances to make our apartment habitable again, I began to clean with desperation, anger, and true aggressiveness. Protecting my nose and mouth with a mask, spreading disinfectant substances everywhere, I removed the filth.

The boys were waiting for my frantic work to finish; I must have looked like an exorcist to them. They looked at me suspiciously; they had never seen me like this. I think I scared them. But they completely panicked when I uncapped a bottle of alcohol and poured the contents all over the bathroom—sink, bathtub, toilet, floor, also down the hallway and on the living room floor—in short, all over the areas that had been in contact with the filth. And then I set it on fire.

"Mommy, noooooo, stop, the house is going to explode! Dictys, we have to call the fire department! Our house is on fire! Mommy, you've gone mad!" screamed Dani, and both boys, like chickens with their heads cut off, ran to fetch water to put out the flames.

"Stay right there! The flames will be over in a minute. Can't you see that only the alcohol is burning? It's not enough to burn down the house. It only serves to disinfect the entire bathroom and the floor that was covered in filth."

Paralyzed with fear and terror, they stared at the show. And, indeed, the flames went out once the alcohol burned away. Of course, it was crazy of me, irresponsible, to disinfect the floor by setting the alcohol on fire. My children were right to call me mad, but anyone who had seen the monumental amount of filth that had been flowing through the house could understand my attack of insanity. Disgust and revulsion were stronger than reason. Fortunately, the house was left intact and clean, without any trace of the past horror.

Three months after the disappearance of my husband, and during all that time without having received any notice from any official institution about his whereabouts, I received a visit from a lieutenant in the Revolutionary Armed Forces. If I hadn't found out the same night about my husband's departure to Africa (it was strictly forbidden to notify relatives, but I knew the truth, because in Cuba you can never keep a secret), I think the appearance of the officer who carried a black bag in his hands would have caused me a fit of hysteria.

The good man recited a speech and ceremoniously handed me the bag, which contained a pair of pants, a shirt, socks, shoes, boxer shorts, a watch, my captain's identity card, that of his workplace, his driver's license, a document proving ownership of our Volkswagen Beetle, and a handkerchief. He gave me a pouch that contained money corresponding to three months of my captain's salary and also informed me that during my husband's mission in Angola, he would regularly receive his salary, which he himself, the friendly officer, would hand over to me every month from now on, as he was the person in charge of caring for the families of the internationalist combatants.

CHAPTER TWENTY-EIGHT

WHAT DOESN'T KILL ME MAKES ME STRONGER

Dictys, now twelve years old and in secondary school, was completing his first week in a program called "from school to field": forty-five days of agricultural work in a cooperative located about forty miles from Havana, housed in a barracks built next to the farm.

I had to go on a tour of the eastern part of the island with a foreign delegation, visiting women in several municipalities in the province of Santiago de Cuba. At the Santiago airport, the secretary of the Communist Party and members of the Provincial Committee of the Women's Federation were waiting for us. Three brand-new Peugeots, still covered with the grease that protected them against the saltwater spray during the crossing from Argentina to Cuba, were waiting in single file, ready to take us to Pinares de Mayarí, the first stop on our tour.

The drivers of the cars, happy as little kids displaying precious Three Kings Day gifts, were eager to start so they could show us that these vehicles had the right to be called "cars." They ran smoothly, had brakes that worked, and the engines didn't quit on every hill: in short, they were impeccable. It was a pleasure to drive them.

"But they don't have license plates yet," I said. "If we have a collision, no one will know where the cars are from."

This silly comment made them slap their thighs in fits of laughter.

"Can't you see they're brand new? Today is their debut. How can you even think about a collision if these vehicles work perfectly?"

Indeed, for years I hadn't been in a car that was in such perfect condition. We were supposed to travel to Pinares de Mayarí to learn about a Special Plan for growing fruit—mainly strawberries—that had been adapted to the microclimate of that town, which was situated at a relatively high altitude. The Europeans, our foreign delegation, had to see for themselves that we also have strawberries in Cuba. The drivers, euphoric with their new toys, drove much faster than allowed and weren't giving the road their undivided attention, so they missed the turn they were supposed to take.

"You went past the turn; you should have gone right on that road," the Secretary of the Communist Party reproached our driver.

As if to save someone from being run over, the driver hit the brake pedal, hard. The car came to a screeching halt, and the car following us hit ours. That driver was so scared that, instead of braking, he accelerated, hitting us again, twice. The third car, luckily, managed to stop a few feet away, so it was the only one that was unscathed.

My head, like a batted ball, flew back and forth, from front to back. I felt a sharp pain in the back of my neck, as if an awl had been driven between my vertebrae, but this sensation lasted such a short time that afterwards I hardly remembered it. I lost consciousness for just a brief moment, and when I came to again, I saw that my seatmate, next to the window, was bathed in blood that was oozing from a large cut on his temple. He was bleeding, and I tasted blood. I thought I was imagining this because of the shock, the thunderous noise, and the sight of so much blood. Obviously my gray cells weren't working well; the violent shaking must have produced some disorder in my brain, for this idea was totally absurd. I also felt my strength leaving me. I was weak, and it was hard to move my arms and legs. *It's the scare*, I told myself, and I tried to help the man next to me. I pressed a handkerchief over his wound, made him put his head back, and got out of the car, at the speed of an old tortoise, my legs shaking, and my body slowed down, as if I had lead weights on my feet.

Our driver had a fractured tibia; the Secretary of the Communist Party, an injured right foot; the driver of the car that hit us, a bruised tibia. We put the wounded in the undamaged car and took them to the nearest hospital. I knew I had a cervical spine injury from my previous experience of diving off the Concha beach bottle, but I didn't want any unfit doctor to ruin my neck even more than necessary. I told the injured to go to the hospital without me, that my injury wasn't important.

The foreign delegation was unharmed because they had been in the last car. Our group, now halved, set out walking to the strawberry plantation. A Soviet jeep, without shock absorbers but with a strong engine, gave us a lift. The people at the farm showed us the miraculous strawberries, with leaves the size of toilet lids and sweet little fruits. Every twelve square feet we found a strawberry. What madness, what a complete lack of common sense to go by plane and travel for hours by car (and risk your life) to see some stunted strawberries. My neck was stiff and sore; my head was spinning and buzzing, and I kept tasting blood, unable to explain this phenomenon.

This is how things were happening in the country: we spent time praising, admiring, celebrating our miracles, our wonders, our achievements, our feats. Cuba: world medical power; world sports power; owner of the world's largest ice cream palace and the most productive dairy cow in the world, White Udder; the highest nickel production in the world; the most advanced biotechnology in the world.

At the end of the visit to the Special Plan, we said goodbye to the miraculous strawberries and the other plants, which, with true revolutionary fervor, were growing despite the sun, humidity, torrential rains, hurricanes, and rocky, arid soil. After impressing on the foreigners how privileged they were to be able to admire such achievements, that Cuba was on the right path to overcome all the obstacles imposed on it, we took a short break in a country restaurant in Pinares de Mayarí.

We were served a rich tomato salad and, as a main dish, an exquisite lamb *chilindrón*, a stew with a spicy sauce prepared with regional products. The diners didn't complain about the abundance of spice or the acidity of the tomato; I was the only one who found the apparent excess of spices not to my taste. After lunch, looking at my tongue in the bathroom mirror, I found the explanation for the taste of blood I'd been experiencing from the shock. My jaws must have closed violently, and my back molars punched two holes in my tongue. My oversensitivity to the acidity of the tomatoes and the spiciness of the sauce required no further clarification. These wounds hurt, and it was logical that they were bleeding.

There were still hours of torture ahead before we could go to bed. We drove through bumpy streets. To avoid damaging shocks, I tried to protect the back of my neck by supporting it with one hand, while with the other I held onto the door frame. Fortunately, I didn't know that I was putting my life in danger with every movement of the car, with every bump and jolt.

When the political activity finally ended—a report on the work being done by the Mayarí women—we went to a motel. The beds were a true disaster. My mattress didn't deserve the name; it was a miserable hammock with countless indentations, and it was impossible to get comfortable in that thing. My roommate helped me put the mattress on the floor, and I tried to sleep. As is often the case in such circumstances, with the darkness and calm of the night, the pain in my neck and head worsened, so that even with several aspirin, I couldn't sleep. It was a terrible night. *A cold shower will do the trick*, I thought. The trickle of water coming out of the pipe wasn't even cold enough to wake me up. I was still giddy; I was in pain, I felt nauseated, and I had little desire to continue the pilgrimage with the foreign delegation. Finally, at four in the afternoon, we started the trip back to Havana, by plane. The flight was an ordeal for me. The vibrations from the propellers exacerbated the sensitivity of my injured neck. The two hours on the plane seemed endless, a real torture.

Back home, after a shower that didn't have the expected effect, I went to bed. I spent a night of one nightmare after another, interrupted by getting up to take more aspirin. I woke up in the morning feeling like a dog that had been beaten. It was Sunday. Gathering up my last reserves of will and strength, I prepared my things and picked up Dani, Pilar, and Gonzalo to go out to the country to visit Dictys, who was eagerly awaiting us. In the course of the first week of hard work in the fields, he had accumulated a fierce hunger. In the camp they only served rice with split-pea soup or split-pea soup with rice. A supply of condensed milk, bought on the black market, and bread with roast pork, also obtained from an illegal source and brought by the boys' aunt and uncle, was essential. It provided a lifeline that enabled the boys to continue another week, and the delicacies prepared by Aunt Pilar disappeared in the blink of an eye. Full belly, happy heart.

Dictys and Dani went to play for a while in the open field to work off some of the after-lunch drowsiness, while Pilar, Gonzalo, and I sat on the grass, resting. The farm looked like a gigantic refugee camp. Hundreds of the boys' relatives were pulling food, painstakingly collected for the survival of their youngsters, from their bags. Has there ever been a calculation of the resources spent in Cuba during each "from school to field" period? I think it's impossible to know for sure how much was spent on gasoline, on vehicles diverted from their true function, illegally used to transport students' family members to the countryside, and on food obtained on the black market at exorbitant prices. I'm sure they didn't keep a record of the boys' production compared to the resources diverted to make their lives superficially bearable in the camps.

Three days had passed since the crash in Mayarí, and I still hadn't seen a doctor. Monday morning I showed up at the office, feeling terrible. It was *la Presidenta* herself who requested an appointment with Dr. Rodrigo Álvarez Cambra, the best-known orthopedic and trauma doctor in the country, to see me. Dr. Álvarez was a professor and the director of the university orthopedics hospital. I drove myself to the hospital and had to spend hours in the waiting room before they saw me. They took x-rays of the cervical area of my spine, and when the plates were ready, I went back to Dr. Álvarez Cambra's office with them in hand. He glanced at them, and I could see that he was shocked. He called all his assistants and aides, giving them a speech in gibberish. Incidentally, in the accident it seems that my hearing was also damaged, because since that date I haven't been able to hear well.

Finally, they all looked at me as if they were seeing a ghost and sent me back to the radiology department. This time I was accompanied by a young specialist who constantly repeated:

"Mónica, walk carefully. Don't trip."

We returned with the studies, and the group again concentrated on analyzing the x-rays. I heard comments of astonishment and disbelief from afar, but I couldn't understand the relationship between these comments and my problem. I was too giddy and in too much pain. Only one sentence stuck in my head:

"Here you can see it clearly, on this x-ray with her mouth open, and she is standing, walking, moving as if nothing had happened."

I was not interested in their discussion. I wanted to get out of there, lie down, and rest.

"We have to put you in a cast," Dr. Álvarez Cambra told me.

"What are you talking about? With this heat, you want to put me in a cast from my head to my thorax? No way!"

"Well, then we'll have to restrain you. You must not move your neck for any reason at all. And if you've already waited this long, it won't matter if you wait another hour. We'll put a Minerva brace on you that will perform the same function."

That said, he picked up the phone and instructed the technicians in the orthopedic workshop to take my measurements and prepare the "cage" for me.

With the Minerva on, I couldn't drive the car. Without the car, I couldn't return to work. So I took it off, put it on the seat next to me, and went back to the office. Once there, I put it back on and finished the workday without having done anything productive. Back home, instead of eating, I filled my stomach with aspirin, because the discomfort continued, and I was annoyed. The next day, my coworkers decided to take me back to the doctor to do something and—above all—to hear what they had found, because I couldn't say what the diagnosis had been: They hadn't told me. But yes, with one of my co-workers as custodian, the female doctor who attended me spoke to us clearly.

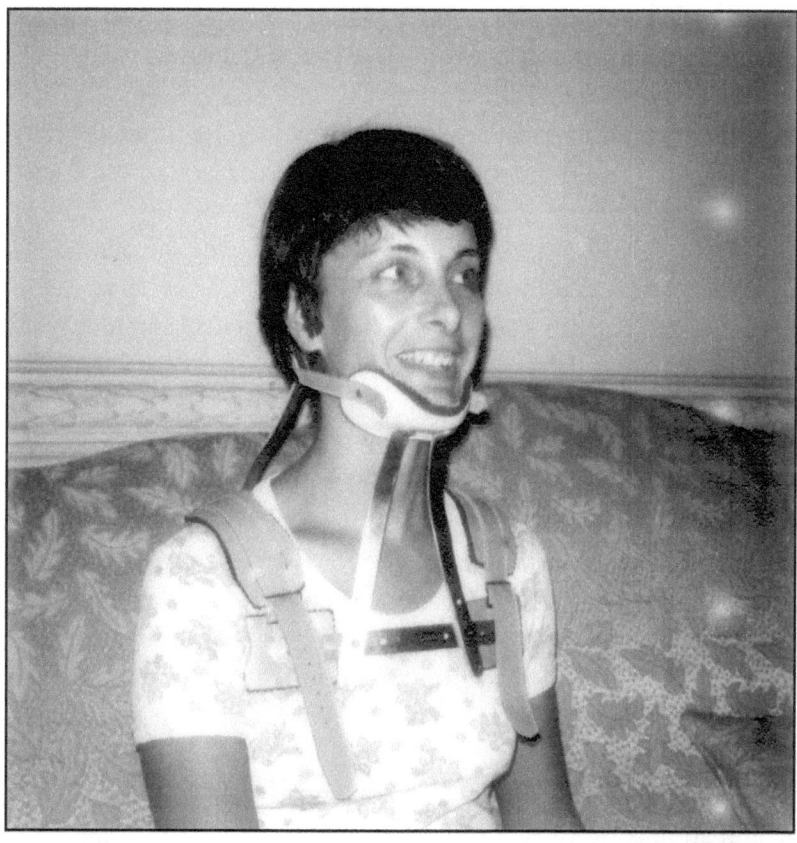

13. *Monika wearing a cervical brace (Minerva) after the horrific car accident*, 1976

"The first vertebra, the atlas, is fractured. You broke your neck. It's an unusual case. With this fracture you should be dead or paralyzed from the neck down. One person in a million with a fracture like this survives and keeps walking. You were extremely lucky. You should be lying down on a board, and you must permanently wear the device to keep your neck immobile. And be careful not to stumble, not to suffer any shock, because your life is hanging by a thread," was the explanation of the specialist.

My colleague and I looked at her with shocked faces. I couldn't believe what the doctor had just said, so I asked:

"Are you sure it's my neck? Me with a broken neck? Since the accident I've traveled by jeep, by plane, and have driven the car to my son's camp and to work. If I had a fractured vertebra, I couldn't have done all this."

"This woman is absolutely crazy! How has she done all these stupid things? She's gambling with her life!" exclaimed the doctor incredulously.

"I absolutely wasn't aware of the seriousness of the damage."

They'd had scaffolding made to prop me up like a house in Old Havana, but not a single word had been said about a fracture.

"Well, let me tell you now: In order not to aggravate the misfortune from which you were miraculously saved, you have to sleep on a board. You have to avoid all movement that could displace the fractured ends and mentally prepare yourself to interrupt all your activities for several months—all your usual activities, because this is for a long time."

She called Dr. Álvarez Cambra to confirm her diagnosis.

"Well, now you know how to carry out the instructions. Get the board today. It's very important, and don't think about carrying it yourself. After what we've seen, I imagine you'd be capable of doing something else stupid. In addition, you'll have to go to the hospital once a week to control the growth of the corpus callosum, which should heal the fracture."

My coworker dropped me off at home. On the way she kept scolding me, calling me irresponsible, stubborn, and hard-headed for all the foolish things I'd done in the days after the accident. Her speech went in one ear and out the other. I was upset because the doctors hadn't spoken to me clearly. How could I act responsibly if I didn't know I was in danger?

Through all this I kept ruminating about how to get a board. The doctor had given the order to use it without further delay but hadn't told me where to get it. Nowhere in the whole of Cuba could you buy a board. In Cuba there was nothing to buy, and there was everything. It was important to have access to resources that didn't officially exist, through friends—to have relationships of *sociolismo*. And we had them.

I called Tomás, my husband's number one friend, a Cubana de Aviación pilot, who had declared himself the godfather of the family since the disappearance of my captain.

"Any problem you have with the children, with the house, whatever, just call me."

"Tomás, my neck is broken, and I have to sleep on a board. The problem is that I don't have a board and no way to get one."

Tomás screamed, listening to my story:

"Don't move from the house! In half an hour I'll be there with the board and other things that you'll surely need. Luckily, I don't have a flight today, and my station wagon has just been repaired. Don't do anything stupid. Wait for me to get there."

Indeed, in less than half an hour the entourage arrived: Tomás, his wife, and an assistant who carried a large piece of wood on his shoulder: the board that from then on would be my therapeutic bed. Tomás's family took over my care. On Sundays, they picked up Pilar, Gonzalo, and Dani to drive to the farm and take food to Dictys, and they took me in regularly for medical check-ups. A friend of the family, formerly a professor of medical sciences, now retired, declared himself my protector and insisted on accompanying me to the specialist so there would be no sort of neglect or lack of information about the recovery process and the therapeutic steps I needed to follow.

Weeks passed, then months, but the fracture wasn't healing. They would have to intervene surgically to repair the damage. During the weeks I was in the hospital, I had time to study the tons of books about sexuality and family planning that *la Presidenta* had accumulated in the FMC library. I took to my bed with material that I requested, and I killed the obligatory rest time by reading, taking notes, summarizing, and thinking up projects.

Once again, my belief that bad things happen for a reason was confirmed, although a less serious problem would have sufficed. But thanks to my fractured neck, I was able to free myself from a world of tedious work obligations that didn't satisfy me, and to direct my professional life toward sex education, counseling, and therapy. Everything that I had to squeeze into a few hours at night before the accident, I could now do taking all the time I wanted. I could determine for myself what kinds of activities I was spending my time on. In spite of everything, I felt lucky.

With the permission of the doctors to restart my work gradually and carefully in the office, *la Presidenta* decided that I could dedicate myself entirely to my new calling, specifically to the development of a national sex education program. *La Presidenta* also selected for this task Dr. Celestino Álvarez Lajonchere, a renowned professor of gynecology, who would be my tutor so I could acquire broad medical knowledge, especially in the fields of endocrinology, gynecology, and andrology, and be able to work, on a footing of near-equality, with medical professionals.

The Lajonchere-Krause team turned out to be highly effective from day one; together we would develop and implement an ambitious, complex national program of sex education, counseling, sex therapy, and family planning. We would enlist doctors, educators, psychologists, sociologists, lawyers, and journalists throughout the country to aid us in our project. This program would be successfully implemented despite a thousand difficulties, moral barriers, *machismo*, and prudery. It would achieve great visibility, have a profound social impact, and be internationally recognized.

In this initial stage, we understood "sex education" to be the transmission of knowledge about the biology of reproduction, contraception, and abortion. In order not to reinvent the wheel or rediscover fire, we were prepared to investigate other countries' experiences in this area. That was how we learned about various initiatives that had been undertaken in Latin America. Despite the embargo, we began an exchange of information and experiences with prestigious American scientists and publishers on the medical aspects of contraception, surgical techniques for abortion, and therapies for sexual disorders. We also had access to the Swedish sex education program, which was reputed to be the quintessential example.

We found the advanced East German sex education program, which had already been going on for ten years, the most suitable for many reasons: the similarity of our political systems, my origin, and my ability to translate. *La Presidenta* entrusted me with an exploratory trip to East Germany. I was commissioned to exhaustively appraise their program, learn about the activities the country was engaging in, collect all the corresponding literature, and evaluate it. I realized that the practical work there corresponded closely to our own plans. The various well-defined programs that existed, such as marriage courses, sexual consultation, therapy centers, lecture cycles, and mass media support in orienting and educating the population on issues of sexuality seemed reasonable, effective, and relevant to our work.

I was especially pleased to see that the popular scientific literature available to all groups of people would be perfectly applicable to our situation, requiring only an adaptation to our particular situation and our particular problems. This literature could serve as excellent, truly effective, work material. During this trip, the bible of sexual enlightenment fell into my hands. It was the book *Man and Woman in Intimacy*, by the German psychologist Dr. Siegfried Schnabl. I felt I had found a treasure, since the book contained the broadest, most complete, updated, and scientifically-based information available: in short, a working instrument par excellence. The author of this work was the director of a center for counseling, guidance, and sex therapy for couples. He did a great deal of publicity on behalf of his clinic and his work, and he was a professor of extraordinary prestige. We were very fortunate in having chosen East Germany for our "sister country," because at this time relations between Cuba and East Germany were at a peak, specifically in the fields of education and health. So I had no difficulty in awakening the interest and enthusiasm of Dr. Schnabl for our cause; on the contrary, I received from him a guarantee of collaboration whenever I needed it.

14. *Monika, Dr. Siegfried Schnabl from East Germany, Dr. Celestino Álvarez Lajonchere, and journalist Natacha Herrera*

Dr. Schnabl was the first international expert in sexology we brought to Cuba. He gave an intensive workshop to the professionals who were going to constitute the "breeding stock" for our program; we would address the training of other professionals at a later stage. We managed to produce and broadcast a television program with Dr. Schnabl, the first program on sexuality on Cuban television ever. Many other prestigious experts from Europe, the u.s., and Latin America followed, who came to Cuba to share their knowledge in workshops and conferences. Several special organizations of the u.n. supported our project by providing part of the funding.

After having located and interviewed the most appropriate foreign specialists and receiving approval from international organizations that financed the training of Cuban specialists, we began a series of intensive courses, in which I acted as interpreter and also as a student. Eventually, I acquired specialized training, together with my tutor, Dr. Lajonchere, who also took part in the courses. We were able to share our new knowledge with all the faculties of medicine and psychology in the country; teacher-training centers; the FMC cadre school; numerous boarding schools; centers run by the National Institute of Sports, Physical Education, and Recreation; health brigade members; and in activities with journalists (to mention only the most important venues). Thus, we played an important role in the education of the teachers that were urgently needed to ensure professional training in sex education, guidance, sex therapy, and family planning throughout Cuba.

Destiny provided a horrifying car accident that fractured my neck and almost sent me to the Great Beyond to mark the beginning of a new stage of my life in Cuba: a life dedicated to sex education, a life of enormous sacrifice and great professional satisfaction.

The immense difficulties, the maddening maneuvers of detractors, the most diabolical obstacles that stood in the way of my work had, contrary to what one would have thought, a stimulating effect: They were a challenge that I was ready to face with all the energy I could summon. With each complaint (and there were many), with each insulting letter or pamphlet, with each accusation of being immoral, of corrupting minors, of spoiling women, who suddenly demanded of their husbands behavior and sexual skills that they didn't even know existed before, I was indirectly benefiting. And every thank-you letter (my office was full of them), every request to give a lecture, to speak on television or radio, every encounter with a total stranger who stopped me in the street asking me for advice on their most intimate problems, which they had never communicated to anyone before, not even to their own partner, served as proof that I had found my vocation and encouraged me to continue, even to increase my "crusade."

CHAPTER TWENTY-NINE
MY CAPTAIN RETURNS FROM THE WAR

MY CAPTAIN, after a year and a half in Africa, suddenly showed up at home without notice, dressed in a dirty, foul-smelling olive-green uniform. His eyes were sunken, his skin was darkly tanned, and he was very thin. He hardly spoke. He looked, in fact, like a lost soul. He must have had horribly traumatic experiences that he had not yet assimilated. Many of the friends who had gone to Angola with him were dead, others seriously ill. He was alive; no physical injury was visible, but who could know the nature of his psychological injuries?

We grew further and further apart every day. On weekends and nights after work, he insisted on directing all his energies toward the completion of a second university degree, which had been interrupted when he was sent to Angola. At the same time, he held positions of ascending importance that increasingly demanded his absence from home. But the most serious problem, the one that definitely led to the breakdown of our relationship, was his inability to accept my new work. At that time, I didn't understand his conflicts, his aggressive position and behavior, his teasing, his bitter and even hurtful comments when he saw me on a television program or found pages of books I was editing on my desk.

Sometimes, when we were at receptions, I would hear sarcastic and hurtful whispering:

"Look who's here. It's Mónica, Jesús's wife." They didn't say, "Look, Jesús came with his wife."

I learned that some high-level officials were blaming him, because no man should allow his wife to say so many outrageous things in public. The conflict came to a head when, proud and happy, I presented him with the book, still hot off the press: *Man and Woman in Intimacy*, by the German psychologist, Siegfried Schnabl. I was responsible for this publication; I had found the author and requested his approval to publish his works in Cuba. I had carried out the technical revision and corrected the translation. Together with my tutor, Dr. Lajonchere, I had written the final version, even circumventing the censorship, and I considered this book to be invaluable material not only for the training of professionals but also for the information and instruction of the common reader.

My husband threw it to the ground, with a gesture of contempt and hatred, screaming that he didn't need to learn anything from a book, he knew what to do. We remained married, but work began to play the role of a drug, an escape valve for both of us, and it was becoming the reason for our existence.

I was not surprised by these follies, these escapes, this impossibility of leading a normal life, because that situation was normal in Cuba, a country turned upside down. Very similar relationships were seen throughout the country. Normal life meant constant mobilizations to perform "voluntary" work in the cane fields, join construction micro-brigades, or train in the territorial militias. Thousands of professional couples were separated because one or both of them were away from home on an internationalist mission, or because their workplace required a prolonged stay in another location. I'm thinking, for example, of the many teachers in boarding schools. Most couldn't go home every day. The true unfortunates, whose schools were located on the Isle of Youth, led a barracks life, isolated, in the middle of the savannah, without their family, without privacy, and without any way to cultivate relationships.

Moral laxity, irresponsibility, and stealing from work gained ground, accompanied by promiscuity, often causing irreparable physical and psychological damage. This social deterioration was reflected statistically in the increasing numbers of teenage pregnancies and single mothers, the vertiginous increase in sexually transmitted diseases, abortions, divorces, school dropouts, and other truly deplorable occurrences. The difference between the official "line"—statements that the Cuban Communist Party and the FMC adopted in congresses and disseminated as official positions—and reality; between the Constitution of the Republic and the Family Code, on the one hand, and real life on the other, became larger and larger. Rifts were everywhere, along with endless, antagonistic self-contradictions.

Our world seemed more and more schizophrenic. Like brainless beings, we repeated the slogans regarding the "socialist family," the "New Man," the "responsible couple that lives its life in equal conditions." But where the hell was a family, a man, a woman, or a couple to be found with these characteristics? On paper, it was all there. At the same time, as if to justify the disastrous results, the lack of concordance between speech and reality, from morning to night we heard, read, and received instructions from our *Comandante en Jefe* to make our contribution, to be willing to sacrifice, to not be tempted by the "easy" way. Socialism and sacrifice, socialism and permanent scarcity or even lack, socialism and rationing, socialism and mobilization, socialism and resignation: With the passing of the years, they meant the same thing. The patience, endurance, and tolerance of the Cuban population, myself included, was admirable.

My children, who are learning about many experiences and many events of our life in Cuba by reading these pages, often ask me:

"Mom, how could you put up with all this for so long?"

I don't know what to say to them. Perhaps my common sense went awry; perhaps the dream of a different society overshadowed my reasoning. I had nothing to compare it to. I didn't know how much time was needed to effect change, the extent to which harmful traditions, backwardness, real and artificially-created complications were acceptable. For many years, the optimism, the hope of being able to contribute to change, and the confidence that thousands and thousands of Cubans gave me through their letters of thanks and their calls to the radio program cushioned the setbacks and difficulties. They kept pushing for me, giving me renewed strength.

"You're committing suicide," some told me.

I didn't listen to them. Yet.

CHAPTER THIRTY

THE NATIONAL SEX EDUCATION WORKING GROUP

During the second national congress of the Federation of Cuban Women, held in 1974, the issues of the family and the young couple were widely debated. The obstacles that prevented the realization of equality for women were analyzed, and resolutions were passed to specifically demand the implementation of a sex education program. The Plan of Action approved in 1975 by the U.N. World Conference of the International Women's Year was assumed by Cuba as the basis for sex education. To fulfill these objectives and formal commitments, and to provide help and an institutional boost to the development of the national sex education program that we were developing, the National Sex Education Work Group (GNTES) was founded in 1977. *La Presidenta* entrusted me with the position of coordinator and scientific collaborator, and later director, of GNTES.

It was extraordinary luck that GNTES was organized at a high level of the government. Formally, GNTES was attached to the National Assembly of People's Power, but I reported directly to Vilma Espín Guillois, *la Presidenta*, the President of the Federation of Cuban Women, Raúl Castro's wife and the country's First Lady (in the absence of an official wife of Fidel Castro), a member of the Council of State and the Politburo of the Communist Party of Cuba. *La Presidenta* belonged to the

15. *Monika in her office at the National Sex Education Work Group (GNTES), Havana, late 1970s*

small circle of people who actually made the country's decisions. This opened the possibility for us—under the conditions of an authoritarian state—to overcome difficulties and pitfalls of the most diverse nature and not only to demand the participation of all the actors required by the national program but also to force them to participate constructively, even if they preferred to block us (as often happened, for example, with the Ministry of Education).

Our brief was to impart modern, scientifically-based sex education to the country. Our most urgent task was to tackle the problem of teenage pregnancy and its many negative consequences: girls dropping out of school, indiscriminate use of abortion as a contraceptive method, marriages between immature couples, and girls giving birth without being prepared for motherhood. Our ambitious goals were to prepare the new generations for love, a relationship as a couple, marriage, and the family; to enable individuals to develop a sexuality that contributed to their physical and mental well-being; to encourage sexuality based on full gender equality, mutual responsibility, and respect between the partners on the basis of mutual affection, caring, and love; and to promote society's acceptance and respect of an individual's sexual orientation.

Achieving these goals would require substantial changes in the attitudes and behaviors of the entire population—a gigantic, if not impossible, job. Even so, we launched the program with enthusiasm and idealism. We prioritized the systematic training of professionals; education in schools throughout the country; education through the mass media; the preparation and publication of specialized literature for professionals and popular science for the entire population; the manufacture and/or importation and distribution of contraceptives; the deployment of skills; and attempting to diminish the effect of institutions that blocked our work, in particular, as I've said, the Ministry of Education.

CHAPTER THIRTY-ONE

A PILOT PROGRAM IN THE BOARDING SCHOOLS

ONE OF THE FIRST MAJOR TASKS that we embraced was to carry out a pilot program of sex education in selected centers of secondary and pre-university education, all boarding schools. We wanted to demonstrate the need for this type of education and, above all, to show that students can talk about sex as long as they are told the truth, are taken seriously, and their desire to know about sex is satisfied. They also, of course, needed to receive help in solving their sex- and sexuality-related problems. But a mountain of obstacles stood in our way.

In 1979, Dr. Lajonchere and I drew up a rough draft of a series of lectures to be given in the target schools. A commission of experts carefully selected by the top management of the Ministry of Education (MINED) had to analyze the content of these lectures and ensure that they were aligned with established policy. The attitude of the MINED representatives can be summed up in three words: fear, ignorance, and prudery. They would have given anything to abolish the sexuality of all students in the national education system. They would have awarded us the medal of honor of the Republic of Cuba (which doesn't exist, but they would have created it for these purposes) if we had invented a vaccine against sexuality.

The head of the pedagogical team, a mother of two children—we wondered how she came to have them, since it was hard to believe that so much modesty and prudery could exist in one person (we called her "Sister Margarita")—destroyed our lectures. She prepared her texts herself, which had nothing in the way of guidance, and the word "sexuality" was banished from her lips. Her "lectures" filled pages and more pages, a catechism built around terminology from the official Marxist-Leninist dictionary. They were, in short, tedious harangues that put everyone to sleep. She read us her texts in an angelic, soft, sweet voice. Without once having to resort to my vivid fantasies, I imagined her with the halo of Saint Margaret, giving a lecture on sex education without sex, directing pleading glances toward heaven, as if the help required to carry out her evangelical mission—to exterminate the demons in every boy and girl in the country—came from above. Sister Margarita spent great time and energy on her conviction that her sermons could bring light to the minds of the lost sheep.

Dr. Lajonchere and I had to summon all our patience and remind ourselves to be polite, not to laugh or fall asleep during these tedious, totally ineffective lectures. I could never accept Sister Margarita's attitude and position, but I have to admit that the poor thing found herself at an impasse: MINED had imposed conditions on her. Her prudishness, her acceptance of *machismo*, and her condition as an obedient woman with no opinion of her own helped her bear this burden. Or maybe she didn't feel this "mission impossible" as a burden at all.

After months of debates, the development of new texts, corrections, and approval of the final versions, we began to give the first cycle of lectures in a vocational school, a teacher training school, a school for educators in daycare centers, and a pre-university center, all located in Havana Province. Not surprisingly, the students awaited us with great expectation and the teachers, with great suspicion. Boys and girls in the eleventh grade and those in the third year of teacher training had been designated to participate—that is, adolescents about fifteen to sixteen years old. In each of these schools, a mailbox was installed so that students could deposit their questions. On the day of the lecture, I would open the mailbox, take out the letters, and answer them during the discussion.

This system never worked well. We realized that on several occasions the teachers, in order to satisfy their curiosity and not lose control, took the letters from the mailbox to read and delivered them to us later, which was a violation of the agreement and, of course, was not accepted by the students, for good reason. They gladly accepted my proposal to write down their concerns on small pieces of paper that I gave them before starting the formal activity, without having to reveal their identity to us. To save time and make it easier for the lecturers to answer the questions, I classified them by topic, as many were the same but with different words. The first lecture dealt with the ethical and moral aspects of sexuality, preparation for marriage and family, male-female equality, and the responsibility of a couple.

MINED had placed the responsibility of teaching this topic on a professor of Marxism-Leninism, who was inhibited, timid, and dogmatic. Even Sister Margarita was worried, because her colleague never took his nose out of his notes, reading them in a droning, monotonous voice. The poor man became a victim of the boys, and how they abused him! They endured his sermon but from time to time someone would insert a joke, which made the other boys burst out laughing and forced the lecturer to look at them. Then they would fall silent, staring at him quizzically, as if to ask why he had interrupted his speech. All these acts of sabotage increased the professor's insecurity. Sweat ran down his face, dampening his shirt, and his voice was failing him. Frankly, we were filled with anguish to see this painful spectacle.

After the reading, he announced to the boys that the discussion would begin, and there the catastrophe was unleashed. Especially the students in the vocational school—brainy little geniuses, some with a tremendous load of mischief and the spontaneity and audacity of kids who think they know everything—cornered the philosopher. They peppered him with questions, and he, like a slippery eel, tried to answer them without coming to the point. His answers satisfied no one, because they were collections of empty words, a boring continuation of his dull lecture. The boys enjoyed watching him fumble. The final thrust was given by a boy who decided to see whether the teacher was able, to the slightest degree, to "talk straight." Could he give a direct answer to the simplest question? So the student asked:

"My friends and I are eager to know the precise rules of the game. Please tell us, short and sweet: can we do it or not?"

Obviously, he was referring to having sex. The philosophy professor turned as red as a ripe tomato and stuttered:

"Well, look, you must know that ..."

"Yes or no?" interrupted the young man.

We had a hard time restoring order because the laughter, the screaming, and the rain of comments had turned the discussion into a comedy show for the boys, but one that was unbearable and outrageous for the teacher.

The philosophy professor stopped taking part in the lectures. He informed us that he was very sorry, but he had to dedicate himself to finishing an urgent project. It was fortunate that he gave up, because more confrontations with the young people would have unhinged him. This experience showed us that inhibited people, for whom sexuality is a forbidden subject synonymous with indecency and debauchery, weren't suitable for sex education; on the contrary, they could cause harm. It also showed us that the professionals in charge of this work had to demonstrate a number of very specific characteristics; they couldn't be selected simply because they were loyal and obedient to MINED.

From now on we ourselves would choose lecturers suitable for this work, reputable professionals whose personal conduct conformed to the ethical and moral principles at the foundation of our work. At the same time, they should have a positive attitude towards sexuality, free of prejudices, inhibitions, taboos, hypocrisy, and *machismo*. Furthermore, they should know from the beginning that this work required a great deal of sacrifice, that we wouldn't allow pretentiousness or arrogance, and that no reward could be expected. They should have a high tolerance for frustration and disappointment. Some became true pillars of sex education; others couldn't overcome their limitations and left the project. Unfortunately, we also had to exclude more than one person from the team because we couldn't accept or tolerate arrogant and opportunistic attitudes and behaviors.

Over the course of a year we gave almost a hundred lectures. On each occasion, the participants would be waiting for us in a packed auditorium. Many students, finding all the seats full, would sit on the steps or stand. Some would sneak in because they didn't want to miss this opportunity, and many complained because they considered it unfair that their class was not on the list.

"If you have a free period now, you can come in. We don't want to discriminate against anyone, nor did we make the selection. Anyone who wants to participate should do so," we assured them.

Most of the teachers in the schools where we offered our lectures didn't participate. Obviously, they didn't want to look bad. As sex educators, they were against the wall. The only recourse they had had before now was the usual: countless prohibitions, which didn't solve the existing problems. With this new program, they were unmasked, and embarrassed; they fled so as not to have to show their faces. Others, dying to know what the lecturers would tell their devilish pupils, stayed, but with their hands on the doorknob so they could make a quick escape if they felt they needed to. Usually by the time we opened the discussion to the students, no teachers would be in the venue. The boys, however, had no qualms about discrediting their teachers. It was clear they didn't trust them when it came to sexual problems.

Beginning with the first lecture, I kept notes on anything and everything that could help to update the educational authorities on the situation in their centers: They could learn to communicate to adolescents of all ages through direct contact. They could gain their trust and thus be able to correct, complete, and improve the lectures by having a brief overview of the students' sexual knowledge, attitudes, and behaviors. My written minutes, full of questions, problems raised, doubts, complaints, and requests for help, both collective and individual, constituted a rich source of information that allowed us to carry out our work much more effectively. We could develop teaching programs with content adjusted to real needs and carry out sociological research for a bibliography that could be used by professionals and ordinary citizens alike.

The highest authorities of MINED didn't give too much importance to the overwhelming, indeed worrying, results that I presented to them after the pilot program ended. In my final report to the leaders, I emphasized these aspects: the pedagogical principle of co-education applied only in the classroom and in the productive work in the field. Invariably, we found that the boys delegated cleaning tasks to the girls, and the girls did the laundry while the boys relaxed, chatted, or entertained themselves. They didn't even carry the buckets of water for the girls.

The girls assured us that they—because they were girls—had to fulfill this responsibility, that they had to be available to the boys. It was a question of destiny, a given, a natural law, that woman was born to serve man. For them, speeches about equality were pure fantasy; the principle itself was limited to the right to be in the classroom with the boys, to have vocational training, or to work outside the home, but nothing more.

"A girl who respects herself and wants to start a relationship with a boy she likes, asks him: 'Do you want me to wash your clothes?' so he knows she's interested in him. If he likes her, he hands her his bundle of dirty clothes, and everyone knows then that they're a couple."

As they themselves told us, the girls who didn't abide by these rules of the game were "useless," "bad," or in the worst case, "dykes."

When we discussed the subject of contraceptives and family planning, the men, in droves, would leave the amphitheater. We would ask them to come back. They would tell us:

"This lecture has nothing to do with us. Men can't get pregnant.

Contraceptive measures are up to them, the women. They have to take care of themselves. We're not going to take pills or wear a condom, or anything like that."

What about their macho attitude of considering themselves not only authorized, but required by teachers and parents to use women as objects to satisfy themselves? They assured us that the man has to prove his manhood; he has to practice in order to know what to do at the moment of truth.

"Practice is the test of truth: this is a Marxist-Leninist principle, isn't it?"

They spoke to us with the gestures of those who are owners of the absolute truth. The girls themselves would tell us that males had greater sexual needs.

"If they don't have sex, they get sick, and we girls have to give them proof of our love."

The boys topped it off by saying:

"I need a different girl for every day of the week, but when I get married, my wife has to be a virgin. She has to be new, right out of the package, wrapped in tissue paper."

"My wife, used? No, man, where do we go if we accept that? I don't buy used shoes: I buy new ones. It's the same thing."

My alarming stories caused amusement and laughter among the senior officials in the Ministry of Education. I was angry and outraged over the submissiveness, the acceptance of discrimination against girls, the thinking that it was a woman's duty to wash clothes, to care for and take care of men, which was not only tolerated by teachers of all the classes and schools we visited but was even encouraged by many. They found our reaction exaggerated and made comments like, "But Mónica, the girls like to spoil the boys; they like to wash their clothes. Let them do it; they're not doing anything wrong."

At times like these, I frankly questioned the true intentions and the very ability of the Ministry of Education to educate Cuban youth. I felt I was facing an impassable wall. And like a small child covering her eyes to avoid seeing something horrible, I kept trying to diminish the wall. I had the persistence and patience of the lost optimist who harbors the vain hope that someday things will change.

In the following years, the sex education program in schools was extended and refined throughout the country. The backward attitude and ingrained *machismo* that we observed in the pilot program continued to prevail, however, showing that tradition and morals don't change overnight.

PART FOUR
THE EIGHTIES

CHAPTER THIRTY-TWO

BOOKS ON SEXUALITY HIT THE MARK

OBTAINING AND DISSEMINATING information on sexuality turned out to be a critical task, since Cuba was a desert in that regard. We were urged to supply modern, specialized literature to professionals, the future disseminators of sex education and counseling, and we were also urged to offer popular scientific literature for those who didn't dare approach the subject. We wanted to reach the entire population, the old as well as the young. The preparation and publication of scientific and popular-scientific works became, for years, one of my most important activities, to which I dedicated a large part of my energy.

In 1979, as I have mentioned, we translated, adapted, and edited *Man and Woman in Intimacy*, by Dr. Siegfried Schnabl. This book was intended for specialists and students in the last semesters of their studies in medicine, psychology, and sociology. The first edition of this scientific treasure underwent significant censorship that we could do nothing to prevent: the chapter on homosexuality was deleted.

After Dr. Lajonchere and I reviewed the final version of the text, as well as the drawings and illustrations, I was also charged with supervising the printing, where a different problem would crop up every day. Dr. Lajonchere and I often went to the printer to follow the work. We would perch on a platform, in front of the roaring monster, the printing machine, wrapped in a cloud of corrosive fumes, shouting at the operator: "Give it more red ink, a little more yellow, the green didn't come out well, put in a little more blue," until, after the tenth time the proportions and contents were adjusted, we obtained a somewhat acceptable result. The operators in charge of printing the text consulted us sheet by sheet to avoid making errors.

We learned that after finishing each chapter, the operators would meet in small groups to discuss the content. The next day, when we were reviewing the sheets again, they would consult us about aspects that they didn't understand or that caused them doubts. These spontaneous "study circles" were, without a doubt, one of the most interesting, stimulating, and fruitful sex education exercises in my entire career. In all the printing houses, in the workshops, even among the top management of the Cuban Book Institute, we always found an atmosphere and a work climate of formidable collaboration in the printing of this and subsequent books. It was a pleasure to work like this; it made us forget the countless daily difficulties, such as the lack of paper and ink and fact that the ancient machines were unable to reproduce illustrations with the required clarity.

The demand for *Man and Woman in Intimacy* was so enormous that coupons were required to purchase the first edition. At the beginning of the distribution, we would constantly receive calls of protest from people who questioned the privilege of those who had been chosen to purchase the book. Several pallets of books that had just been bound disappeared from the printer, and some galley proofs vanished. I received an anonymous phone call:

"Monica, your book is being sold for ten pesos in Havana's Central Park. But it's not worth going there—you'd be late, because they're selling like hot cakes and are being ripped out of the hands of the sellers."

Fortunately, a second edition was produced years later, reaching a total of 150,000 copies. With the second, revised and updated, edition, we also managed to circumvent the censorship. We handed over the manuscript without giving the detractors time to mutilate it, and so it happened that for the first time in Cuban history, a book was published dealing in very broad terms and with a scandalously modern approach with the subject of homosexuality, which had been censored in the first edition, exposing the baselessness and backwardness of the official discourse advocating discrimination against and condemnation of homosexuals. We had taken an important step toward promoting a humanistic, scientific, and civilized approach to homosexuality, although the censorship on this issue continued for several more years.

In 1980 we began to prepare a new publication: *Are you Now Thinking about Love?* by Dr. Heinrich Brückner, also a German. This was a popular-scientific work aimed at adolescents. To obtain authorization to print this book, which dealt broadly and in detail with the topics of interest to this population group, we needed the approval of "experts" from the Central Committee of the Communist Party, the Ministries of Public Health, Education, and Culture, the Union of Young Communists, and the National Assembly of People's Power. This inquisition committee, with its prudishness, inhibitions, prejudices, and fear of having to decide on a subject that they considered controversial, forced us time and again to make modifications, and to remove and substitute one text for another.

Given this process, the publication took much longer than should have been necessary. To research the effect that photos of childbirth and naked boys and girls would have on adolescents and adult readers, I conducted an experiment, using people of different ages as my test group. The photos of the naked adolescents—taken from the original book—were classified as pornographic by those over thirty. The older participants condemned them, with comments such as: "How horrible!" "And this is what you call teaching photos?" "How immoral!" The series of childbirth photos caused even greater revulsion.

In 1982 the book came out. Two nude photos, one of each sex, managed to survive the censorship, but not the childbirth photos. Even so, we were happy with the result, as the text was published with little mutilation. In numerous letters to the publishing house, readers expressed satisfaction and joy that such a comprehensive book, so full of information for adolescents, had finally been published. One young man, happy to have the book, wrote to us: "My eight-year-old nephew came running to the house screaming that they were selling pornography in the bookstore. I immediately ran there, and, indeed, I believed it was true. But when I held the book in my hands, when I looked through it and read it calmly, little by little, I realized what a wonderful book I had acquired. This book deals with all the aspects, absolutely all, that young people want to know and which have never been explained to us until now."

The 100,000 copies of the first edition of *Are you Now Thinking about Love?* sold out right away. In early 1983, another 150,000 copies were printed. Even so, many young people complained because they hadn't been able to get a copy. They requested a new edition. The *Juventud Rebelde* newspaper and the monthly magazine *Muchacha* published the book in chapters. The publication and sell-out of 250,000 copies of such a complex work in an underdeveloped country was a hitherto unknown event. This was followed by the preparation of *In Defense of Love*, by Dr. Schnabl, and *Mother, Father and I*, by Dr. Brückner, both published in 1983.

Mother, Father and I was geared toward preschool children. The book begins with the presentation of a young girl and boy, both naked together in the bathtub. A woman is lathering them. The book continues with the story and corresponding illustrations of the birth of a child and ends with the silhouettes of a naked man and woman whose aim is to teach the little users of the book what adults are like.

Faster than I could imagine, I received a negative response from the Ministry of Education: the publication was blocked. They argued that the book suggested topics to children that weren't suitable for them, that the illustrations were totally inappropriate. Finally, the direct and tenacious intervention of *la Presidenta* of the FMC allowed us to continue and finish the project.

Part of the adaptation of this and all the books involved redoing the photos and illustrations to correspond to Cuba and the Cuban society. The publishing house proposed several illustrators, one of whom we were immediately drawn to. Apart from some inaccuracies that required fixing, we really liked his illustrations. An example of a failed illustration was the drawing of a mother breastfeeding her baby; it had several errors. I took the illustrator to a nearby maternity hospital and asked a young mother to allow the illustrator to observe her while she was breastfeeding her baby. The mother, very willing and proud to serve as an example for a book, agreed. I asked the illustrator to pay attention to the position of the hand, especially the mother's fingers when she places the nipple in the child's mouth, and I explained in detail the reason for this position, which was what he hadn't drawn correctly. For the first time in his life and very astonished, the illustrator consciously observed this act. There are so many important things when it comes to breastfeeding. Care must be taken that the nipple is completely in the baby's mouth, that the mother places the baby on her arm in such a way that the baby can find it without pulling, that both are comfortable, and that the child can breathe freely while it suckles.

The new version of the drawing of a mother breastfeeding her child was not only correct but also beautiful. The acceptance of *Mother, Father and I* was wonderful. And—miracle of miracles!—I even received a note with a positive and encouraging message from the Minister of Education herself. She excitedly told me that her little nephew had *Mother, Father and I* on his nightstand and didn't allow anyone to touch his treasure, except for his mother, who had to read a chapter from the book to him every night.

In 1986 I was invited by the University of Florida's College of Medicine, in Gainesville, to give a lecture on family planning in Cuba. My audience consisted primarily of professors and teaching staff from that university, as well as sociologists, psychologists, and anthropologists invited by their medical colleagues. A long discussion followed the lecture, demonstrating the participants' enormous interest in the subject, as is often the case when professionals from Cuba visit the U.S.

On the next day, I had until only about noon to snoop around the university library, always looking for new literature titles that might be useful to us. They told me that the director of the anthropology department wanted to talk to me, that he was waiting for me in his office. The professor showed me a book and said:

"It's hot off the press; they gave it to me this morning. I know you're looking for books for your national sex education program. It's a gift!"

It was Masters and Johnson's book *On Sex and Human Loving*. It was the most comprehensive book ever written on human sexuality. The authors were world-class sexologists, and their book was an invaluable source of information, also very objective and easy to read. A few weeks later I found out that Masters, Johnson, and Kolodny's *Textbook of Sexual Medicine*, the 1986 revised edition, had also just been published in Spain. I asked an acquaintance at the Cuban Embassy in Spain to send me a copy.

I proposed that these two works be published in Cuba. To our great amazement, decision-makers endorsed their immediate printing without any censorship. Obviously, by 1986 we had reached a certain degree of maturity on the subject. Both books, *Textbook of Sexual Medicine* and *On Sex and Human Loving*, were published in 1987, with a printing of 50,000 copies each. These wonderful works were the most up-to-date and scientifically-based material at the moment, and we made them available to doctors and medical students.

CHAPTER THIRTY-THREE
MÓNICA, QUEEN OF CONDOMS

THE INTERNATIONAL PLANNED PARENTHOOD FEDERATION (IPPF) was for many years the only international institution that supported the Cuban program for women's reproductive health. The effect of the U.S. embargo against Cuba, especially in the 1960s and 1970s, limited the possibilities of obtaining the necessary equipment for family planning clinics, even though the U.S. was only a half-hour flight away. The IPPF used diverse tactics to supply us with the most essential materials for our work. The officials, on their trips to Cuba, frequently carried in as personal luggage a suitcase full of intrauterine devices, surgical instruments, and other valuable things that allowed us to continue working. These items were distributed throughout the country until they were depleted.

The IPPF informed us of its intention to support the national sex education program and of its willingness to cooperate with us. I was sent to London to present our program to IPPF officials and to negotiate the details of the possible cooperation. Before leaving for London, I met in Havana with the head of family planning in the Ministry of Public Health, who was the coordinator in Cuba for cooperation with the IPPF. He was the one who managed the IPPF budget for Cuba (about $100,000 a year at that time); he approved or rejected the purchase of any contraceptives through the IPPF. I set out to convince this colleague to agree to order high-quality condoms from the IPPF, in order to improve and update our family planning. Scared, indignant, and insulted, he responded:

"You're crazy, totally crazy! No preservatives! (He shied away from the word *condom*). I won't spend a *centavo*, not a single cent! You know perfectly well that no Cuban will use those things. We have millions of them in drugstores, rotting in the tropical sun in shop windows. Our kids use them as balloons at birthday parties, but no one uses them for birth control. Mónica, please, don't be ridiculous."

Indeed, all the country's pharmacies offered Chinese condoms of poor quality, made of rough and porous rubber, without lubricant. Their acceptance among the population was nil.

"The millions of condoms (I said this terrible word, and my colleague made a face as if he wanted to vomit) that are rotting in pharmacies are actually rubbish. They're not condoms; they're sticky pieces of rubber. Furthermore, they're stored in totally inappropriate conditions. They can't even be inflated on birthdays because they're porous."

"They've rotted because nobody wants to use them!"

"Not true. People don't use them because they're garbage. I ask you, be reasonable. You know that there are very good quality condoms, and you also know that people would accept them if we had them here in Cuba."

"Mónica, this is my irrevocable decision: not a single cent of the IPPF budget will go toward the purchase of preservatives. This product will not be in Cuba! I maintain my position: NOOOO!"

A few days before leaving for London, I had to brief *la Presidenta* about the status of our project and the preparatory work for the meeting with the IPPF. I mentioned the condom discussion to her and asked for her support. I considered it extremely important that condoms be distributed and made available, especially to young people who frequently change partners. *La Presidenta* agreed with me.

"But I don't have a single cent for that," I said. "The coordinator in the Ministry of Public Health won't allow even a symbolic sum to be diverted for this purpose."

"Don't worry. I'm sure I'll be able to convince the Minister of the need for this investment," was *la Presidenta's* firm expression of support.

In London, our national sex education program not only was of great interest but also won the approval of the IPPF. Among other concrete cooperation agreements, we agreed that the institution would send us quality condoms for our sex education program. I was happy with the result, but not entirely happy about having had to score this success by abusing my power and circumventing the opposition of my colleague from the Ministry of Public Health.

Weeks after my return to Havana, the Vice Minister of Public Health, who was also in charge of the distribution of medical products, called me one day and yelled at me on the phone:

"Mónica, get yourself a truck and pick up *your condoms*, as soon as possible. But make sure you find a big truck, because there are ten pallets; in total there are several million of them."

"What are you talking about?"

"Yes, *your condoms*! The IPPF sent you ten pallets of condoms from London. *They're yours!*"

"Please don't say that. Of course they're not mine. They must be distributed throughout the country as soon as possible. And I ask you to pay attention when they are sent to the provinces. They must be kept in a cool and dry place, and we must ensure that all pharmacies in the country receive a reasonable amount and don't put them in the sun!"

"Mónica, I clearly told you that these are *your* condoms. I'm not going to distribute them; they don't belong to the Ministry of Public Health; they belong to you. Before the day after tomorrow they must have disappeared from the warehouse. I don't have space to store them, so do me a favor and pick them up; if not, we'll throw them away."

I had no choice but to order the cargo to be transferred to the

GNTES headquarters, a large house in El Vedado. We set up a conference room about thirty feet long and twenty feet wide with air conditioning, and we filled it with the pallets of condoms. All the seminars, lectures, and other educational activities that were to take place at this site during the next few weeks would have to be held on the terrace, until the ten pallets were distributed to all the provinces in the country.

All of this happened one day before New Year's. I had an idea. I found some sheets of wrapping paper. My collaborators and I packed several dozen boxes, each box containing one hundred condoms, and each one hermetically wrapped in a packet with lubricant. They looked like blue pillows, with a heart painted in the middle. We loaded up our gift packages and went to the central OB/GYN clinic near the GNTES headquarters. On the second floor, I met the head of the clinic, who was changing shifts with a colleague. Around them stood a large group of nurses, students, and interns.

"May we disturb you for a moment? My colleagues and I are from the National Sex Education Working Group, and we want to wish you a Happy New Year. We have a small gift for each of you that we hope will contribute to many happy hours."

The head doctor received the first package. He glanced at it, full of mistrust, and then at me, without an iota of confidence. He had no idea what might be inside.

"Thank you, very nice of you to give me a New Year's gift," he said.

"With pleasure. Why don't you open it?"

He suspected that it was a trick of some sort and didn't want anything to do with the package. His colleagues kindly asked him to open it. He carefully removed the wrapping paper and held a very attractive and decorated box in his hands. There were blue hearts with silver arrows painted on the package and a phrase printed in nice big letters: "Only with me will love be perfect!"

As if asking for help, the doctor looked at me.

"Mónica, what does this mean? What is this?"

"You don't have to be afraid of a cardboard box. Open it and you'll see what's inside!"

At last he brought out from its extraordinarily delicate, fine, even beautiful, wrapping something that resembled a miniature pillow. He held it with the thumb and index finger of his right hand: a finely textured condom, delicately lubricated. The doctor was furious; he felt we were making fun of him. Putting on a serious face, he placed the box on the table and prepared to leave. I cut him off.

"Please, don't be a spoilsport. Stay and listen to what I have to say!"

The director felt insecure, and I admit to having acted a bit indelicately when starting this show. I never, ever wanted to provoke the head doctor's displeasure. In the end, he became my faithful ally and an excellent specialist who deserved all my respect. But now, it was too late for a retreat. Addressing the group, I removed another packet from the box, opened it, took it out of the wrapping, unrolled it, and showed it to the participants.

"Check it out! I bet you've never seen anything like it. They're high-quality condoms! They're super resistant and ultra-thin at the same time, made in Sweden with the latest technology. Each one has been electronically tested to rule out the smallest defect. They're lubricated, and each one is packaged in an airtight packet. We've never seen condoms like this in Cuba."

Nervous laughter, explosive laughter, and protests.

"Well, Monica, I don't need them," said the director, and he began to leave.

"Okay, but if you happen to change your mind, no problem. I'll save you some boxes," I replied.

I had caused a real riot, a great uproar. My colleagues forgot that they were in a hospital, and we began to distribute our gifts. Some made faces as if they were holding a box of filth. However, most were curious and took the boxes home. A few days later a wave of requests began. The hospital dermatologist demanded a whole palette for her special area of venereal diseases, because for the first time since the beginning of her career, she saw the possibility of achieving the definitive cure of her patients with gonorrhea, protecting them from reinfections by using quality condoms.

Word spread across the island, and in just a few weeks all the pallets had been distributed. Reactions were unexpectedly positive, because it was a premium product, and the doctors who ordered them did an excellent job of outreach. As a result of this success, the Ministry of Public Health decided to import reasonable quantities of these condoms, so that all over Cuba, quality condoms suddenly became available in pharmacies.

This ideal state of affairs lasted only about two years; then the importation and distribution of condoms became irregular, as happened with all products in Cuba. But the effective blow had been dealt. The condom, which in Cuba until then had been unanimously and irrationally rejected, came to enjoy wide acceptance.

And with this act, I earned the nickname "*Mónica, La Reina del Condón*; Mónica, Queen of Condoms."

CHAPTER THIRTY-FOUR
STAR OF RADIO AND TELEVISION

A VERITABLE TIDAL WAVE of sex education flooded the island in the 1980s. Everyone wanted to participate, and sex education was all the rage. Newspapers and magazines held competitions to see who best informed, instructed, and educated Cubans about sexual matters. Radio and television followed.

After lengthy negotiations, the President of Cuban National Television approved our proposal to do an educational series on contraceptive means and methods. They also accepted me as the instructor who would elaborate on the subjects. A group of young amateur actors received permission to collaborate with me. Everyone wanted to be a part of this series; there was tremendous enthusiasm. They knew that by putting these issues out front, there would be answers to many questions that until then no one had even asked.

Unfortunately, neither the cameramen assigned to the program nor the director that had been chosen were the least bit interested. On the contrary, working with me on this matter was a burden, which they had to comply with grudgingly. Their prejudices and ignorance, which often bordered on the grotesque, were for me and my young collaborators a sometimes unbearable test of stamina.

Filming the first episode took forever, and was, to my mind, a disaster. The director insisted on his absurd idea that the most appropriate setting for our series would be beautiful parks, bucolic landscapes, and historic buildings. Pure kitsch, as if we were producing music videos. I protested, but my protest had no effect. Thus, the filming of the vaginal ring, an intrauterine device, began in a rowboat in a pond on the outskirts of Havana.

The young actors sat with me in one boat and the camera crew and director were in another one that followed us. The sun beat down on us relentlessly, and we had to constantly swat away the clouds of mosquitoes. In that situation, it was hard to talk about the effectiveness of the ring and how it is used. I didn't have the space to set up my illustrations and mock-ups, my plaster models, the many pictures, and also the samples of the various types of IUDs that exist. To top it all off, we were constantly interrupted by the infernal noise of low-flying MIG fighters, as the location chosen by the director was close to the San Antonio de los Baños military base.

After a wasted day, with a hundred mosquito bites on my legs, arms, neck, and face, and with no useful footage, I was able to twist the director's arm, and he gave in to my insistence that we film in my office. My office was quite nice, with enough space to put up my illustrative materials, and there was no noise, MIGS, or mosquitoes. The next morning we began rehearsals there. Everything went wonderfully well, and in less than an hour we had completely filmed the chapter on the vaginal ring. For the chapter on the pill, the director had chosen a wonderful park with royal palms, hibiscus bushes blooming in beautiful colors, antique garden furniture, and the ruins of an old farm. My arguments in favor of filming in my office, saving resources, and avoiding unnecessary journeys, were ignored.

I said I needed two girls for the filming. They were supposed to ask me the most frequent questions that thousands of young people asked us in the programs, in national surveys, and in relevant research. My role was to answer the questions. One of the girls froze. She was speechless when she had to ask me a question.

We had to interrupt and start over several times, until she finally asked to speak to me alone.

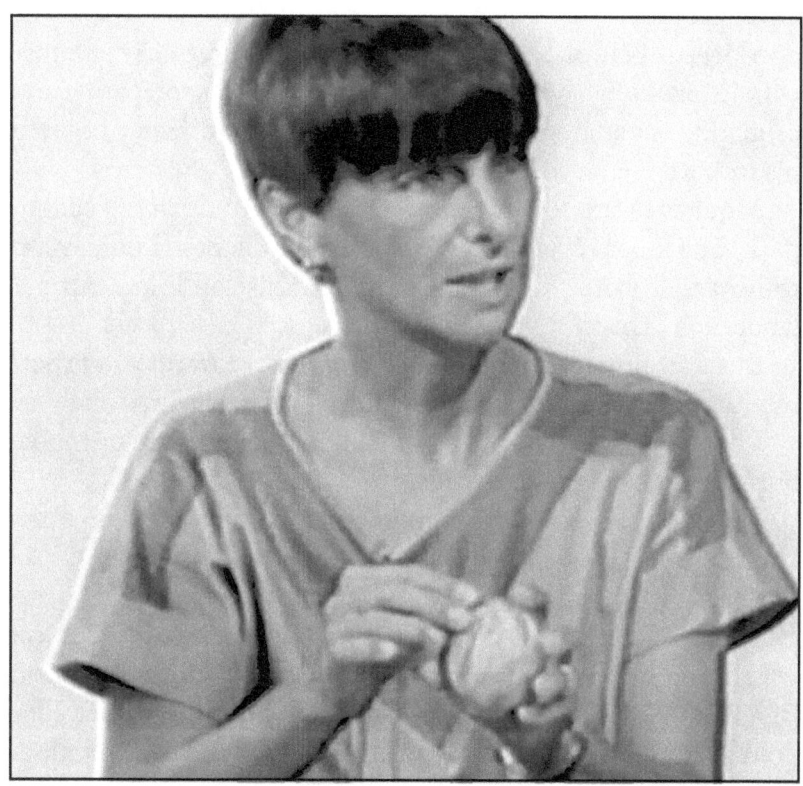

16. *Monika on Cuban TV demonstrating the diaphragm*

"Mónica, I can't, I just can't. I keep thinking about my mom, who doesn't miss a television program I'm acting in. I'd be looking for trouble. What if my mother sees me when I ask you about the pill? That would be horrible. What will her conclusion be? She'll think, *If my daughter is asking the doctor about the pill, it's because my daughter is taking the pill. She's doing it, and we have to find out on television!*"

I released the girl from her commitment to act in this episode, and we finished filming. The really curious thing was that she had no qualms about participating in the filming about the IUD and the diaphragm.

We concluded the series on contraceptive means and methods with the thorniest issue: the condom. The director and I reached a compromise: We wouldn't film in my office or in a park on the outskirts of Havana. We would film on the terrace of my house, with its plants, bushes, and flowers. I was finishing preparing and arranging my material on the table when the director pointed his index finger at me and said very seriously:

"Mónica, I want to tell you one thing: the word *condom* cannot pass your lips. During the filming of this chapter I don't want to hear that word. If you don't agree to this condition, our collaboration is over."

"But the subject is precisely the condom. How do you expect me to explain it if you forbid me to call it by its name?"

"I don't care, it's your problem. Call it a preservative or rubber, but the word *condom* is forbidden."

Reluctantly, I accepted the imposed condition. I had no other choice.

I began my presentation by pulling a condom out of its wrapper. As I unrolled it, I was describing the texture of the object, explaining that it was made of very fine latex and was covered in a thin layer of odorless lubricant. I asked the assistant cameraman to fill it with water from a watering can. The condom I was presenting with so much praise kept growing as it filled with water. Everything was going as planned, when suddenly the assistant interrupted:

"Cut! Turn off the camera. Sorry, but I can't show my hands. There are people who might recognize me by my hands, and I don't want to have anything to do with this show, nothing, but absolutely nothing. I will gladly pour water into that thing, but my hands have to stay out."

And yes, we finally shot this scene again, being careful not to show the assistant's hands.

The complete series on contraceptive means and methods was broadcast twice on Cuban television during 1986. The broadcast schedule guaranteed a maximum number of viewers: on Sundays, late morning, and not during the season when people went to the beach.

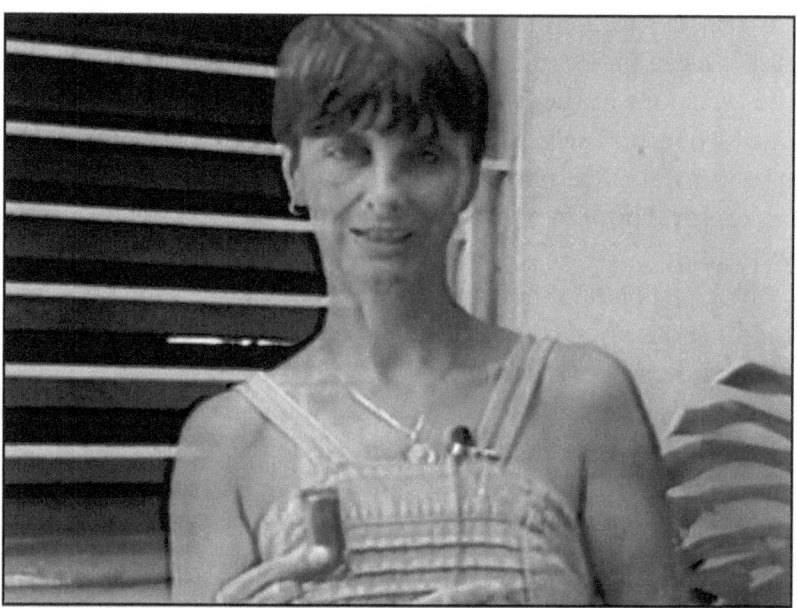

17. *Monika on Cuban TV advocating condom usage*

The public reacted with an avalanche of letters to our center, to the radio and television stations, and to the country's newspapers and magazines, not to mention with countless telephone calls. We received many expressions of approval, but also of disapproval. Some people, including some at the top level of leadership in the country, believed that the chapter on the condom was terribly shameful, that a decent Cuban woman would never dare speak about *that thing*, much less touch it, and that I was a threat to Cuban morals.

My title of honor, "Mónica, Queen of Condoms," received a new layer of varnish with the program, throughout Cuba and in a lasting way.

After the successful television series, one of the most popular radio stations in Cuba, *Radio Rebelde*, offered me the opportunity to present a weekly two-hour program on sexuality. Dozens of letters from the public expressing a desire for a program with this content had showed the station's director that there was a need for this type of program. I readily agreed, and I presented my concept to the program director. I wanted to do a live and direct radio program, and so did he. He would start by reading the questions in the listeners' letters, and I would answer them one by one, precisely. Then I would invite the audience to ask me questions over the phone, which I would answer spontaneously.

Approval by *la Presidenta* was pending. Her reaction was overwhelming:

"No! Responding spontaneously, live and direct, is too risky. You might suddenly start to stutter, or you might not know what to answer. No, and I repeat, no!"

The program director and I agreed on a format that attempted to comply with my boss's order, while maintaining a certain spontaneity. We decided to give the audience the possibility of phoning in with topics of interest. I'd take notes, and after a short pause to prepare, I'd cover the subjects on the air. Thus, as ordered by *la Presidenta*, I wouldn't be directly answering questions.

The weekly show quickly reached a large audience. When the telephone line was opened for listeners' questions, they would call in non-stop from all corners of the country. At first, the callers were mostly young women with questions about contraception. They were also interested in treatments for the genital-tract infections that abounded in Cuba. There were also questions about problems related to pregnancy, childbirth, and menopause. Soon men also began to call in with their questions. The center of interest shifted to conflicts in a couple's relationship. There was an enormous deficit of up-to-date information on the sexual response of men and women, standards of conduct, each partner's rights and duties, and the ethical and moral aspects of sexuality.

There were opponents who constantly presented their complaints to the higher authorities about the "indecent issues that Mónica discusses on the radio." *La Presidenta* called me in to tell me. The meeting made me feel I was on trial.

"I've received complaints about the program," she said. "They say you're talking about indecent things on the radio; for example, that you speak in great detail about masturbation."

"It's true that I've talked about masturbation because I've received many questions about it. It seems wonderful to me that people are overcoming their inhibitions and asking about what interests them."

La Presidenta repeated her concerns but then implied that the reaction of the audience was tremendous, that the program has already become an institution. She wavered between approval and disapproval. I interpreted this indecision in my own way—in my favor, as a call to continue my program as it had been until now. And so I proceeded.

Six months or so after starting my radio program, I was given good news. In the annual analysis, when the audience's correspondence was evaluated and the most informative programs were selected—those with the largest audience, the most liked and appreciated—they informed me that my program on sexuality had been declared a "Star Program of Cuban radio."

My last program took place the very week of my return to Germany, in November of 1990.

CHAPTER THIRTY-FIVE

THE UNEXPECTED VISIT OF A WOUNDED MALE

A YOUNG MAN BURST INTO MY OFFICE ONE DAY, brandishing a book in one hand, as if it were some sort of disgusting weapon, while with the other he tried to hit me. Yelling insults, he kept swinging at me, and I didn't have much room to dodge the blows. With my back against the wall and his aggressive hand almost slapping my face, I managed to stop him.

"I can't believe you're seriously thinking about hitting a woman. Don't you think it's better if we talk like civilized people? I'm backed against the wall, dodging your fist, and if you knock me out, you're not going to feel good about punching a woman who weighs half what you do and can't defend herself. May I invite you to have a cup of coffee and tell me why you're so angry?"

The man looked at me dumbfounded, shook his head several times, and sat down, deflated, his chin touching his breastbone. I poured him coffee and left it for a little while until he recovered from the crisis that had caused him to lose his temper. Then, like an unstoppable torrent, with barely contained rage, frowning and clenching his jaws from the effort he made not to jump up again, a truly dramatic speech came out of his mouth:

"*Doctora*, you're guilty of the many divorces, the destruction of so many couples. It's your fault that women suddenly demand things from us that they didn't even know existed before the appearance of this cursed book. Look, I have a lot of experience. I've had many women, and now mine is on strike. She throws in my face that I'm like a rooster that rides a hen, humps her two or three times, and, after coming, gets down and goes to sleep. She says she feels nothing and that she also has the right to pleasure, like this shitty book says. She tells me I'm selfish and clumsy—yes, she called me clumsy!—and since then I haven't been able to get it up. It's dead; there's no way it will rise. No one can take this. You're to blame for turning me into an impotent wreck with my wife demanding something from me that I can't give her."

The man was destroyed. He was shaking and having trouble holding back his tears. I talked to him for a long time, and, miracle of miracles, he listened to me. We finished what started as an attempt to beat me up by his agreeing to begin therapy with one of my colleagues, a highly respected specialist in treating wounded males like the one seated before me in my office. My colleague kept me abreast of the encouraging developments in therapy. Luckily, this couple was saved. I say "luckily" because in many other cases all efforts were in vain.

An individual's conviction that men have sexual rights and women have the duty and obligation to satisfy men was, most of the time, more powerful than all attempts at therapy, which too often became a useless undertaking. In most cases, therapy wasn't even accepted as a real possibility for help. Many women also accepted the sexual demands of their husbands or partners as an authentic need and felt they had to satisfy them, even to the detriment of their own satisfaction—if the woman was even aware of the possibility of sexual enjoyment. I received calls and letters from women who reproached me for inventing things that didn't exist, such as equal sexual needs, orgasm, and fabulous sensations, arguing that all this was a fairytale, pure lurid fantasy.

Some even told me that these phenomena might exist in Germany, where people weren't ashamed, where men and women went to the beach together naked (outrageous!), but for decent Cuban women who had some self-respect, all this was unacceptable, and I should stop trying to turn them into animals. Others, however, felt very satisfied because, finally, not only was there written information available about all aspects of sexuality, but people were talking openly about issues that they had never dared to mention before, because "you don't talk about these things."

Uplifting gratitude. Condemnation to the most horrible hell. These were the extremes, the honey and the bile, the daily seasoning of my professional work for years. I can't complain of having led a boring and monotonous life in Cuba, quite the opposite.

CHAPTER THIRTY-SIX

MISADVENTURES OF THE BOYS IN BOARDING SCHOOLS

DANI FINISHED ELEMENTARY SCHOOL in July of 1978 with the best grades in his class. He earned a place in the Vladimir Ilyich Lenin Vocational School, which made him happy. Before starting his new life, no longer in his ordinary school in the Miramar garage but in the most coveted institution for Cubans who aspired to an exceptional education for their children, he was lucky enough to spend, with his brother, summer vacations with their German grandparents, aunts, and uncles. There they filled their bellies until their clothes got too tight.

The day before returning to Cuba, Dani dislocated his right elbow. He was going to be admitted to the hospital to put the joint back in place, and they had to give him general anesthesia. When we told the doctor that the child had to take a plane in less than twenty-four hours to cross the Atlantic, she told us to forget it, unless the child agreed that the intervention could be done without anesthesia, using only one local anesthetic. Dani was so eager to get out of the torture that already had him on the verge of despair that he replied:

"Go ahead. It couldn't hurt any more than it already does."

With hardly any local anesthesia, the doctor pulled his forearm and put the bone back in its place. He came out of this with his arm in a cast and permission to fly back to Havana. He then began his first year at the Lenin, leaving every afternoon to attend a physiotherapy program in an orthopedic hospital at the other end of the city. This made it easier for him to adapt to the military regime in his new school. But once the mobility in his arm was fully restored, the good life was over. Like all the other students, he lived in the dormitories all week, sharing with his new companions, in eighty-bed shelters, the total lack of privacy, affection, and love. They all developed a self-protective defense mechanism to help them withstand, hopefully without major damage, both the sometimes hostile relationships between students (the law of the jungle) and the often anti-pedagogical behavior of teachers who seriously believed in the possibility of producing the New Man in these monstrous factories, these experimental workshops in which human material was subjected to their Machiavellian methods. Once again, that old adage "the road to hell is paved with good intentions" was tested, and found to be true.

For Dani, the Lenin was a place of psychological torture. In a matter of weeks he lost weight so dramatically that he looked like a kid from a concentration camp. He learned the tricks that allowed him to eat twice at each meal, and he ate everything, including the weevils and larvae that often "enriched" the meals. When the only teacher capable of motivating him and making him feel good, the physics teacher, a well-prepared, affectionate, and sensitive young woman, moved to another educational center because she was pregnant, life in the Lenin became unbearable for Dani.

The departure of the revered teacher coincided with national events that deeply wounded Dani's sensitivity, events that today still give us chills: the exodus of thousands and thousands of Cubans through the Port of Mariel in 1980 and the state terror unleashed against them. Every day, relatives of Lenin students arrived to request their withdrawal, because the family had decided to leave Cuba by boat to Florida. When they would show up at the office to take away their children, nephews, or cousins, loudspeakers throughout the school would blare a call for an "act of repudiation." All, absolutely all, the usual activities of the school would immediately be interrupted while the act of repudiation was performed. This act consisted of calling the students together so that they, with their teachers, could yell at the "deserters" the most horrifying and denigrating things imaginable: "traitor, sell-out, worm, scum, lumpen." The "deserters" would be cornered and physically attacked, spat on, threatened with sticks, and then the vehicle in which they were leaving would be set upon and damaged. It was a truly deplorable Roman circus, an ignominious show, fired with irrational hatred, that always left both sides wounded in body and soul.

Children, teenagers, who until yesterday were excellent students, an example for their peers, friends at heart, today were declared despicable scum, enemies, and garbage, and this took place at the Vladimir Ilyich Lenin Vocational School, the most prestigious educational institution in the country, just as it took place throughout the entire island, for weeks. What difference was there between the witch hunts, the public burning of heretics at the time of the Inquisition, the pogroms of the Fascists, and these acts of repudiation at the Lenin school and throughout the country? And the same question could be asked about the Marches of the Fighting People, organized from east to west to reaffirm hatred towards others.

A brutal fanaticism spread throughout Cuba; rational thought was frozen. The brutality was not just permitted but actually organized and instigated from the top down. The open display of contempt for every human being who dared to think and act differently from the Party line had become the order of the day in Cuba. As a result of these humiliations and rampages, deep fissures formed in our faith and confidence in the Revolution's justice. And yet, once the hysteria subsided, life went on.

The Lenin was divided into six units, three for secondary school students and three for pre-university students. Each unit had its own dorms and educational buildings. The entire school, all six units, stretched for almost a mile. The director of Dani's unit never missed a chance to humiliate, degrade, and insult the students, and he developed a special animosity toward our son. The children called the director "Puss-in-Boots" because he wore military boots and had green eyes like a cat. He considered all children subversive elements, customary liars, and, true to his conviction, he punished them without taking the trouble to find out whether his suspicions were true or not. I will never forget the day I received a call from the school to pick up Dani and take him to the hospital. The doctor suspected that he had pneumonia, and the school infirmary didn't have the resources to treat him properly. On the way to the hospital where his great friend, Dr. Valladares, our family's pediatrician and his godfather, worked, he told me:

"Mom, I need to have the diagnosis confirmed. I need a good pneumonia to be able to stay home for at least a week. I can't stand having to see Puss-in-Boots' face. Every time I see him, I have an irresistible desire to kill him."

I was speechless; I didn't recognize my son. This affable, happy boy, a friend to all his little companions, a friend to animals, was harboring a killer instinct?

Another incident intensified the hatred that Dani developed toward the school. One Saturday, on the way home from the pickup point, Dani didn't speak. With his distant gaze, he seemed lost, in another world. He didn't take part in our conversation, and he didn't answer our questions. At home, alone with me, he told me what had happened: Rubén, a boy from his group and a good friend, was caught showing his penis to another boy in the bathroom. No one knew for sure whether the two boys were involved in homoerotic games or not. The fact is that a third student entered the bathroom, saw that the two were showing each other their genitals, and went down the hall screaming so loudly that you could hear it on the moon:

"Fags! I caught them with their hands in the cookie jar!"

In a matter of seconds, all the students in the unit had entered the dorm and gathered in front of the bathroom, threatening the boys with screams and sticks, a horrifying scandal. It was a miracle they didn't lynch the two surprised boys; luckily a teacher, alarmed by the screams, arrived and managed to get the two boys out, made them get dressed, and locked them in the office to protect them from the mob. Moments later, all four thousand students at the school gathered in front of the office, shouting with hatred.

"Fags, kill the fags!"

That same night—it was a Friday—the school administration decided on Rubén and Aníbal's immediate expulsion. They advised the parents to pick up their children from campus on Saturday morning, before the other students were sent to the pick-up point. When Rubén's father arrived to pick up his son, who was moving like a zombie, a convict condemned to be hanged and on his way to the place of execution, the students and teachers at the famous elite school formed a chorus of maddened animals that had cornered their prey, yelling at the boy:

"Faggot, get out! You fucking faggot, get out of this school!"

They pounded like frenzied beasts on the buses with their fists, spoons, key rings, and other metal objects, to the beat of their war song. For Rubén and his father, this demonstration of blind hatred, contempt, and condemnation was the most humiliating event they had ever endured. Father and son were devastated.

I proposed to Dani that he leave this deformed institution "of the noblest human values" and continue his pre-university studies in an ordinary institution. Dani gladly accepted. He himself had not brought this up to us because he didn't want to go through the shame of confessing his disappointment and total disillusionment. To this child, the pride of his beloved teacher and also of his parents, other relatives, neighbors, and friends; to this boy, who had felt so enormously happy at being selected to be part of the elite as a student at the Lenin school, to bring up that he wanted to leave seemed like a confession of failure, an insufficiency incompatible with the characteristics of a good student.

Thus, Dani continued his education in an ordinary pre-university institute in El Vedado. He managed to get on practically the last train, because a year later it was determined that all pre-university students in the country had to study in a center with a boarding school. He had three happy years, with new classmates who, unlike those in the vocational school, were true friends that he still maintains close contact with today, no matter what country they ended up in. He graduated from high school with flying colors, and having achieved that success, was given the opportunity to study mathematics in Germany. His dream, his dearest desire, was going to come true.

Dictys had the (bad) luck of being selected to go to the Ministry of the Interior's José Carlos Mariátegui Vocational School, which was located on the Isle of Youth, off the south coast of Cuba. The students would remain on campus for six weeks, then spend four days at home and return to the barracks. The remoteness and difficulty of going back and forth to the island and then getting to the school, which was located in the middle of a swampy area infested with mosquitoes, without a decent road or a bus or train line, turned the problems of life in the boarding school, already horrible in itself, into a real catastrophe.

This school was a ghoulish spawn of the most old-fashioned and anti-pedagogical minds of bureaucrats sitting on the top, air-conditioned floor of the Ministry of Education, in cahoots with senior Ministry of the Interior officials equally unconnected to reality. Calling that institution a "vocational school" was a joke. It was the center with the highest rate of teachers with health problems—mental health—in the entire system. None of them lasted long in that imprisonment before requesting a transfer to a school in Havana, after showing a medical certificate. Students who didn't withstand those inhuman conditions were ridiculed. They were branded as "lazy" and "weak" and were reminded that the combatants of the Sierra Maestra had sacrificed so that boys like them, the New Men of socialist Cuba, could have wonderful schools like this one, so they should stop "pussyfooting" and complaining.

The authorities in the Ministry of Education denied the existence of the great number of serious problems, regularly violating the most elementary norms of the physical and mental health of the students. For half a year the school was without water. Not in their wildest imagination could anyone who has not seen that disaster with his own eyes believe that some six hundred students and their teachers lived in this hell. A tanker truck filled a cistern twice a week. On these days, the boys could wash up a bit, and the dining room, which gave off such a smell of fermented peas and rancid fat that you wanted to vomit, would be at least partially mopped.

The toilets were sewers. In the toilet bowls, roasting over low heat, the foul-smelling human waste accumulated for days, weeks, and months. Thousands of fat black flies with bright green bellies banqueted on this disgusting mess. Nor were they in the least interrupted when some boy, impelled by the pressure in his gut, squatted on the bowl and dropped another turd on the accumulated shit. The flies, almost paralyzed from the heat and the fullness of their bellies, moved slowly, like drugged bugs.

Scabies, lice, and bacteria thrived, finding a breeding ground in this filthy center. At five in the afternoon, religiously, the walls of the classrooms, bedroom, dining room, and other premises would be covered with thick layers of mosquitoes. In the bedroom, at the boys' headboards, the walls were painted with the blood of their remains. Mosquito nets? There were none. Soap, detergent, disinfectant? None, or, in the neo-vocabulary of the Revolution, "they were missing." On one occasion the school was given insect repellent of the kind used by the border guard; any other type of repellent was ineffective.

It was only logical that dengue would also make its triumphal entry into this school. The *Aedes aegypti* mosquitoes, which transmitted this disease, felt at home in that dirty swamp, which offered unusual amounts of young human blood to guarantee not only their survival, but also a truly prosperous development. The Mariátegui mosquitoes must have been the happiest insects in the world. Dictys, like many other boys, was hit hard by dengue. There was no doctor at the school and the nurse couldn't cope with the multiple skin lesions caused by lice, scabies, and crabs without effective remedies, so she didn't realize that he was seriously ill. For days Dictys didn't eat. Instead of ingesting food, he filled his stomach with aspirin. The result was a bleeding stomach ulcer that allowed him to leave for a week to heal in a hospital in Havana.

This was a week of comfort for Dictys. It meant having water at all times, clean clothes, being able to sleep without battling swarms of mosquitoes, and being able to read without being criticized for preferring reading to rough games and "fighting for a chick," the entertainment par excellence of the alpha male students. Unfortunately, the week of unofficial vacation passed too quickly, and reluctantly, but with the disciplined Teutonic spirit that characterized our first-born, who underwent all the tests, torture, and punishments that were handed out in large amounts at his school, he returned convinced that there is no evil that lasts a hundred years, not even that horror called José Carlos Mariátegui Vocational School.

At each home leave, every six weeks, we parents received an "informative letter" from the school principal. The students had to return to the boarding school with the letter signed by the parents. In one of these letters, we were told the dire results of a test to measure the political knowledge of students. Practically no student knew the names of the members of the Politburo, nor of the ministers and other important figures of the Cuban Communist Party and the Cuban state. On the contrary, they did have extensive knowledge of musical groups in the u.s. and Western Europe. It was evident that the students were made of Teflon in the face of the perpetual drip-drip-drip of indoctrination they received all day through the campus audio system. The sermons went in one ear and out the other.

The school administration demanded that we parents take effective measures to correct this unacceptable state of affairs, especially in this school, which was founded to forge future cadres of the Ministry of the Interior. I couldn't believe this absurd criticism, this crude attempt to hold parents and students responsible for the failures of the educational system. If the students spent six weeks in a row in that wonderful school and only four days at home, whose fault was it? Who was responsible for what they should know? The school or us, the absent parents?

In another letter, the principal complained of serious deficiencies in the students' spelling. This letter was a true feast: It contained at least ten spelling mistakes. It was a joke. What were we supposed to do? Could we return the letter to them marking the mistakes with red ink, so that they'd realize that those who teach badly cannot reap good results? I said to Dictys:

"Here, check the letter and tell me how many spelling mistakes you find; let's see if you miss any."

It was a fun game for both of us. At least the letters were good for something.

Dictys was in the eleventh grade when, suddenly, he was made into a teacher of two subjects for tenth graders. The crisis due to a lack of teachers had worsened to such an extent that in order to guarantee the continuity of classes, the campus administration was forced to resort to this tactic. This freed Dictys from the daily "productive work" in the grapefruit orchards. While his classmates were completing their day in the fields, he was teaching math and biology, or preparing the classes. In order to perform his work with a bare minimum of knowledge, he was given a veneer of expertise, a few hours of basic training, and then he was released on the tenth-graders. He spent many mornings correcting and grading his students' written assignments and preparing to master the next day's lesson. It was a tough year, but Dictys had the satisfaction of feeling useful and recognized.

Exams for the first semester of the last year of pre-university had arrived. These were the most important tests; they actually carried more weight than the final exams since the results of the first semester served as the basis for distributing the places available in the country's universities and abroad. It was discovered that a group of students had committed massive fraud by gaining access to the sealed envelopes kept in the principal's office, which contained the exams sent by the Ministry of Education. Thus, they knew the questions in advance and were able to prepare and answer them perfectly on the exam. The strange thing was that the teachers didn't notice any irregularities when they graded the exams. It didn't surprise them that precisely the worst students—the slow and lazy ones, who had passed the previous courses by a hair—had answered all the questions perfectly. It was the other students who expressed their doubts about it.

The Ministry of Education sent a special commission to the island to investigate. The results were terrible. Most of the seniors had taken part in the fraud. To tell the truth, the ringleaders had to be recognized as experts in picking locks without leaving traces and opening, closing, and leaving the violated envelopes like new. Wasn't it a question of forging young talent to be the future agents of the Cuban state security apparatus? As they couldn't expel all those involved from the school—the last year then would have had less than half of the students—they expelled only the ringleaders. All the exams were nullified, and new, more difficult exams were made. Everyone—all those who had participated in the fraud and those who hadn't—had to take the new exams. This was a well-known application of the communist collectivist concept: equal punishment for innocents and sinners alike. It was difficult for the boys to acquire a correct idea of justice and responsibility.

I spoke with Dictys shortly after the discovery of the deception. Sad and disappointed, with an expression of terrible disappointment, he told me:

"Mom, not only is this school a big fraud, the whole of Cuba, from San Antonio to Punta de Maisí, is a gigantic fraud."

Dictys managed to finish high school with an excellent record. But even those fantastic results didn't dispel his pessimism. His disappointment and frustration reached their peak when he was informed that he had been "awarded" a career in international journalism in Moscow, as if it were a raffle. Like his brother, his desire was to study in East Germany, and he had a special attraction to biology. Now they were sending him to study for a career in which he felt no interest, and in a country that didn't appeal to him either. If he didn't accept, he ran the risk of having to remain in Cuba to clean floors or cut cane. If he accepted, he did it knowing that he had to stick it out, because you couldn't exchange one career for another.

CHAPTER THIRTY-SEVEN

MY FATHER'S DEATH AND MY MOTHER'S LAST VISIT

IT WAS THREE IN THE MORNING on May 26, 1981. The persistent ringing of the phone woke me up. I was half asleep. Who would call at three in the morning? I heard the voice of my older brother in Germany among many noises and interruptions:
"Monika, our father just died."
The voice disappeared. I felt like I had been slapped. *It can't be*, I told myself. *Just a few days ago I received a letter from him announcing his arrival in Cuba for the month of September.* He'd had an operation, but in his letter he assured me that he'd come out of it in good shape. Of course, the letter was dated sometime in March; it had taken eight weeks to reach me. Was I dreaming? Did I have a nightmare? I still had the phone in my hand. I kept hearing sounds, as if the waves of the Atlantic were in the receiver and, again, from far away, the voice of my brother, repeating his message, confirming the death of my father. A blood transfusion, contaminated with the hepatitis virus, had caused a raging infection that destroyed his liver and killed him. Now I was awake, and I realized that it wasn't a dream but a real nightmare.
I couldn't be with my father on his last trip to the cemetery; I didn't have the right to purchase a plane ticket in Cuban pesos like I had two years ago. The minimum time allowed me between trips, paying in Cuban pesos, was three years. If I had greenbacks, I wouldn't have a problem buying a ticket, but I didn't have any,

and if I had had, I'd have been thrown in a cell, because having foreign currency was a serious crime in Cuba. *What a shame, Dad. Your favorite daughter couldn't be with you to say goodbye. Luckily, you never knew.*

18. *Grandpa Herwig and Grandma Berta with Dani, Dictys, and Monika in Germany, Summer 1979, the last time they met Herwig alive*

My mother had to go through a long and painful process of learning how to cope with her sudden widowhood. At almost seventy years of age, she was forced to become independent, to be responsible for planning and using her time (no longer with a partner), to decide what to do with her savings and pension. But this freedom, which she wasn't accustomed to, gave her no satisfaction. She felt overworked, tormented by the bureaucratic obstacles that were my father's daily bread and butter, but which had never interested her. She felt pressured by any form she had to fill out, any notice from the bank or the insurance office, because she didn't understand the language they used. It took her a long time to adapt to being alone, to claim her rights, and to take responsibility.

With some difficulty, I convinced her that she should disconnect and spend some time with us. A month of rest in Cuba, we thought, would do her good. Not two days had passed after her arrival in Cuba when suddenly, at seven in the evening, all the lights went out and the anti-aircraft siren on the roof of an adjoining house started blaring. All the cars on the street turned off their engines and came to a halt at the curb. Mom was frozen with fear, white as a sheet. She didn't understand anything that was happening. Poor thing, she didn't know that for a long time in Cuba, we had been playing war games, practicing evacuation, defense, counterattacks, and other warlike activities against the Great Enemy.

"Don't be scared, mother; it's nothing, just an exercise."

My mother grabbed my arm. Her hands were shaking. She saw herself, suddenly, in a very similar scenario, only it wasn't an exercise. It was the brutal reality of the two wars that she had lived through—the First and Second World Wars. She had lost relatives in the wars. Her husband, my father, had been a prisoner of war. She experienced the terror of the bombings and the shortages of food, clothing, and the most essential things for life. She managed to save her own skin and that of her five children, but she lost her house with all her belongings, and she had to agree to go live with her mother-in-law, who accommodated her and her children in exchange for my mother's unconditional subordination. Mom, who in her youthful years had enjoyed singing, playing the piano, learning English and French, moving freely in society, and enjoying the delights of the arts, now had to learn how to cook, do laundry, sweep and wax floors, and even steal potatoes and chunks of coal from wagons on the way to the stockpile near the house. Fortunately, she lived long enough to be able to put the horrors of war behind her. And now, in her daughter's house in Havana, she was in another war?

Shocked by that hyper-realistic military exercise, my mother began counting the hours until she could return to Germany. Nothing was going right for her. Her first trip to Cuba, in 1963, had been a disaster, and now, twenty years later, it was happening all over again. She didn't dare set foot outside the house. There was not another military exercise in our neighborhood during her stay in Cuba, but there were other phenomena that were equally unbearable. Her vacation was ruined for good by a veritable chain of storms with powerful thunder and lightning, tropical downpours that gave her the impression that the world was coming to an end. Since she was a child, when there were no lightning rods yet and a storm entailed the real danger of destroying a house and killing everyone in it, a visceral panic at such a natural event had been instilled in her.

Of course, every storm meant a long blackout and several days without electricity, water, or refrigeration. Through all this, I couldn't take time off to keep my mother company and make her stay in Cuba more bearable. On the contrary, in preparation for the Fourth National Congress of the FMC, I had to take several business trips to the eastern provinces, leaving at dawn and returning late at night. Those days of travel meant enormous torture for her. She felt abandoned and defenseless, in the face of unknown dangers that took on unimaginable dimensions.

Her imagination, as rich as mine, instead of helping her to cope with her problems and loneliness, provided her with images of dramatic events of horrific content. My mother was a master at brooding about calamities and living them in advance, almost masochistically. There was no remedy; she was allergic to Cuba. On the day of her farewell, we all felt relieved.

CHAPTER THIRTY-EIGHT
AT THE PEAK OF MY CAREER

M\Y WORKLOAD WAS CONSTANTLY INCREASING, with radio and television programs, teaching activities in the Faculties of Medicine and Psychology, the FMC Cadre school, the Ministry of Education's continuing education centers, and Middle Medical Teaching schools. I was also involved in implementing research (such as on teenage pregnancy), doing editorial work, and attending international conferences. There were never enough hours in the day.

In 1983, I defended my doctoral thesis at the University of Rostock in Germany, acquiring the scientific degree of Doctor of Philosophy, based on my sex education work in Cuba. It took me months of intense labor to gather the necessary bibliographical material, write, and review my thesis. I worked into the dawn and on weekends and strained my eyes in the dim light of countless candles during nocturnal power cuts. I passed the rigorous exams with *summa cum laude*, and I returned to Cuba, now with another title, that of Doctor, to continue wasting energy and effort, always hoping that some seed would fall on fertile ground.

During the Fourth Congress of 1985, I was elected to membership on the Federation of Cuban Women's National Committee and reelected during the Fifth Congress in 1990. The National Committee was the body responsible for adopting and applying

FMC policy. This new responsibility meant having to attend a good number of additional assemblies, meetings, and events.

In 1986, the School of Medical Sciences gave me one month to prepare and present myself before a commission to take the state exam to become a full professor, which was a requirement if I were to continue teaching classes to health professionals and medical students. I had plenty of material for another thesis, but not much time. I spent entire early mornings and weekends writing a thesis on teaching and preparing a master class. The oral examination, in which the jury picked apart and analyzed my thesis, ended in a heated debate. There were abysmal disagreements between my position and that of the five male members of the jury, seated across from me. We all—examiners and examined—forgot that this was a state exam. We raised our voices, gestured, defended, and attacked each other. Three hours after starting the exam, which should have lasted an hour at the most, we were still arguing about procedures, provisions and their practical implementation, deficiencies of the health system, and problems in our corresponding professional occupations, so that it was difficult for us to return to the reality of the exam.

I passed the oral exam, but they set a trap for me in the master teaching exam. I was sure that the ten pieces of paper on the table, supposedly with different subjects, all had the same one: homosexuality. I knew that was an issue of great interest to the jury, and I knew that they would never accept my well-known position on homosexuality. My demands for tolerance, an end to the marginalization, criminalization, exorcism, and persecution of homosexuals—in compliance with the notorious resolution of 1971 (discriminatory and inhumane with respect to the treatment of homosexuals) that was still in force—clashed head-on with the convictions and opinions of the jury in charge of evaluating me. I also knew that the jury was hoping to see me fight like an upside-down beetle, kicking the air, with arguments and justifications that they, the omniscient and irreproachable gods, were surely going to refute.

I had been fortunate to have access to the most recent books by Masters, Johnson, and Kolodny, with which I had prepared myself. I based my position on homosexuality on these recently published scientific works that had been researched and written by world-renowned specialists. The jury, however, was not yet aware of the books, as they were only available in English and in libraries to which the jurors didn't have access. They were careful not to show that they were woefully out of date. Seeking confrontation would have meant contrasting the latest, scientifically based data and knowledge with beliefs, myths, half-truths, and personal opinions that had no place in this exam. They behaved with discipline during my presentation, summoning all their patience and self-control, and I was not intimidated by their frankly hostile looks and gestures. I finished my master class, and they asked me to wait outside the classroom.

While the jury deliberated on my grade, I waited in the hallway. After two hours, I was worried and uneasy, and also indignant, because with all due respect to the High Examining Commission, this was no way to treat a candidate. I knocked on the door so that they would give me the news once and for all. I was convinced that they'd forgotten about me and that they surely had disqualified me. One of the members of the jury came to meet me.

"Don't worry, Mónica. You passed the exam, but you can't imagine the discussion that broke out when you left. It was like a riot, a street fight. You said a lot of things that fell on them like bombs. Some were offended, and some wanted to disqualify you. Fortunately, the detractors didn't win. You can go away calmly; you're now a tenured professor. The official document will be prepared and sent by the Ministry of Higher Education. Congratulations!"

What a relief and what luck. Now I could continue my work without having to divert time and effort to acquiring any more degrees.

In 1988, the National Sex Education Working Group (GNTES), founded in 1977, and of which I was the director, became the

19. *Monika, Havana, late 1980s*

National Center for Sex Education (CENESEX), in recognition of the importance of our work and the magnitude of its impact. CENESEX was also given a broader mandate, particularly for research work and the training of professionals. I was appointed the first director of CENESEX, a position that I filled with all my energy until the day of my return to Germany.

To crown the honors, I was elected a member of the Scientific Council and Advisory Council of the World Association for Sexology and an honorary member of the Polish Academy of Sexological Sciences.

At this point, the famously witty Cuban *vox populi* had awarded me several titles of honor. For those who sought my help it was "*La Doctora* Krause," "Mónica of sex education," or simply "Mónica." My adversaries called me "the corrupter of minors," "the sex-obsessed German" and "that dreadful woman." For both sides, I was also "Mónica, the Queen of Condoms."

Our sex-education work in Cuba transcended borders. I was often interviewed for television in various countries in Latin America and Europe, and my articles were published in the press of these and other countries. I took part in congresses, symposia, and workshops in Latin America, the U.S., and Europe. I was respected and admired.

I traveled to congresses without even having the resources to pay for a lunch or a decent hotel. Since I was the director of a U.N. Fund for Population Activities program, the U.N. financed almost all my professional trips, but I couldn't use the money they gave me at the U.N. office: MINSAP kept the bulk and allowed me to spend such a ridiculously limited sum that I had to be a magician to pay all the taxes, registration fees, and other fees that must be paid at an international congress. Since post-war times in Germany, when I was still a little girl, everything had been rationed, from food to clothes to school supplies. I acquired masterful skills in managing scarce resources to solve countless problems, and I applied these experiences to my numerous professional trips.

I would arrive, for example, at the little hotel where I was to work. From my large suitcase I would take out a discreet-sized briefcase to go shopping at the nearest, least expensive supermarket. I would buy a loaf of whole wheat bread or canned biscuits, smoked salami, and hermetically sealed cheese (which didn't taste like anything, but gave me the feeling of being fed), plus products that didn't spoil easily: instant coffee, condensed milk, canned butter, and fruits that could be stored without refrigeration for some time. In my luggage I always carried a little electric water heater to boil water with. I never dared to drink water without boiling it first. Neither in Mexico nor in Nicaragua nor on the steppes or the African desert, in the worst times of terrible heat, lack of hygiene, and lack of clean water did I have intestinal problems that destroyed the health of many people. When the representatives of "normal" countries met in restaurants for lunch or dinner, I would stay in my little room to prepare my scant meals—which, incidentally, compared to the monotonous and rudimentary diet of Cuba, constituted real feasts—and continue to attend work sessions. My prodigious imagination always helped me to bear the humiliation that this terrible limitation often imposed on me.

I couldn't even invite colleagues from other countries to have coffee, let alone invite them to lunch. I missed invaluable opportunities to chat with them, to update myself. The well-known Cuban hospitality with which I had been associated since the beginning of my life in Cuba suffered permanent hardships. I was ashamed, but I told myself that the mendicant friars spent their lives begging for alms to carry out their works of Christian charity. Unlike those friars, however, I was acting on behalf of the U.N. and MINSAP, and none of my foreign colleagues could imagine or suspect that most of the money that the international organization paid me had to be returned to MINSAP. Surely they must have thought many times that this Cuban-German woman was the world's biggest cheapskate.

When I walked along the main streets of Caracas, Buenos Aires, Sao Paulo, Rio de Janeiro, Madrid, Frankfort, Mexico City, San Juan, Berlin, San José, Heidelberg, and many other cities, without a penny in my pocket, and saw the storefronts full of things that make life more pleasant for human beings—some totally useless, grotesque, or bizarre—I imagined winning the lottery and being able to buy paint for the peeling walls of my house, new sinks to replace those that had been broken for a long time, a stove and a water heater that worked, slip covers for my furniture, some clothes for the family, and rich food to satisfy my decades-old hunger. But what made me suffer most were the bookstores. Even knowing that I didn't really need those books was no remedy against temptation and my vehement desire. I spent hours browsing through them, writing down titles (what a useless task), dreaming about them, and hoping to be able to purchase them one day.

PART FIVE
THE NINETIES

CHAPTER THIRTY-NINE
THE SPECIAL PERIOD: *MACHISMO* AND UNDERDEVELOPMENT

DESPITE ALL THE RECOGNITION inside and outside Cuba for my work, I increasingly felt I was getting nowhere. To make matters worse, in 1990 the country plunged into economic, political, and moral bankruptcy. The Special Period in Time of Peace began. This was the official euphemism used to describe the severe crisis caused by the end of Soviet subsidies, and the crisis showed, in a really painful way, that most of the achievements, social advances, and programs (not only sex education) that had been so exemplary worldwide were built on sand: They had been supported for decades by the enormous subsidies that came in as if by pipeline from Moscow. The Cuban economy, inefficient like none other, didn't produce the wealth necessary to sustain itself. And the u.s. embargo did the rest. The Special Period suddenly catapulted us into the lowest ranks of the Third World.

At this time, the problem of teenage pregnancy was at its peak. About thirty percent of the babies were born to teenage mothers. Between thirty and forty percent of the women who underwent an abortion—a surgical intervention performed more than 160,000 times (as opposed to 180,000 deliveries) per year, according to official statistics—were adolescents. Even the doctored official statistics on this situation were appalling. I met girls who bragged about having had five abortions.

"But *Doctora*, it's nothing; it's more uncomfortable to have a tooth filled," they assured me.

The shortages exacerbated the situation. Our budget was constantly being slashed. The construction of a birth control pill factory that had been inaugurated in the presence of distinguished representatives from the U.N. months before was halted. The production of the much-needed birth control pills did not begin. The constant increase in prices of the machinery, raw materials, and construction material impeded completion of the work.

"I take pills, but where can I find them? In my province there haven't been any for a long time," I was constantly asked.

"*Doctora*, could you get me the pill for my daughter? She can't use an IUD, it hurts her; the doctor recommended that she take the pill, but they can't be found anywhere."

Every day, invariably, I received requests for help to get the products that should be available to the population. They should be, but weren't. Intrauterine devices were like a prize in the lottery. We re-made nylon fishing line into intrauterine devices, as the good-quality copper IUDs were too expensive.

We had managed to get the population to accept and request condoms, because the ones we distributed caused unexpectedly positive reactions. But from the moment the budget was reduced, condoms were crossed off the list of goods to be imported; there were more important things that had to be done first. The first cases of HIV had been reported in the country. The first AIDS center was established in 1989, a clinical center outside Havana where people who tested HIV-positive were confined by law and isolated from the rest of the population. Condoms would have helped prevent more than one infection with HIV.

Why were we wasting energy spreading information about family planning and protection methods if there were no resources to make them available to the people? Underdevelopment, in collusion with the dislocation of the socialist economy, hindered us on every front. We were helpless witnesses to a society and economy devolving, moving backward, and it had us on the brink of despair. I felt like I was grasping at straws. On several fronts where we had believed and hoped for profound social change, we were frustrated to perceive regression.

In 1989, a complaint of a suicide by a girl from Holguín led us to request an in-depth investigation. The investigation found that in many hospitals and polyclinics in the eastern provinces, virginity tests were being carried out against the will of the girls, often under the threat of angry parents who forced the doctor to examine their daughter. Doctors, faced with the alternative of being killed with machetes or doing the required examination, preferred to save their skin, knowing that such a practice would have dire consequences for a stigmatized girl, not to mention that it was a violation of both professional ethics and the girl's rights. Under the law, a virginity examination was justified only when there was a suspicion of a sexual offense committed against the girl, and in such a case, there had to be a police charge and a court order to carry out the examination.

Likewise, it was unacceptable that the Cuban specialists attending the 1989 Latin American Congress of Forensic Medicine should demonstrate their incomprehension and non-acceptance of the legal term "rape in marriage" to their Latin American colleagues.

A 1990 investigation yielded data so inconceivably catastrophic that they were kept out of the public eye: hundreds of thousands of underage Cuban children, whose mothers were single or separated, received not a penny of support from their fathers, let alone the affection to which every human being is entitled. How was it possible that in a country that strictly enforced laws when it suited it, the law that obliges every father to pay child support was not enforced if he divorced or separated from his partner and left his children with their mother?

The increasingly chaotic and desperate economic situation was accompanied by a persistent deterioration in ethical and moral values. When there are no prospects, when no one knows what new misfortune the next day will bring, it seems that the mechanisms that guide reasoning and civic behavior stop working. A dislocation, a sexual anarchy, a "to hell with the consequences" attitude characterized our society. Most worryingly, top-level leaders, unscrupulous practitioners of *titimanía*—throwing away an old partner to show off with a *titi*, a young, sexy one—set the worst examples. The frequent change of partners had become a sport practiced ostentatiously, reaching the most remote corners of the country. One of the results of this trend was a skyrocketing rise in sexually transmitted diseases.

People kept getting married and divorced as if it were a game. Not infrequently, young people got married in order to obtain the few privileges that were granted to newlyweds: a few days in a hotel, the opportunity to buy a case of beer, a set of towels, sheets, cutlery, and dishes. There was no other way to have a vacation or obtain essential items for the home, and the divorce cost only a hundred pesos and was taken care of in a matter of days.

Cuba experienced what, only five years earlier, seemed unthinkable: the rebirth of prostitution, which, especially for teenagers, acquired troubling proportions. With the increase in international tourism (Fidel Castro's hedge for facing the Special Period), this ages-old occupation received the influx of clients that allowed it to prosper.

The Fifth National Congress of the Federation of Cuban Women, held in 1990, was dedicated exclusively to defense and production in the Special Period, totally disregarding the original issues that had been discussed in countless provincial assemblies prior to the Congress. During the Congress, in which I was ratified as a member of the National Committee, I dared to ask for the floor to draw attention to the deteriorating situation of families, ethics, and society. They allowed me to speak for three minutes on the subject. It was the last passionate and desperate speech that I presented before a select audience: Fidel Castro was presiding over the session. The official newspaper, *Granma*, which reported in detail the debates in the Congress, gave no mention of my statement.

"You know? *El Jefe* didn't like what you said," those who were close to *El Máximo Líder* whispered in my ear.

I realized more and more every day that our voices of alarm didn't find an echo, especially since, as a result of the Special Period, the budget for CENESEX, already short, was cut significantly further.

Our small production of educational films almost came to a halt due to a lack of materials and spare parts for the existing equipment. Our gasoline quota was cut. We couldn't get spare parts for the two vehicles that transported the teaching team and the researchers to their respective workplaces, thus interrupting the research and teaching programs throughout the country. The photocopiers and the computer—a real treasure that was cared for like a newborn—were idle for much of the time, due to lack of ink or spare parts. We couldn't continue to meet our commitment to the provincial specialists to supply them with brochures, posters, or miscellaneous informational material because of the chronic lack of paper and printing possibilities.

Friends from abroad would give me pens, pencils, notebooks, and reams of paper. When I went abroad to take part in scientific events, I would collect office supplies that the sponsors sometimes left scattered on the tables and bring them back to my office. My team members received some of these materials, but they weren't enough to also satisfy the most basic needs of our colleagues in the provinces. Every sheet of paper, every videotape, every piece of equipment (tape recorders, video cameras), every pencil, every spare part for our vehicles, every book, every liter of gasoline, every scheduled seminar meant a struggle. We wasted energy time and again.

The occasional help from friends outside —crumbs, though given with much love and in a spirit of solidarity— was not enough to continue implementing the Cuban national program on sex education. Financial support from the U.N. and other international organizations, which considered our program worth reproducing in developing countries, couldn't close the huge gaps. The limitations crushed us, and we couldn't act efficiently, rigorously, and consistently.

CHAPTER FORTY
THE BOYS BECOME MEN

IN 1987 DICTYS RECEIVED HIS MASTER'S DEGREE in Journalism from the Moscow Institute of International Relations, the breeding ground for the elite foreign service of the Soviet Union and "friendly" (socialist) countries. He experienced the spring of *glasnost* and *perestroika* and learned about new ideas and modern approaches that were at odds with stagnant Stalinism. Dictys had conflicts with the Cuban representatives in Moscow, who tried to ensure that Cuban students weren't infected with the new ideas. Those who dared express their own views were sent back to the island without appeal. Cuba was protective of its students' "revolutionary integrity" and "purity" and wanted them to distance themselves from these new, poisonous currents of "ideological diversionism" that had begun to gnaw at the firm, flawless substance of future Cuban foreign service officers. This new wave—so feared by the Cuban authorities—could have the effect of a malignant cancer.

Back in Havana, the news agency Prensa Latina offered Dictys a permanent position. There he consolidated his abilities as a journalist. In 1989 he was informed that he was going to be sent to Angola. I almost had a heart attack when he told me. "Angola, again? O my God!" They had already summoned him to receive instructions and the documents required to leave without delay.

I moved heaven and earth to postpone the departure date. With great luck, since that decision was beyond my power (and my captain, at that time, was no longer holding any public office), Dictys was able to save himself from having to go to Angola.

Meanwhile, Prensa Latina had posted him to the regional office in Nicaragua, where he would be a correspondent and observer of the first electoral process that was beginning under the Sandinista government. His boss preferred to work in his mansion in Managua, and this opened a great opportunity for Dictys. He assumed the responsibility of Prensa Latina and spent a year of intense work, not without danger, in a country where even the children carried Kalashnikovs. He traveled all over Nicaragua, from the Atlantic coast to the Pacific Ocean, through mountains and plains, on foot, by helicopter, truck, car, and oxcart. He knew and passionately loved this Central American country and interviewed practically all its politicians, both from the Sandinista government and from the opposition. He reported up close, first-hand and from the inside, on the elections that Violeta Chamorro would eventually win. His reporting was accepted and appreciated in the journalistic world, and Dictys had the satisfaction of feeling recognized. In the end, it was worth having endured the five hard years of study in Moscow that were imposed on him.

Dani returned from Germany in August of 1989, at the age of twenty-two, with an M.S. in Mathematics with honors and the offer of a scholarship to pursue his doctorate—all expenses paid by the Dresden University of Technology. The Minister of Higher Education in Cuba, acting on the orders of *El Comandante en Jefe*, strictly prohibited him from continuing his doctoral studies in Germany, alleging that recent graduates should go to the jobs assigned to them by the Revolution, that he was "already good at messing around and enjoying the good life"—as if studying mathematics in Germany meant a permanent party.

The prohibition on Dani's acceptance of the university's offer, the order to work in an agricultural institute where the Revolution (the Ministry of Higher Education) assigned him, and the flat rejection of the request from the Faculty of Mathematics at the University of Havana to place him as a member of the team of specialists in artificial intelligence awakened in Dani an insubordination and rebellion that had been until then dormant.

Dani began working at the Institute for Fundamental Research in Tropical Agriculture (INIFAT) in Santiago de las Vegas. The INIFAT colleagues, scientists, and botanists were in love with their profession, using no other resources than their brains, carefully preserved old books, a precious seed bank, and a large dose of willingness to pass on their knowledge and experience to new generations, with the hope that someday an interest in valuable plant species that had ceased to be cultivated due to collectivization, monoculture, and neglect would be recovered in Cuba. They managed to stimulate Dani's interest, and during the months that he worked at INIFAT, he fell in love with Cuban flora, dedicating himself to the study of botany. He continues the cultivation of this love to this day.

The absurd dictum "you will work where the Revolution assigns you" never stopped haunting Dani. Once, he was sent for a month to repair the palm roof of a warehouse in San Antonio de los Baños. Every day, he would travel by bus from El Vedado to Santiago de las Vegas, and from Santiago de las Vegas he would be taken to San Antonio de los Baños in a Russian SIL truck, the kind that consumes more fuel than a Sherman tank, along with a worker who had been given the same task. Day after day they would climb up onto the rotten roof of the warehouse, scare off rats with a crowbar, and firmly hold on to the least rotten trunks to tear off decaying palm leaves, one by one. Once the day was over, they would return to Santiago de las Vegas on the gigantic truck, with no other load than the two "roofers"—a mathematician and a worker—plus the driver at the wheel. Then Dani would return to El Vedado by bus.

Months later, in the framework of a war simulation similar to the one that had scared my mother years before, Dani was sent off with a brigade for two weeks to dig trenches on the outskirts of

Santiago de las Vegas. The first few days he had bleeding blisters on all his fingers and palms, which soon turned into calluses. In those two weeks of intense physical work, the brigade dug several yards of trench in rocky terrain. Just a week after the action ended, Dani saw, as the bus that took him from home to INIFAT in Santiago de las Vegas passed right in front of the place, that a bulldozer was filling in and leveling the holes. Dani felt a deep disappointment, and not a little resentment.

"That I had to go pull off palm leaves—well, deep down it was a useful job. But for them to give me a pick and shovel for two weeks for the fun of it and then immediately close up the holes, that's both Kafkaesque and disrespectful."

At INIFAT there were two computers, a donation from the U.N. Food and Agriculture Organization for the institution's scientific work, but Dani didn't have access to them. Why? They belonged to a different department than Dani's and could only be used by members of that department, as if one department were separated from the other by a national border. Dani managed to "resolve" the issue and got permission to use the computers from other centers with better equipment: the National Institute for Sugar Cane Research and the National Botanical Garden. In that way he could occasionally do scientific work with modern equipment.

CHAPTER FORTY-ONE

MY LAST STAND AGAINST INSTITUTIONALIZED HOMOPHOBIA

Homophobia in revolutionary Cuba, both societal and institutional, has always troubled sympathizers with the Cuban Revolution. In the 1960s, French writer and philosopher Jean-Paul Sartre is reported to have said: "What the Jew was for the Nazis, the homosexual is for the Cuban revolution."

In the 1960s in Cuba there were even forced labor camps, the Military Units to Aid Production (UMAP), with the supposed purpose of re-educating homosexuals through hard physical labor, thereby converting them to heterosexuals. This was slave labor, in subhuman conditions, and the treatment of homosexuals as if they were animals led to the death or suicide of more than one. A few years later, after massive protests from progressive voices around the world, this sad chapter of the Cuban Revolution was closed.

For twenty years, a resolution with the force of law was rigorously applied in all centers of middle and higher education, all state institutions, the Communist Party, and the Union of Communist Youth. This inhuman resolution, passed in 1971 during the First Congress of Education and Culture, institutionalized the repression of homosexuals and demanded the cleansing of "these antisocial, weak, and easily corruptible elements" from education and work centers. This resolution declared that homosexuals should be denied access to university studies and to leadership positions and that they were not to be allowed to join the Communist Party or the Communist Youth, since they were untrustworthy people of questionable integrity.

In all educational and work centers, purification and cleansing activities took place annually, with the mandatory participation of the entire group. Each individual had to criticize himself in front of those gathered and openly respond to accusations or questions about his integrity when suspected of being homosexual. Horrifying scenes of blatant contempt for human beings happened within the framework of these witch hunts. Many homosexuals who had barely managed to keep their condition hidden, who had earned the recognition and prestige of their peers, suddenly found themselves branded as perverse, pitiful, weak, and a traitorous monster. Suicide was often the only way out.

From the beginning of my role as director of GNTES and then of CENESEX, I had compiled extensive, scientifically based, and up-to-date information on homosexuality.

I had an explicit order not to speak publicly on the subject, much less in the media. Even so, I always considered it my duty to relentlessly bring up the subject in my teaching activity and in my exchanges with political leaders. It was a crusade in which I had to endure the most unhinged calumnies. "She defends these degenerates because she must be one herself," they said. To carry out this work I could only count on the help of a very few brave people, like Dr. Lajonchere.

In 1990, I committed the most daring transgression of all. And the last.

A well-known journalist from the University of Havana's monthly publication, *Alma Mater*, visited me to do an interview. We had a six-hour session and spoke at length and in detail about many aspects of human sexuality, particularly about the taboos that existed in Cuba. Of course, we also talked about homosexuality.

"I want you to know that I'm not authorized to speak publicly on the subject of homosexuality, much less publish articles about it," I told the journalist.

"At *Alma Mater*, we're going to make an attempt," he said.

"I've tried to do this with others before you. For months I've kept a series of articles in my drawer that address this issue straightforwardly and academically. They've been held back, and I'm waiting for the green light, but it seems that the traffic light that has to give it to me doesn't exist."

"But I'm an optimist. I'm sure the article will be published in full, including the parts on the prohibited matter."

"If you manage to pull that off, it would be great. I ask you that when you've written your article, when it's ready to go to press, please allow me to take a look at it to avoid any error in the text. Not that I doubt your abilities as a journalist, no, but you aren't a specialist in sexology. Any misinterpretation—even the slightest—or any incorrect definition will harm us. Our adversaries would like nothing more than to find mistakes in our work. And another thing I have to tell you: the paragraphs on the subject of homosexuality have to be printed verbatim, without any literary interpretation."

During the weeks that followed this interview I had a lot of work. I was constantly traveling to the provinces, so I forgot about it until the day the storm broke, with lightning and thunder.

Attending a reception of the Academy of Sciences, in which *la Presidenta* was also present, the disaster was unleashed.

The personal bodyguard of *la Presidenta*, a woman who looked like a human tank, just smart enough to fulfill her obligation of permanently watching over *la Presidenta*'s physical safety, headed straight for me.

"This tops everything! What were you thinking? This is defamation; you use the same arguments that the enemy uses! Everything you're saying discredits our country. Come on, are you nuts?"

It was August, the hottest time of the year, and icy waves were running down my back. I knew that *la Presidenta*'s bodyguard parroted everything our mutual boss said. But at this moment I didn't know the reason for these terrible accusations. I wasn't aware of having committed any crime, and I didn't feel guilty about anything.

"What are you talking about?"

"What audacity! I've never seen anyone with more nerve than

you in my life. Don't play the innocent, like you don't know what this is about: that in Cuba we discriminate, humiliate, and deprive men of their rights."

Suddenly, I understood.

"Where did you read that?"

I couldn't believe that the interview with *Alma Mater* had been published without censorship.

"Are you telling me you didn't give the interview to *Alma Mater?*

"Yes, I did, but …"

"No buts. There it is. And here you are playing dumb, as if you're surprised. Listen to me: the boss is foaming with indignation. Hopefully you can come up with something to get out of this."

"Please, show me the article. I have to see it."

Shortly afterward, she appeared with a copy of *Alma Mater*. I almost snatched it out of her hand. And indeed: there was the proof of the crime. Everything, but absolutely everything that I had said on the prohibited subject was printed in black and white, including my open criticism of institutionalized homophobia in Cuba. Magazine in hand, I retired to a corner of the patio to read the article from start to finish. The article was well done, although it had two or three small conceptual errors that could have been avoided if I had reviewed the manuscript before it was delivered to the press. But they were minor mistakes.

The publication of the interview in *Alma Mater* in 1990 cost me severe disapproval for violating strict, explicit orders. But it filled me with satisfaction to see that it had unleashed a change, a process of critical discussion of the homophobic policies in force throughout the country. The days were numbered for the infamous homophobic resolution of the First Congress of Education and Culture in 1971.

One month before my departure from Cuba in November of 1990, Dr. Lajonchere and I received approval to prepare a document that would serve as a basis, a working instrument, to develop and implement new guidelines on homosexuality based on socially humane principles and corresponding to the most up-to-date scientific knowledge in this regard.

CHAPTER FORTY-TWO

THE CIRCLE IS CLOSED

IN 1990 MY MARRIAGE WAS DEFINITELY BROKEN. We had divorced the previous year, and my ex-husband was now living with his new wife, with whom he had just had a daughter. Ours was a civilized separation, without violence, without claims to power or intent to destroy each other. In Cuba this way of separating was the exception rather than the rule. Crimes of passion continued to occur quite often. These horrendous events were never reported in the official press, where there was room only for positive news, but through *"radio bemba"* (the grapevine, gossip's underground railway), the whole country learned about the most talked-about events in a matter of minutes.

Among those who committed such crimes were people from all social levels, intellectuals and peasants, laborers and high officials. The most common weapon used was pouring gasoline on the poor wife or girlfriend and setting her on fire. (This method also continued to occupy first place for suicide.) Those who had a firearm—legally or illegally—used it. In the countryside, the machete was usually the instrument of choice for carrying out an execution.

Dictys and Dani met the beginning of political change in Eastern Europe and the former Soviet Union with great expectations. The initial euphoria of seeing one totalitarian regime after another collapse like a house of cards and the hope that at least a breeze of reform would arrive in Cuba faded, though, with the passing of the months of 1990. Once again, the condition of being an island surrounded by water and the counterproductive hostile policy of the U.S. worked in favor of the orthodox Cuban Communist Party.

In the mid-1990s, the two boys told Jesús and me that the political system of unitary thinking was suffocating them. They had received their German passports in November of 1989, handed over by the East German ambassador himself, which put them in the privileged position of having a country where they could go, legally, to live. The other variable in the equation was being able to leave Cuba, which in 1990 was (almost) impossible.

And what about me?

One day in June of 1990, a woman came to the CENESEX headquarters in tears and asked to see me. Sobbing, she painted a picture of her miserable life and asked for my help. She had been married for fifteen years. Always, day after day, even when she felt unwell, even when she was menstruating, she fulfilled her "marital duty." Never, until the day she came to see me, had she questioned this procedure, the meaning of this life. She simply did what her husband told her to do.

"I've felt sick for weeks, but my husband gets on top of me, demands my submission, and has no consideration. He's abusive, and I can't talk to him. He rides me as if I were a bicycle, regularly, at the same time, always doing the same thing, always the same, always the same. If it didn't hurt so much, I'd continue to put up with it, but yesterday I refused for the first time. I got up the courage to tell him: 'Not today, I'm sick, it hurts!' And what do you think he answered me? Well, just so you know, he said: 'You have to do it with me, I need it. Or do you want to send me to the street? No, girl; no way! Did you marry me so that I can go to the street and get AIDS? That's not going to happen!'

"Suddenly I saw him as a monster, an animal. My throat tightened, and at the same time I felt angry, an anger so strong that it blinded me. He threw himself on top of me. I ran away from the house, and here I am. And even if the divorce costs me, I won't continue to accept these conditions; I can't take it anymore."

We talked for a long time, and the woman had a catharsis. She also told me that after she listened to some programs about sexuality on the radio, where I spoke several times about problems similar to hers (although, to tell the truth, they were never that terrible), she wrote down my address and decided to talk to me. I was able to direct this poor woman to one of our best specialists in couples therapy. My colleague managed to get the husband to appear and take part in the therapy sessions as well.

Ever since the boys expressed their firm desire to continue their lives in Germany, I had been torn apart. I understood that it was my mission, my destiny, to help individuals like the crying woman who came to see me in June, and to contribute—for example, with each radio program—to the dismantling of archaic myths and traditions, just as a drop of rain sculpts a mountain.

On the other hand, every day I felt less strong. The country had more pressing problems than sex education, and funding for CENESEX and the National Program had dried up. Also, at almost fifty years of age, my health was far from good. And most importantly, I couldn't imagine continuing to live in Cuba alone, without a husband, without my children.

The logical decision was to return to Germany with my sons. How we managed to get out, being three Cuban citizens (our status as Germans was olympically ignored by the Cuban authorities), is told at the beginning of this, my Cuban story.

Looking back at my life in Cuba and my professional career, many have asked me (and I have also asked myself) whether the sacrifice was worth it—Was it worth giving thirty years of my energy and youth to Cuba? Was there anything left of my timely, small, ephemeral contribution to the cause of women's equality in Cuba, of my fight against *machismo*? Did I do anything more than sprinkle a few drops of water on the fire? Was I blind to reality?

And I answer them, and I answer myself:

If I managed to make one person think and question an attitude, it was worth it. If I imparted one solution for a problem, it was worth it. If I managed to avoid a single catastrophe, a single suicide, it was worth it. If I helped break one taboo, it was worth it. If the positive consequences of my work outweighed the negative ones, it was worth it. If one seed sown by me germinated, surviving the cyclone of traditions, time, and underdevelopment, and managed to take root, it was worth it.

I believe that our commitment to changing many people's attitude toward sexuality was successful. When men or women begin to question and revise their value systems, I think this can be considered an enormous accomplishment. It was wonderful to see men, women, and children in a Latin American country begin to talk seriously about sexuality.

Adiós, Cuba, my heaven and my hell. *Adiós*!

AFTERWORD

Our mother passed away on May 20, 2019, in Flensburg, Germany, surrounded by her husband, Harry, and the two of us. Her ashes are buried in Glücksburg in a forest facing the Baltic Sea. Mum and Harry lived happily for twenty years in the North of Germany, with a view over the Sea to the Danish islands. We remain in regular contact with Harry.

The idea to publish our mother's memoirs in English emerged from our desire to keep our mother's legacy alive.

We, her children, are an intrinsic part of this story. We experienced the vicissitudes of the young mother in the circumstances of the Cuban Revolution. We enjoyed together the relaxing— almost magical— swims in the Gulf of Mexico and shared the bliss when we were a complete and happy family in Chile. We witnessed her years in the Federation of Cuban Women, constantly traveling in and out of the country. We suffered the anguish of the car accident that almost killed her while our father was in a futile war on a distant continent. We admired with amazement and pride Mom's fervent turn to her new mission and professional passion: sex education, through which she became a well-known, respected, and beloved figure throughout Cuba.

Beyond her unusual and eventful career and accomplishments, there is the self-sacrificing, compassionate, loving, creative, funny, singing, and steadfast mother who gave us the best possible education and transmitted love and principles to us. There is the honest and consistent woman who broke down walls for her convictions. There is the bold and determined woman who grew through all obstacles. This brave woman and mother inspired us to produce this English edition.

The Spanish translation was a true labor of love by Regina Anavy of San Francisco. The work of art she created is simply magnificent. Regina soon became a partner (if not a member of our family or vice versa) in this project, participating in the decision making. Regina, in all humility and gratitude, thank you so much!

DICTYS JIMÉNEZ KRAUSE, *Hamburg*
JULIAN DANIEL (DANI) JIMÉNEZ KRAUSE, *Brussels*
March 8, 2022

www.ingramcontent.com/pod-product-compliance
Lightning Source LLC
Chambersburg PA
CBHW022028290426
44109CB00014B/796